SPECULUM
MENTIS

or

The Map of Knowledge

Oxford University Press, Amen House, London E.C.4

GLASGOW NEW YORK TORONTO MELBOURNE WELLINGTON
BOMBAY CALCUTTA MADRAS KARACHI LAHORE DACCA
CAPE TOWN SALISBURY NAIROBI IBADAN ACCRA
KUALA LUMPUR HONG KONG

FIRST PUBLISHED 1924
REPRINTED LITHOGRAPHICALLY IN GREAT BRITAIN
AT THE UNIVERSITY PRESS, OXFORD, 1946, 1956,
1963

SPECULUM MENTIS

or

The Map of Knowledge

by

R. G. COLLINGWOOD

βλέπομεν γὰρ ἄρτι δι' ἐσόπτρου ἐν αἰνίγματι

OXFORD
AT THE CLARENDON PRESS

TO

MY FIRST AND BEST TEACHER

OF

ART, RELIGION

SCIENCE, HISTORY

AND

PHILOSOPHY

CONTENTS

PREFACE

THIS book is the outcome of a long-growing conviction that the only philosophy that can be of real use to anybody at the present time is a critical review of the chief forms of human experience, a new Treatise of Human Nature philosophically conceived. This is a project which in itself is not new ; but its possibilities are very far from being exhausted. We find people practising art, religion, science, and so forth, seldom quite happy in the life they have chosen, but generally anxious to persuade others to follow their example. Why are they doing it, and what do they get for their pains ? The question seems, to me, crucial for the whole of modern life, and I do not see the good of plunging into the systematic exposition of logic or ethics, psychology or theology, till it is answered.

Nor can I, even at the outset, conceal my suspicion that a philosophy of this kind—a philosophy of the forms of experience—is the only philosophy that can exist, and that all other philosophies are included in it. In the present state of opinion, I hesitate to acknowledge a belief in the possibility of a philosophical system, and to confess the crime of offering the reader, in the present volume, a crude sketch of such a system. I do not expect the critic to spare his blows : I only say ' strike, but hear me '. The hatred of systematic thought is not in my opinion a fault ; it is based on recognizing two important truths, first, that no system can ever be final, and secondly, that a coherent system is so difficult a thing to achieve that any one who claims to have achieved it is probably deceiving himself or others. I do not claim to have achieved it. I only confess that I am aiming at it as at a counsel of perfection, and that

I regard the deliberate renunciation of this ideal as the degradation of philosophy to a game, one of the most tedious and stupid of games.

This book is only an outline, and I have tried to reduce detail and sketch in my main forms as boldly and emphatically as possible, not sparing repetition of the essential points if I thought they could be usefully placed in a new light. The conventional limitations to the size of books have more effect upon the choice of their contents than readers are apt to imagine ; and the internal capacity of his expected guest imposes an absolute limit on the hospitality of any host. I would venture to dwell on the parallel. The reader is partaking of a meal set before him by the writer, and is bound to him by the tie of hospitality given and received. Let him be content to eat what is set before him in the order in which it appears, and not call for the cheese when the fish is being served, or complain of not being given three different entrées instead of the joint. The host has done his best for his guests' comfort. He has not wittingly flouted any one's taste, and wishes only to speak even his enemies fair, should they appear at his table. But he, and no one else, has the responsibility for choosing the viands and directing how they shall be served, and the reader is asked not to be offended if the writer's choice of arrangement and terminology differs from his own.

For arrangement, I have tried to make the subjects with which I have dealt arrange themselves in an order natural to them. For terminology, I have recognized one aim only, to write English that a well-disposed and intelligent reader will understand if he tries. No writer can protect himself against the verbal pedant who tears two sentences from their context and sets them together in the hope that, infuriated by the pain of transplantation, they will fall to fighting.

And it is my strong belief that a philosophy which cannot be written in plain terms, without reliance on the jargon of any school, must be a false philosophy. I have not avoided such jargon altogether, but I have seldom used it except with the intention of reminding the reader of some technicality as an illustration to my argument.

But I may here call attention to one or two words which, though I think my use of them is natural and correct, may be a stumbling-block to others beside the malicious. When I call a thing subjective I mean that it is or pertains to a subject or conscious mind. When I call it objective, I mean that it is or pertains to an object of which such a mind is conscious. I do not call a real rose objective and an imaginary one subjective, or the rose objective and its colour subjective, or the molecules in it objective and the beauty of it subjective. A real rose I call real, and an imaginary rose I call imaginary ; and I call them both objective because they are the objects of a perceiving and an imagining mind respectively. Similarly, the molecules are objective to a scientist and the beauty to an artist. Again, where formal logic uses the words judge, judgement, I have permitted myself, out of respect for English use, to substitute assert and assertion, or state and statement, where no confusion could result. Again, when I speak of a sensation, imagination, thought, or the like, I sometimes mean an object sensated, sometimes the act, habit or faculty of sensating it, and so on. If any critic is so unaccustomed to the English language that he finds himself confused by this usage, I can only commend him to the mercy of heaven. To suppose that one word, in whatever context it appears, ought to mean one thing and no more, argues not an exceptionally high standard of logical accuracy but an exceptional ignorance as to the nature of language.

It would be pleasant to attempt an acknowledgement of my debts, but this is a temptation which must be resisted. There is hardly any philosopher whom I have read from whom I am not conscious of having learnt something ; and indeed one learns what one has it in one to learn, not what one's teachers have it in them to teach. But whatever view of life is contained in this book has been acquired in the main neither from teachers nor from books, but in the course of working at things which are not called philosophy. Looking at pictures and reading books about them qualifies nobody for discussing the philosophy of art. For that, one must spend much time and trouble in the actual practice of the arts, or at least one of them, and learn to reflect on the experience so gained. The same applies to the other forms of thought which I have discussed in these chapters ; for to write a philosophical book is to write a commentary on human life, and a commentary compiled out of commentaries on an unread text is a thing of shame. I should like to be able to persuade the reader that the things I have said about this or that form of experience are not ingenious objections to theories but plain information as to where in one or other kind of life the shoe pinches. But then the stage philosopher who does nothing but sit and think is a person whom, if he exists, I have not met.

On the other hand, to write a commentary without consulting previous commentaries would argue not scholarship but ignorance, not sincerity but frivolity. And by greatly adding to the bulk of this volume I could easily have pointed out the affinities of my position with that of eminent writers past and present, and so, perhaps, have recommended it to readers who rightly shrink from any philosophy which is advertised as new. If I have consistently refrained from doing this it is only because I want my position to stand on its merits rather than on names of great men cited as witnesses for its defence. But if the reader feels that my thesis reminds him of things that other people have said, I shall not be disappointed : on the contrary, what will really disappoint me is to be treated as the vendor of new-fangled paradoxes and given some silly name like that of ' New Idealist '. I do not, with presumptuous mock-modesty, claim that the philosophy of this book is a poor thing but mine own. Rather, with what I hope is the arrogance of humility, I claim that it restates to the best of my power the essence, or what I take to be the essence, of every great philosopher's teaching. The bickerings of philosophical sects are an amusement for the foolish ; above these jarrings and creakings of the machine of thought there is a melody sung in unison by the spirits of the spheres, which are the great philosophers. This melody, *philosophia quaedam perennis*, is not a body of truth revealed once for all, but a living thought whose content, never discovered for the first time, is progressively determined and clarified by every genuine thinker. To have contributed anything substantial to that process I dare not claim ; but I at least know that by this test, and no other, the value of my work must be judged.

R. G. C.

Stapleton's Chantry,
North Moreton.
August, 1923.

I

PROLOGUE

ALL thought exists for the sake of action. We try to understand ourselves and our world only in order that we may learn how to live. The end of our self-knowledge is not the contemplation by enlightened intellects of their own mysterious nature, but the freer and more effectual self-revelation of that nature in a vigorous practical life. If thought were the mere discovery of interesting facts, its indulgence, in a world full of desperate evils and among men crushed beneath the burden of daily tasks too hard for their solitary strength, would be the act of a traitor : the philosopher would do better to follow the plough or clout shoes, to become a slum doctor or a police-court missionary, or hand himself over to a bacteriologist to be inoculated with tropical diseases.

Nor can we silence these reflections by arguing that the passion for truth, the desire to know, is planted in the human breast by Nature herself, and must be satisfied no less than the demand for food and clothing. The philosopher may try to defend his position by comparing himself with the producer of any commodity necessary to the health and decency of mankind ; but he knows very well that his thoughts are not quoted on the Stock Exchange along with corn and rubber, and that when he offers them to the world, the world is frankly uninterested. Except by professed students, his lectures are unattended and his books unread. If the great public cried out for philosophy as it does cry out for novels and cinematograph-shows, it could very soon get all it wanted. But the demand is not there, and the supply dissipates itself like an ' earthed ' electric current. The philosopher cannot justify his existence as the writer of popular novels can, by saying that he satisfies a need universally felt.

If the philosopher pipes to a generation that will not dance, he is in this not alone. Religion to-day is in much the same state. There is, thanks to our various communities and sects, a steady supply of religion laid before the public, and a supply so varied that one would expect all tastes to find satisfaction. But we actually see everywhere empty churches, or churches filled only by the popularity of a preacher or for some other personal reason, not because the religious principles for which they stand are such as give peace and consolation to the people who attend them. A man who devotes his life to religion, like one who devotes himself to philosophy, is offering wares in a market that cannot absorb them.

Nor is art, in spite of the popular novels, in a better state. Thousands of men and women are trying merely to live by artistic production, and failing. It is not that their work is bad, nor even that there is too much of it for the demand. The actual output of pictures and statues, poems and string quartets does not fail of its market because of its own low quality ; for the purchasers do not buy the best, because they have not the skill to distinguish it ; and any one who doubts this can prove it to himself by merely walking round an exhibition of pictures and observing which of them are marked with red seals. Nor are these things unpurchased because there are too many of them ; a rich man will spend in cigars alone a sum that would purchase the whole output of a promising young painter. But the rich man wants cigars, and he does not want pictures. He may buy old masters, Rembrandt etchings, Sheraton sideboards, and early Chinese porcelain, but why does he buy these, and not the work of his contemporaries? 'Because his contemporaries cannot turn out such good work as the old masters.' If this is true, is it relevant? If young Jones cannot etch as well as Rembrandt, is Sir Gorgius Midas so exquisitely sensitive to refinements of the etcher's art that he values the purely aesthetic superiority of a Rembrandt over a Jones at the difference between £1,000 and nothing? Every one knows that this is not so; and the disputes about the genuineness of 'antiques' are flagrant proof that the buyer does not buy old masters because they are masters, but because they are old. The craze for old masters is merely a symptom of the failure of modern artists to reach the ear of the public, and the correlative failure of the modern public to appreciate its artists.

Is this a peculiarity of our age, or was it always so? In part, it is a permanent and necessary feature of human life; but in part it is a special failing of our age. It has always been true that prophets are without honour in their own country; that the great man, when he appears, is more likely to be despised and rejected than to be crowned as king. This is inevitable, and one would not have it otherwise. A really great man does not take pleasure in admiration, except it be the admiration of those whom he respects as equals; he would not thank us if we offered him the adulation of all the contemporaries whose incapacity to judge his work is to him only too evident. There is in all greatness something forbidding and inimical to the small, and all great men have their enemies. It is only after many days that mankind resolves upon canonizing them and enters their names on the roll of those who may be invoked and must not be criticized. It is only of the dead that nothing is spoken but good.

Great men can look after themselves. We are rather concerned with the journeymen labourers in the fields of art and religion and philosophy. It is these who in our age seem out of touch with the world, unable to give the public what it wants. And this is a new and a serious matter. We are apt to defend our present inattention to art, to religion, to philosophy, by bewailing the present lack of great men. Ours, we say, is an age of little men : how can we care for their work ? Our little poets—how can we have patience with them ? Send us another Keats, and we will listen. Good sirs, if the soul of Keats could be re-embodied upon earth, you would treat him as your fathers treated him before. You have learned by now to like his Odes ; but if he came to earth again he would not repeat them, but write something as far in advance of this age as his Odes were in advance of that. The lack of great men, if it is true that we lack great men, is no excuse for our lack of interest in art, for a great man is never recognized by his generation for what he is, and is accepted only because he—for instance —writes plays in a generation that cares for plays, not because he is William Shakespeare. Indeed, this harping upon great men is simply a parrot-cry designed by indolence and folly as a defence against the humiliation of self-knowledge and a means of evading responsibilities. We are tempted to regard the great man as a miracle sent by Heaven to extricate us from sloughs in which, till he appears, we may wallow at our ease, cursing God for not sending us a great man to pull us out, but in the meantime doing nothing towards climbing out by ourselves. If God does not send us great men, we may be sure that it is only because we do not deserve them ; in other words, because we have made ourselves a world in which no great man could reach maturity and keep his greatness unimpaired. The greatest painter will not do much for modern art if you keep him all his life in a coal-mine ; the greatest philosopher will not go far towards teaching you the truth if you blow him to pieces with a shell at the age of twenty.

Our concern is therefore with the ordinary artists, the ordinary ministers of religion and students of philosophy, who exist among us in great plenty and yet fail to justify, in the world's eyes, their very existence. These people are not incompetent or insincere or vicious as a class ; they include men and women of every degree of virtue and ability ; yet they fail, and fail with a thoroughness which is a new thing in the world's history. The general public, and that class of rich people whose taste on the whole faithfully represents that of the general public, is not apathetic in matters of taste. It is keenly and wholesomely interested in football and racing, business and wages, even politics. But in art and religion and philosophy it is not interested, and for the people who practise them it cares not a straw. It is not moved to excitement by news of an event in the world of painting or of metaphysics, as it is by a new idea in the technique of Rugby football or a move-ment of prices. We do not say this in any spirit of con-tempt. The man who despises the poor for their interest in football or the rich for their interest in grouse-shooting is a man whose opinion on any important subject is likely to be worthless. We say it because it is a fact which we are concerned to analyse. For it is a new fact. It was not so when young men of every degree crowded to Oxford to hear Duns Scotus, or when Cimabue's Madonna went through the streets of Florence, or even when London society fell to quarrelling about the merits of Handel and Buononcini.

But the great public is not really indifferent either to art, or to religion, or to philosophy. Everybody wants a pretty house to live in, pleasant furniture and crockery to put in it, and nice clothes to wear. Everybody wants to see his public-house and his town-hall well built and handsomely decorated. Everybody wants some faith that will guide him in his difficulties, support him in his temptations, and comfort him in his sorrows. And everybody wants some answer to the riddles and mysteries that beset him on every side, some reply to the question whence he comes, whither he goes, and what he is. These are permanent needs of mankind, and our age is not free from them : or why do the rich spend great sums of money on pictures and ornaments, and why is the cult of spiritualism and exotic religions a very disease of society ? The demand for art, religion, philosophy, is a real thing to-day, as real as ever it was. Nor is it a demand incapable of at least partial and provisional satisfaction ; men have surrounded themselves with beauty, they have found peace in God, they have come appreciably nearer to a solution of the world's mystery. Art and religion and philosophy are not vain quests, they are normal activities of the human mind.

This is the special problem of modern life. On the one hand, there is an unsatisfied demand for art, religion, and philosophy. On the other, there is a crowd of artists, philosophers, and ministers of religion who can find no market for their wares. Every street and every village in the country contains people who are hungering for beauty, for faith, for knowledge, and cannot find these things. And those who have them are starving for mere bread, because no one will buy. The producers and the consumers of spiritual wealth are out of touch ; the bridge between them is broken and only a daring spirit here and there can leap the gulf. If one of the consumers finds his want intolerable, he can satisfy it, no doubt ; he can win scholarships and go to universities and schools of art to the admiration of those who believe in education as an end in itself ; but he has only escaped one horn of the dilemma to be impaled on the other. He has satisfied his soul's desire, and it only remains for him to starve in a Chelsea attic or a slum curacy, with the knowledge that he is perfectly useless to those whom he left in his village at home. He has merely joined the class of unwanted producers.

This coexistence of overproduction on the one side with unsatisfied demand on the other I have ventured to call the special problem of modern life. Our age is often accused of superficiality and shallowness. It is significant that those who so accuse it are precisely those at whose piping it will not dance. They reveal to it their own magnificent plans for its betterment, and it brushes them aside : they implore it to behave in this or that way, and it persists in its old courses. This is enough to annoy any prophet ; but a prophet scolding to empty benches is not an edifying sight, and one may be forgiven for suspecting that the fault lies, at least in part, with the prophet himself. An engineer whose engine will not go does not plead that Nature's stores of energy are exhausted ; but the social reformer who cannot get society to obey him is too ready to explain the fact by accusing his age of spiritual poverty. He ought to know better. He ought to know—or his licence as a prophet ought to be taken away—that the spiritual energy pent up within the breast of his own boot-and-knife boy is enough to overthrow empires if the word were spoken that released it. Our age suffers from no lack of spiritual energy. We are as capable of shunning delights and living laborious days as the subjects of Elizabeth or Pericles ; we have been nursed upon the self-same hill with men who have proved, not by argument but by action, that honour and duty, courage and endurance to death are not gone from us. There is no degeneracy in the human breed as yet, for all the rantings of our unsuccessful reformers.

And yet the fault is not all the prophet's. He is the son of his age ; and a generation that produces crazy prophets must be a crazy generation. Every one knows that our civilization is in difficulties, and the stupidity of the suggested remedies only indicates the gravity of the disease, for a sick society has to diagnose and cure its own complaint, and the worse the complaint, the wilder the diagnosis is likely to be. But no one denies the disease. On this our philosopher-novelists, our politician-divines, our Utopia-mongers and religious revivalists, are agreed. One sect thinks we shall be well if we redistribute our property ; another, if we are married by professors instead of priests ; another, if we stop drinking wine or eating meat ; another, if we abolish machinery or war ; and there is always, by healthy reaction against all these proposals, a party which maintains that the disease is better than any suggested cure. But every one agrees that our present condition is, in some peculiar way, a morbid one.

Is this general belief a mere illusion ? Is our disease nothing but the fitful fever of life itself, that fever from which all must suffer and for which there is only and always a cure in death ? To many critics of our civilization one is tempted to answer that this is so ; that they are seeking to abolish things which are a necessary part of our human lot, evils bound up with our very life. And against any one who thinks that socialism would destroy avarice, or that the abolition of war would put an end to the cruel waste of human lives, this retort would hold good. But there remains a difference between our age and earlier ages, a special *maladie du siècle* which is endemic among us and which we can detect if we compare our own society with that of former times. If, for instance, we turn to the middle ages and ask what was the most striking feature of their life, we shall reply that medieval life was altogether governed by the idea of institutions. The individual counted for nothing except as the member of his guild, his church, his monastic order, his feudal hierarchy. Within these institutions he found a place where he was wanted, work for him to do, a market for his wares. He could devote himself to fulfilling the duties assigned him by his station in this great organism within which he found himself lodged ; these duties occupied his whole energy and his whole life, and thus the institution acted as the safeguard of the individual's utility and happiness. In saying this we do not idealize medieval life or hold it free from defect. We do not forget either the corruptions to which these institutions too often succumbed, their tendency to level downwards, or the hideous fate of those adventurous souls who found their limits too narrow. But the very tendency to level downwards, the very narrowness of medieval institutionalism, secured one great benefit, namely the happiness of those humble ordinary men and women who ask not for adventure or excitement, but for a place in the world where they shall feel themselves usefully and congenially employed.

The men of the middle ages, as we look back on them, appear to us half children and half giants. In the narrowness of their outlook, the smallness of the problems they faced, their fanciful and innocent superstition, their combination of qualities and activities which a reflective or critical society would find intolerably contradictory, they are children, and it is difficult for us to believe that human beings could be so simple. But in the solid magnitude of their achievements, their systems of law and philosophy, their creation and organization of huge nation-states, their incredible cathedrals, and above all their gradual forging of a civilized world out of a chaos of barbarism, they seem possessed by a tenacity and a vastness of purpose that we can only call gigantic. They seem to be tiny people doing colossal things.

The secret of the medieval achievement is undoubtedly connected with the medieval institutionalism. Cathedrals could be built because there were guilds to do it ; because men interested in building organized themselves into a body where work could be parcelled out among competent workers and where the continuity of tradition and the community of training guaranteed that these would not work at cross-purposes. Such guilds, as executive bodies, were called upon to do whatever work in their line was required : as schools, they gave his training to every young man who wished to practise a given craft. Hence the training of workers and the production of works were always, through the agency of the guild, kept in touch with the requirements of the market, and supply and demand balanced each other. The same principle held good outside the guilds. A man who wished to paint could devote himself to painting miniatures in his own monastery ; his work was valued there, and he could live his life as a painter in the knowledge that what he was doing was of use to his world. The systems of land tenure and military and ecclesiastical service were essentially the same. In every case there was an organization which gave the individual his place and duties, told him what to do and—in a rough and ready way, perhaps—looked after him so long as he did it. And the great thing about these medieval institutions is that they actually did find room for good men doing good work, work which endures in stone and on parchment, and in the fabric of our own life and thought.

Now there is no truer and more abiding happiness than the knowledge that one is free to go on doing, day by day, the best work one can do, in the kind one likes best, and that this work is absorbed by a steady market and thus supports one's own life. The man who is rich enough to work unnoticed and unrewarded is by comparison a savage; the man who can only do his own work by stealth when he has won his daily bread elsewhere is a slave. Perfect freedom is reserved for the man who lives by his own work and in that work does what he wants to do. But this freedom and happiness were in principle at least the lot of every one in the middle ages; and to what extent they were actually achieved by no small number of workers we can see when we look at the work they have left behind them. For these works breathe visibly the air of a perfect freedom and a perfect happiness. Chaucer and Dante are no shallow optimists, but their tragedies are discords perpetually resolved in the harmony of a celestial music. The fundamental thing in Chaucer is the ' mery tale ' of human life as a heartening and lovely pageant, diversified with all the adventures that befall upon the course

> Of thilke parfit glorious pilgrimage
> That highte Jerusalem celestial;

the fundamental thing in Dante is not mere human fortitude, the ' gran dispitto ' of Farinata, but

> l' amor che move il sole e l' altre stelle.

The medieval mind feels itself surrounded, beyond the sphere of trial and danger, by a great peace, an infinite happiness. This feeling, so clear in the poets, is equally clear, to those who have eyes to see, in the illuminations of a missal and the detail of stonework, in the towers of Durham and the Vine window at Wells.

But this happiness, characteristically present in the

medieval mind, is characteristically absent from the modern. And if our art, our religion, our philosophy, are dark with foreboding and comfortless in their message, this is not altogether unconnected with the fact that the medieval man could be happy because his church or guild told him what to do and could give him work that he liked ; while the modern man is unhappy because he does not know what to do. One wishes to be an artist, but there is nothing for him to do as an artist except to paint pictures that nobody wants. Another wishes to devote his life to religion or philosophy, and he can only preach sermons to which no one will listen or write books that no one will buy. In the middle ages the first would have worked happily at missals or churches, the second would have passed his life in prayer and meditation, the third would have helped in some nascent university to create that medieval logic which is still the background of all our speech and thought. This fact is so obvious that some of our social physicians are all for reverting to a medieval institutionalism and entrusting our welfare to a system of guilds or a great international Catholic church or the like, thinking that our individualism is the root of our troubles. This is an error. Individualism is a symptom, not a cause ; and the middle ages enjoyed that degree of happiness and success that was theirs, not because of their institutionalism, but because of something they possessed which made institutionalism workable. And it is not difficult to see that the medieval man could only obey his institution because of the childishness that was in his disposition ; that it would be useless to reimpose the medieval institutionalism on the modern world, because the modern man would always be wanting to go his own way in spite of his station and its duties.

The medieval man acquiesced in his institutionalism

because he had firm hold on a principle which we may call
the unity of the mind. No mental activity, for him, existed
in its own right and for itself. Art was always working hand
in hand with religion, religion hand in hand with philosophy.
This is sometimes expressed by saying that art and philosophy were subordinated to religion ; but the subordination
was not, as this phrase suggests, one-sided. Art was the
handmaid of religion, but religion by this very fact acquired
an intensely artistic character. Philosophy was ostensibly
subordinated to faith ; but this gave not only a religious
tinge to philosophy but a philosophical tinge to religion.
Thus religion was coloured by art and philosophy to the
same extent to which they were coloured by religion, the
fact being that there was a general interpenetration of
the various activities of the mind, in which each was
influenced by all.

If art and religion are conceived as separate activities, it
will follow that religious art is a peculiar form of art, differing
in certain specifiable ways from art pure and simple. In
the modern world this is so. A church is built in a style of
its own, and an architect accustomed to working on secular
buildings has to tune his mind to a wholly different key if
he begins designing a church. So religious paintings and
secular paintings follow different conventions, and we are
shocked, without understanding why, when we see a sacred
picture which the artist has treated in a secular style. In
the middle ages all this was unknown. The Gothic style of
churches was the Gothic style of the house and the castle ;
it was simply everyday architecture turned to the construction of one building instead of another. So in the
missal-paintings what we should call sacred and secular
subjects are inextricably blended ; the fact being that the
artist never contemplated the existence of the distinction

which to us is so real. All art was religious art, or, what comes to the same thing, all art was secular art ; there was no special kind of art used for religious purposes, because there was no feeling that these purposes stood by themselves.

The same is true of philosophy. Nowadays we hear of something called ' religious philosophy ', and we distinguish one kind of philosophy as dealing with religious subjects or questions from another which does not. We accustom ourselves to think in a special way when our philosophy concerns religion, and regard theism as a kind of Sunday philosophy as opposed to other, week-day, theories of the universe. And if we required theological students to take a course in philosophy, we should prescribe a theistic philosophy and pass hastily over the others, even if we did nothing so crude as to enter them on an *index expurgatorius.* But to the middle ages it did not occur as a possibility that there could be a distinction between a Sunday and a week-day philosophy. All philosophy was felt to be equally concerned with religion, and the philosophy officially used by the church for its own purpose was selected for that purpose not as having a specially religious tendency but as being the best philosophy on the market.

Thus the medieval church had the advantage of being able to use the best philosophy and the best art for its own purposes, and was not limited to employing in its service those philosophers who specialized in ' religious philosophy ' or those artists who specialized in ' ecclesiastical art '. And because these specialist philosophers and artists are neces- sarily bad philosophers and bad artists—since philosophy and art can only be good when they are just philosophy and art unqualified by any specialization—it follows that the medieval church was well served by both philosophers and artists, with mutual profit. The church got the benefit of service by the best men of their age, and the men got the benefit of working for an institution which encouraged them to do their best work and guaranteed a market for it.

This was in its way a happy state of things, especially by contrast with our modern world. But it was only possible by reason of what we have called the childishness of medieval man. Art, religion, and philosophy are not really the same thing : there are differences between them which need not appear as long as they are at a comparatively low level of development, but appear all too sharply when they reach maturity. At first it may seem possible to be at the same time perfectly artistic and perfectly religious ; but if you develop these two tendencies as fully as you can, if you aim at ever deepening and intensifying both your religious life and your artistic life, you will sooner or later come to the parting of the ways and find that you can be one but not both. The monastery is an excellent place for primitive art ; but the art of the monastery can never be more than primitive. And when the artistic mind of a race has perfected its primitive art, a crisis will come when either the progress of art or its connexion with the monastery must cease. Either the art must remain within the monastery, cramped into a permanent primitiveness, or it must follow its own bent, break away from its old surroundings, and mark its maturity by asserting its independence. In the same way, a primitive philosophy may develop as it were in the womb of religion ; but when it is full grown the very power of thought will bring it to the birth and philosophy will part from religion as the child parts from its mother. Only if the power of thought fails, if the unborn child dies in the womb of its dead mother, will the birth never take place. It is the very success of the first phase in producing a healthy and progressive life in art, religion, and philosophy, that ensures the coming of the moment when they must separate and go each its own way.

In our own history we call this separation the Renaissance. It did not happen all at once ; it was long brewing, and its premonitory tremors were felt throughout the middle ages. But these tremors did not overthrow the medieval compromise, they rather stimulated men to hold more firmly by it, and thus the greatest work of the medieval mind was accomplished, as we can now see, after the death-warrant of medievalism had gone forth. The art, the religion, and the philosophy of the middle ages were all alike tinged with childishness ; primitive, immature. But the medieval mind was a healthy and progressive organism, and its very progress brought it to a point at which these tendencies came into conflict with one another. Art struggled to be free of religion, to come out of the cloister and work for its own hand. Thought claimed for itself the same right, the right to follow its own ideal of truth careless of all else. Religion too demanded its freedom, its separation from art and thought, its recognition as a world to itself. Freedom, the watchword of the Renaissance, meant freedom for all the different activities of the mind from interference by each other. Freedom in this sense means separation, the severance from each other of all man's various interests. It is the exact opposite of the medieval unity of the mind, the interdependence of all these interests. But we saw that the middle ages too had their freedom ; the freedom of occupying an ordained place which one desires to occupy and finds happiness in occupying. This is a freedom in which there is no conflict, a positive freedom, like the freedom of a child at play. The freedom of the Renaissance is the freedom of discovering that one can leave one's ordained place and march out into the world without being struck dead by an offended God. But God is offended ; that is to say, one has bought freedom at the price of an internal conflict, a conflict between the self that wants to wander and the self that wants to stay at home, the artistic self, it may be, and the religious self. The freedom of the Renaissance is a negative freedom, the freedom to outrage one's own nature : it is that impulse of which it is written

> We all possess,
> Like rats that ravin down their proper bane,
> A thirsty evil : and when we drink, we die.

This negativity or conflict with itself is characteristic of the Renaissance and all its fruits. It wins its freedom, but at the price of its peace. In religion, it gives rise to the Reformation with its puritanical and philistinic attitude to art and to thought. The religions of the Reformation set themselves free from art by destroying its works, and from philosophy by banishing it from their presence ; the tendency of puritanism was to make religion an ugly thing and a stupid thing, a thing for the ignorant and the insensitive. The same tendency is hardly less evident in the catholicism of the counter-reformation. This was not all loss ; far from it ; in this violent divorce from art and thought, religion attained a pitch of purely religious intensity quite unknown to the middle ages. Our own puritans may have done permanent and incalculable damage to English art, but when it came to religion they had the root of the matter in them and undoubtedly surpassed the achievement of their medieval ancestors. Similarly, art declared its independence, and went so far, in its instinctive reaction against religion, as to play at reverting to paganism. It did not believe in paganism, but merely used this fashion to express its new-found freedom from all religious connexions. Art became definitely irreligious ; but in this moment it suddenly shot up to a stature previously unimagined, and gave birth all at once to a galaxy of artists whose very names, repeated in a catalogue, make us wonder whether the men of that age can have belonged to the same species with ourselves. Yet these men, without any exception, show in their greatest work the signs of the struggle which their liberty has entailed. Supreme as artists, they know that other claims than those of art press menacingly upon them, and these claims appear in the form of a brooding tragedy that overshadows all their work. To the medieval artist, as we saw, the terror of the world is dissolved in wonder, and fear is but an eddy on the surface of joy ; but the artist of the Renaissance, like him of ancient Greece, peers into a darkness that no eye can penetrate, and is happy only by defying his despair. Nothing is more typical of the Renaissance than the quality of its laughter : the way in which for Shakespeare the dreadfulness of life lurks among the rose leaves of the lightest comedy, or the way in which Molière jokes like a man who watches himself dying by inches and has nothing left to do but laugh at his ridiculous body.

The middle ages thus represent, in their spiritual life, a mind content with its lot, at peace with itself, growing in sun and shower like a tree, hardly seeking ' to know the law whereby it prospers so ' ; the Renaissance represents the same mind coming to a new consciousness of the depth and seriousness of life, realizing that it must choose its vocation, making its choice and thus breaking with the easy life of compromise when it could be in fancy, like a dreaming boy, everything at once. Henceforth all is disunion. Priests and artists and scientists no longer live together peaceably, either uniting these functions in one single individual or at least combining them without thought of friction in a single social organism ; it is now a war of all against all, art against

philosophy and both against religion. Henceforth no man
can serve two masters ; he must give his whole soul to art,
or to religion, or to philosophy, and in choosing his friends
he chooses at the same time his enemies.

Hence arises a curious result. In point of fact, religion
cannot live without art and science. There must be churches
and theologies, and therefore religion must employ both
artists and philosophers. But now that art and philosophy
have parted from religion and gone their own irreligious way,
she can no longer employ them. Only one course is open
to her. She must go back instead of forwards, and use the
art and philosophy of the days before the rupture took place.
Hence when modern religion woke up to the need of in-
corporating art and philosophy into its own organism, it
saw that the contemporary artists and philosophers had
nothing that it could use ; and therefore it invented neo-
Gothic and neo-Scholasticism. This tendency is common
to all our sects ; and it is strange and pathetic to see chapels
of all kinds being built to-day in the fashion of the time when
their sect was born, as if to proclaim to the world their
inability to live either with art or without it. This might
suggest that there is something especially feeble and inverte-
brate about modern religion, incapable as it certainly is of
marching with the advance of art and thought as it marched
in the middle ages. But the failure of religion to make use
of modern art is only correlative to the failure of modern
art to make use of modern religion, and the failure of both
to recommend themselves to the general public. The church
of England affects Gothic because it is old, and the rich man
buys old masters because they are old : modern art is
equally useless to both, and in neither case is one side solely
or especially to blame. They are all suffering alike from the
after-effects of the Renaissance.

C

In the first flush of that dawn, when art, religion, and thought, strengthened by their long medieval discipline of intimacy with each other, broke apart and suddenly began to work miracles, men might be excused for thinking that in their mutual separation lay the secret of their well-being. But the contrary soon appeared. Each, cut off from the others, tended more and more to lead its followers into some desert where the world of human life was lost, and the very motive for going on disappeared. Each tended to become a specialized activity pursued by specialists for the applause of specialists, useless to the rest of mankind and unsatisfying even to the specialist when he turned upon himself and asked why he was pursuing it. This is the point to which we have come to-day. The churches, we are told, have lost touch with the people. It is true ; and it cannot be mended either by scolding the people or by abusing the priests. The artists have lost touch with the people, too ; they work for each other in a vicious circle of academicism which only becomes more academic when it breaks down old conventions and sets up new. This again cannot be cured by extension lectures or by ' arts and crafts ' exhibitions, or by holding up modern art to ridicule. It is only a symptom. The philosophers have lost touch with the people so egregiously that it is hardly worth while insisting on the point, except to remark that it cannot be mended by manufacturing cheap adulterated philosophies to tickle the public taste. And all alike are asking themselves what use they are in the world, and whether they had not better give everything up and start a poultry-farm.

This is the fruit of the Renaissance. If the artist, or the priest, or the philosopher complains, we can only answer ' tu l'as voulu, George Dandin '. He demanded freedom, and he has got it. He wanted a real separation, art for art's sake, truth for truth's sake, religion for religion's sake, each free from all claims on the part of the rest ; and now the freedom has come home to roost, in the form of that disruption of life which we analysed at the beginning.   In the middle ages the artist was perhaps not much of an artist, the philosopher was by our standards only mildly philoso-phical, and the religious man not extremely religious ; but they were all men, whole of heart and secure in their grasp on life. To-day we can be as artistic, we can be as philoso-phical, we can be as religious as we please, but we cannot ever be men at all ; we are wrecks and fragments of men, and we do not know where to take hold of life and how to begin looking for the happiness which we know we do not possess.

In this state of things we are sufficiently justified in turning an eager ear to any one who promises to show us the way out of our troubles.   Indeed, we are justified in asking every teacher and preacher whether he can help us, and going our ways if he cannot.   We can hardly be wrong in refusing to listen to anybody, on any subject, unless he can hold out some hope of bettering our condition.   Hence we may repeat that all thought is for the sake of action, and that every one who offers us a philosophy must answer the question ' what shall we do to be saved from these present distresses ? '

This book does not profess to give an answer ready made. But it does profess to ' explore the avenues ', as politicians say, towards a possible answer.   Some people, whose voice is so sweet that we can hardly refuse them audience, assure us that in the life of art, and there alone, we can find happi-ness and salvation.   Others, men of wisdom and authority, say the same of religion ;   and others, whose gospel is supported by the cogent argument of miracle, say the same of science. From all these we shall find ourselves compelled, with whatever reluctance and respect, to dissent. And we shall dissent no less from advocates of history or philosophy or any other form of experience whose adoption means the denial of some other form. For we now recognize the nature of our disease. What is wrong with us is precisely the detachment of these forms of experience—art, religion, and the rest—from one another ; and our cure can only be their reunion in a complete and undivided life. Our task is to seek for that life, to build up the conception of an activity which is at once art, and religion, and science, and the rest.

In a sense, that is to say, we demand that the work of the Renaissance shall be undone, and that the middle ages should be brought back. But bringing back the past cannot solve the problems of the spirit. The advance from the middle ages to the Renaissance was a real advance ; tendencies that struggled obscurely in the depths of the medieval mind were in the Renaissance set free and blossomed gloriously. If we went back to the middle ages, we should only return to childhood, and the throes of adolescence would still be to come. The middle ages died because their union of the various claims was too hasty, too much of a compromise. If we are to achieve any kind of union again, that only will satisfy us in which the full development of art, of religion, and of philosophy is possible ; no mere medieval compromise, but the full-grown life of a Titian, a Luther, and a Descartes, all attained within the limits of a single corporate mind as truly unified as ever was that of the middle ages.

There is nothing new about this answer. It is the fundamental principle of Christianity that the only life worth living is the life of the whole man, every faculty of body and soul unified into a single organic system. Incarnation, redemption, resurrection of the body, only repeat this cardinal idea from different angles. Again, it is the outer aspect of this same principle on which Christianity insists when it teaches that the individual man, just because of the absolute worth of every individual, is nothing without his fellow men ; that the holy spirit lives not in this man or that but in the church as the unity of all faithful people. It was thus in their institutionalism and their insistence on the unity of the mind—outer and inner sides of the same truth—that the middle ages were distinctively Christian ; and it was just this Christianity that, as we have already seen, made giants of men who taken singly were children. In the denial of this double principle, and the assertion of its opposite, an outer individualism coupled with an inner separatism of the activities of the mind, the Renaissance rebelled not against medievalism so much as against Christianity, and reverted to the pagan ideal. For the separatist principle is the principle embodied in the pagan world and idealized in the pagan philosophies ; whether it takes the form of slavery or the doctrine of the immortality of the soul, whether it appears as a practice of religion in which divine worship is a duty to be discharged and done with, or as a theory of art in which pity and fear are emotions to be got rid of, when they become troublesome, by attending a tragedy. For the Christian, as never for any pagan, religion becomes an influence dominating the whole of life ; and this unity of life once achieved can never be forfeited again. No one who has outgrown the ancient paganism can be content with being everything by turns and nothing long ; he must unify his life somehow, either positively, by bringing every activity into harmony, or negatively, by suppressing all but one. The former was the medieval way, the latter that of the Renaissance. And thus the return to paganism was really an illusion ; it was not paganism, not a real destruction of the Christian unity, that the Renaissance achieved, but only a kind of desperate Christianity, the Christianity of the plucked-out eye and the lopped-off limb.

Our solution, then, can only be in principle the Christian solution ; but it must not be the naïve Christianity of the middle ages or the self-mutilated Christianity of the Renaissance, but something in which the good of both these is preserved, the bad destroyed. And even this is not a new ideal. Ever since the negative aspect of the Renaissance culminated in the eighteenth century, it has been clear that some kind of revived medievalism, some new interpretation of Christianity, was the only hope for the world's future. The Romantic movement which enshrined that new belief made itself a little ridiculous by its assumption that everything medieval was good and everything else bad ; that was the mere swing of the pendulum from the exaggerated respect for pagan antiquity that had marked the Renaissance. But we here claim no more than to be following and working out the tradition founded over a century ago by the great men of the Romantic movement ; purifying it, perhaps, of some things that are worthless to-day, but happy if we can attain anything like the clearness of vision and closeness of thought which they attained, and anxious above all not to pose as repositories of a new revelation, or vendors of any new-fangled philosophical patent-medicine, but to say once more, in words suited to our generation, something that everybody has always known.

II

SPECULUM MENTIS

Our task, then, is the construction of a map of knowledge.

We have already seen, in our preliminary survey, how the field of human experience seems to be divided into provinces which we call art, religion, science, and so forth. How many such provinces there are we do not yet know ; what their relations to one another may be we cannot tell until our map is made. But here we beg leave to make certain assumptions, to be tested, and, as far as may be, justified in the course of our inquiry. First, we shall distinguish the provinces of art, religion, science, history, and philosophy. Secondly, we shall assume that each of these is no mere abstraction but a concrete form of experience, an activity of the whole self in which every faculty, if it is permissible to distinguish between faculties, is engaged. Thirdly, because each is a concrete activity it follows that each is in some sense a kind of knowledge, an activity of the cognitive mind.

The first assumption is of little importance : the number of provinces may be augmented or decreased without affecting our fundamental questions. The second is no more than a refusal, until good reason can be shown, to commit ourselves to the schematism of a faculty-psychology. The third is the vital point. And on this point we must begin by observing that every one of our forms of experience, whatever hostile critics say about it, makes for itself the unequivocal claim to be knowledge. Even art claims truth : a truth identified indeed with beauty but not thereby ceasing to be truth. At times we seem to find in art the one and

only key to the riddle of the universe, the sole true revelation
of the mystery whose concealment is the perennial torture
of the human intellect. The great artists are unanimous in
so regarding art. For them, and for every one whose
experience of beauty whether in art or nature has attained
any kind of depth, the emotional aspect of that experience
is a mere troubling of the surface, an eddy which may or
may not serve to indicate a deep and rapid current : no
more an argument for a hedonistic theory of art than the
mathematician's joy in discovering a new truth justifies
a hedonistic theory of mathematics. Such is at bottom the
attitude towards art of every one whose opinion is worth
taking. It is our business to examine it critically and see
to what extent, in what sense, subject to what reservations,
it justifies itself.

Of religion the same thing is more obviously true. Every
religion claims to tell us something which is not only true
but supremely true, something that lets us into the secret
of the universe. It does other things besides this ; here, as
in art, there are practical and emotional elements ; but this
at least it does. It is the mere recklessness of a disappointed
intellectualism that drives the student of religion to overlook
this claim and to analyse religion as a complex of moral or
emotional contents, a thing of ' the will ' or ' the feelings '
to the exclusion of ' the intellect '. Such analysis is always
in conflict with the view of religion maintained by religion
itself, for that view invariably bases itself on the claim to
truth. After the conflict between religion and science or
philosophy has arisen, and under the influence of the conviction that the truth must lie with science or philosophy,
attempts at such analysis are inevitable ; but they are the
fruit of a sophistication in which the religious attitude itself
has been lost to sight. While that attitude is preserved,

or even vividly remembered, it is impossible to deny that
the heart of all religion is the claim to truth. Here again
we are but quoting the opinion of those whose opinion is
worth quoting : to criticize and qualify it is the task of our
own inquiries.

That science claims to be true will hardly be denied by
any one ; yet here, as in the case of art and religion, the
claim, though admittedly made, is frequently challenged.
And this applies also to history and to philosophy. All
these are believed by those who are engaged in them to afford
truth and indeed absolute truth concerning the nature of
reality ; but each is accused by its critics of being something quite different from this, science a mere form of
practice, history a *fable convenue*, philosophy the exuberance
of a mental intoxication. And here again, our task is to
face these criticisms and see how far and in what ways they
can establish a case against the *prima facie* claim to truth
made by each type of experience in turn.

At the outset, then, we find no less than five types of
experience, each claiming not only to give truth, but to give
the absolute or ultimate truth concerning the nature of the
universe, to reveal the secret of existence, and to tell us
what the world really and fundamentally is. But surely
there is in the last resort only one world, and there can be
only one type of theoretical activity which is really adapted
to solve the problem of its ultimate nature: If the artist is
right, if ' Beauty is truth, truth beauty ', if the world truly
is what the artist believes it to be, then it is true that ' the
rest may reason, and welcome ; 'tis we musicians know '.
The secret of the universe is hidden from the scientist and
the philosopher, to be revealed exclusively to the artist.
Similarly, if religion is right, and if God is the answer to
every question, then art and science are barren quests. If

science is right, if the truth of the world is to be found in
the laws of nature, art and religion are toys. history and
philosophy vain delusions. And so on.

Thus the different forms of experience seem to be competitors for one prize, the prize of truth. Now a prize can be
dealt with in three ways. It can be given to one competitor
and denied to the others. It can be divided between two
or more of the competitors. Or it can be not awarded at all.
So it may be suggested, as the answer to our present problem,
that one of the five forms is the one which gives us real
knowledge : that each gives one type of real knowledge :
or that all are delusions.

We will take the third alternative first. If all the forms
of so-called knowledge are delusive, if the prize is not
awarded, we must reflect that in such a competition as this
an unawarded prize falls to the judge, and that therefore
his refusal to award it is likely to result from a desire to
keep it for himself. In other words, we are asking for a type
of experience capable of giving true knowledge. Now to
say that there is no such type is to imply that one *knows*
both what knowledge would be if it existed, and that it does
not exist. But this is to claim for oneself the possession of
that very knowledge whose existence one is explicitly
denying. That form of experience, therefore, which denies
truth to all the five recognized forms claims to be itself
a sixth form which is the rightful claimant to truth. Hence
the refusal to allot the prize stultifies itself.

But if one of the forms is the true form, how are we to
discover it ? Any one whom we ask will no doubt give us
a reply : the artist will vote for art, the scientist for science,
and so on. And if we say to the artist, ' This is mere professional prejudice ; you vote for art because you are an
artist,' he will reply, ' On the contrary, I choose to be an

artist because I believe art to be the true form of knowledge and the rest illusions '. Every answer that can be given will be vitiated by the suspicion which inevitably arises from the fact that every competitor votes for himself : he does so automatically : he votes for himself by just being himself, for to embrace a particular form of experience and to believe in its validity are the same thing. It is all very well to ask for an impartial judge ; there are no impartial judges. The scientist can judge between art and religion, but only because he condemns both impartially and claims for himself the prize for which they are fighting : the philosopher offers to arbitrate between all the rest put together, but his reign, every one knows, will be that of King Stork. We must have an impartial decision, but no one is qualified to give it.

But even supposing it were given, it would satisfy nobody. Suppose it could be settled that science (say) was true and that all the other forms were errors. This would not satisfy art or religion. For it would not explain them ; it would not show why anybody had adopted such errors. The judge in this competition has not only to allot the prize, he has to account for the existence of the unsuccessful competitors, and this is a very different matter from the mere prize-giving, which if all else fails can be done at the bidding of caprice, prejudice, or bribery.

These difficulties can only be overcome if the judge is himself entitled to speak in defence, and therefore in criticism, of the various forms of experience in turn. The word of a scientist condemning art is worthless ; but the word of a scientist who is also an artist, comparing these two forms of experience from within, is of extreme value. The only slur on its value is the suspicion that in trying to serve two masters, science and art, he is not whole-heartedly committed to either and therefore not fully entitled to speak for those whose entire life is absorbed by one or other activity. This again can be partly overcome if he has spent a definite portion of his life in the specialized cultivation of one activity, if he has been an artist in such a sense as to be acquainted with the life of art not as a relaxation or amusement but as a discipline. If the person to whom is committed the task of judging between art, religion, science, history, and philosophy can prove to us that he has lived these lives for himself, has graduated successively in each of these schools, then we shall listen with respect to his opinion.

Even then, however, it remains a mere opinion. A man may say that he has lived in five countries, and that England is his favourite ; but that choice binds nobody but himself. If he is to show that his choice of a form of experience is not capricious but is a lead which other people ought to follow, he must vindicate the rationality of his choice. He must prove that the choice is inevitable, and that each of the other forms in turn has characteristics which drive him on to the one in which alone he claims to find satisfaction. Now the characteristic mark by which a form of experience is shown to be satisfactory is simply that it is possible. We ask only for a life that can be lived, a programme that can be carried out. Art, science and the rest are schemes of life by adopting which we are promised happiness and truth. Any scheme which is in itself contradictory or nonsensical cannot redeem these promises, because it cannot be put into execution ; but if there is any scheme of life which is inherently consistent and therefore, ideally speaking, practicable, we may safely assume that this is the scheme to adopt.

Self-consistency, then, is our test. It might be suggested

that a better test is suitability to our human nature or the facts of the world ; but this is a mistake, because we are raising the question what is human nature ? what are the facts of the world ? and how are we to discover them ? We are in the position of actually doubting what the real world is, whether it is a world of matter and motion, of beauty, of spirits, and so forth ; and we are equally in doubt as to what we ourselves really are. We cannot assume that, at the very beginning of our inquiry, we possess answers to these questions so securely based that on the strength of them we can organize our whole life. Scientists, artists and the rest claim to possess such answers, but that is the claim which we question.

The true form of knowledge is thus self-consistent, and it must prove its claim by demonstrating the necessary inconsistency of the other forms. It must, that is to say, not so much attack and demolish these forms as exhibit them demolishing themselves through the working of their own inconsistencies. External criticism is valueless ; the true critic is one who can place himself at the point of view criticized, and in his own person live out its consequences to the bitter end. He must vivisect himself in illustration of his own lecture.

But further, such a criticism is not merely destructive. It is a vindication of the very experiences which it refutes, for it exhibits them not as strange and inexplicable perversions of the mind, morbid types of thought indulged by the foolish and depraved, but as stages through which the critic has himself passed, and which he can confess without forfeiting his claim to rationality. Had they been sheer and unmitigated error, only an utterly deluded and imbecile mind could have fallen into them ; and in that case the knowledge that one had fallen into them would be a stain

on one's intellectual record which nothing could remove. If
we find a man whom we respect as a sensible and thoughtful
person confessing that he was once led into materialism or
Mormonism or murder, we expect him to be able to tell us
what it was in these things that he found worthy to attract
him. If he cannot tell us that, we think worse of him than
we did before.

Our map is now beginning to take shape. It is to be
a statement of the essential nature or structure of each
successive form of experience, based on actual knowledge
of that form from within, and concentrated upon the search
for inconsistencies, rifts which when we come to put a strain
on the fabric will widen and deepen and ultimately destroy it.

But where are we to begin ? It may not matter very
much, to all appearance ; and yet the question of order
cannot be altogether irrelevant. We must begin somewhere.

There is an obstacle which we must here remove from our
path. This is the theory of art, religion and the rest as
co-ordinate species of knowledge, species of a genus, each
valid and autonomous in its own sphere but each limited
to a single aspect of reality, each constituting a single aspect
of the mind. Such a theory admits what we have already
shown to be undeniable, that they are all cognitive or
theoretical activities, none merely emotional or merely
practical. The truth of this is shown by the fact that they
all regard themselves as theoretical ; and to regard yourself, even erroneously, as theoretical is to be theoretical,
since nothing but theory can be in error. But it is now
suggested that each is a specific type of thought concerned
with a specific type of object : art with beauty, religion
with God, science with natural law, and so forth. Each is
thus competent in its own field and impotent in any other

field ; for each is merely thought as such, taking on in each case such a specific character as enables it to solve the specific problems with which it is there faced. If this view is sound, the prize is divided. To the question 'Which form of thought gives truth?' it is replied 'Truth about what ? If about beauty, the answer is art. If about God, the answer is religion : and so forth. There is no such thing as truth in the abstract, and every kind of thought has its own appropriate kind of truth.'

This account of the matter is plainly sound up to a point ; but it will not carry us far, and to accept it as a complete answer to our problem would be to make shipwreck of our whole work. For it amounts to this : that art, religion, science, and the rest are all necessary to a complete and full mental life, that each of them occupies one faculty of the mind—a faculty, no doubt, with intellectual, practical and emotional sides to it—and that each serves to acquaint us with one aspect and no more of reality. But if this is so, the medieval view of life is simply right and the Renaissance view simply wrong. The parts of a whole exist in mutual support, and the aspects of an objective reality become more comprehensible when seen in their interrelations. It follows that the mixture of art and religion and philosophy which we described as primitive and childish when we found it exemplified in the middle ages was the only right state of things, and that the specialized life of art or religion or science is nothing but a pure error. Yet to say that science, for example, can best thrive in a mind which equally cultivates art and religion is to fly in the face of evident fact in obedience to a baseless dogma.

The matter becomes worse if we turn to the objective side of the question. Beauty, God, natural law, are said to be aspects of a single reality. But what is this reality ?

For art, it is beauty and nothing else whatever. For religion it is simply God, who is the beginning and the end. For science, it is nothing but natural law. The exclusiveness of these various objects is an essential part of their nature. You cannot combine them, because each of them is an implicit denial of all the rest.

This is a truth which is so often forgotten that we must not hesitate to dwell on it. The parts of a whole, the co-species of a genus, are modifications of a common principle, but modifications of which to assert one is implicitly to assert the others also. Assert the triangle and you assert the square : assert the inside and you assert the outside. Therefore a group of activities which could be described as species of knowledge would imply each other, as the geometry of the triangle implies the geometry of the square ; and a specialist in the geometry of the triangle would regard the specialist in the geometry of the square as a partner in a common work, a contributor to a whole which each recognized as transcending his own work and including with it that of his neighbour. But in the relation of religion and science this is not the case. The scientist 'has no need of God' as an hypothesis, and the religious man has no need of natural law, not because God and natural law are distinct parts of reality but because they are rival ways of conceiving the whole. Religion cannot tolerate the idea that in addition to God there are also laws of nature. The laws of nature, for him, are simply God's will. Similarly science cannot tolerate the suggestion of a God distinct from the laws of nature ; the admission of a divine will into the delicate machinery of natural law destroys the meaning of science as completely as the admission of a physical necessity into God's plans destroys the meaning of religion. So, when a benevolent third party sets himself to arbitrate in the quarrel of religion and science and tries to persuade them that each expresses 'one side of the truth', the disputants reply with perfect unanimity 'God *or* nature, by all means : offer us the choice between religion and science, and we will try to choose, though no doubt the choice is hard ; but do not offer us God *and* nature, for that means offering us neither religion nor science, but the corpse of religion chained to the corpse of science '.

Religion and science know their own business a great deal better than these impartial persons who attempt to 'reconcile' them and only show how utterly they fail to understand either. And the theory which makes them species of a genus fails not only when we thus try to put it into practice, but when we try to think it out coherently. For when we do this, we find that the notion of genus and species is a logical notion, and therefore logic is somehow a master-science having jurisdiction over the whole field of knowledge ; for the notion of species is applied to every one of our five forms of experience. But in so far as logical conceptions apply to all five forms, they are all reduced to the same form and all judged by the same logical standards. There is therefore only one form of knowledge, describable in terms of logic, which is directed indifferently upon five classes of object. This is pure intellectualism, and leads us to look for syllogisms in music, inductions in religion, and so forth : which precisely contradicts the thesis with which this view began, namely the independence of these various fields of thought. This is what really happens when people attempt to maintain this view of the forms of experience as co-ordinate species : they assert, without in the least realizing it, the absoluteness of formal logic and reduce all alike to that Procrustean standard. Of this, however, we shall have more to say in a later chapter in dealing with what we call ' scientific philosophy '. For the moment, it is enough to recognize that the application of the notion of genus and species to the forms of experience is an example of the fallacy which we shall so designate.

We must, then, begin somewhere. The five forms of experience—and whatever others there may be—are not species of a genus, which may be indifferently taken in any order ; they have a natural order of their own.

If we look at the life of individual human beings, we shall find that it normally falls into periods of predominantly aesthetic, predominantly religious, or predominantly intellectual activity. Plato laid down that poetry and fiction were the natural food of the very young. In this he was certainly right. Children do not as a rule crowd round their elders clamouring for mathematical demonstrations or historical narratives ; they seem with curious uniformity to demand a diet of aesthetic products—stories, rhymes, songs and so forth. ' Read to me ', ' sing to me ', and even ' draw to me ' are the hourly demands of the young from about the age of two years. They are not yet particularly religious ; that comes later ; and all parents of young children find the right way of beginning religious education something of a problem. No one ever found the aesthetic education of the young a problem ; they take to nursery rhymes and fairy tales with an ease and a universality which are, if one reflects upon them, rather striking. Religion comes next, and a normal child of four is already tolerably at home in the world of religious imagery ; but scientific thought sets in later, and it is perhaps unusual for a child to interest itself very much even in the simplest mechanical problems before it is about six. But this is only the development of the child ; a little later, beginning at puberty, the same process seems to repeat itself on, as it were, a higher level.

The child, at the dawn of adolescence, becomes fiercely and agonizingly sensitive to beauty ; poetry and music shake its very soul. This is normally followed by a violent awakening of the religious consciousness ; and when adolescence is gradually settling down into maturity, an eager spirit of scientific inquiry frequently displaces both art and religion from their position of primacy. But even beyond this again lies the mature life of the adult human being, the life of professional work ; and here again there seem to be a more childish type of attitude which gives rise to the artist, a more adolescent type which gives rise to the specifically religious vocation, and a more adult type which gives rise to the scientific professions. Childhood, adolescence, and maturity seem thus to correspond with art, religion, and science as their proper spiritual antitypes ; and each phase splits up into the art, religion, and science of childhood, all tinged with the fancifulness of art, the art, religion, and science of adolescence, all affected by the passionate and devotional character of religion, and the art, religion, and science of maturity, all consolidated by the reflectiveness and stability of thought.

Such a scheme of the ' ages of man ' is crude and abstract no doubt, true at best in a shadowy and schematic, kind of way ; and yet there is some truth in it. At any rate, it is true enough to be acted upon by everybody in the practice of education ; we all educate children by developing their aesthetic consciousness, we all believe in the importance of religious guidance for the adolescent, and we all begin a serious scientific training after the age at which children normally leave school.

The same general tendency towards a series of phases beginning with art seems to be at work in the history of mankind. Just as we are often surprised by the excellence

of children's drawing, singing, dancing, and composition of
verses or stories in prose, so we discover with something of
a shock that palaeolithic man was a really great artist ;
a painter, a sculptor, a decorator of genius. At the very
beginning of human history we find the extraordinary
monuments of palaeolithic art, a standing problem to all
theories of human development and a delicate test of their
truth. Certain archaeologists have conjectured that palaeolithic art had a religious motive. There is no evidence for
this : it is simply a confession of failure, on the part of the
archaeologists in question, to conceive a race primitively
and intensely savage throwing its whole soul into artistic
expression for its own sake. Yet no one who has a keen eye
for art can see behind the palaeolithic products anything
but the purest and most spontaneous aesthetic impulse.

Dim premonitions of religion palaeolithic man certainly
had ; and, as we shall see, there is in all art such a pre-
monition of religion. But the evidence of archaeology is
clear that the full development of the religious consciousness was the work of the neolith. All that we know of
neolithic man confirms us in the belief that he was keenly
religious ; and his curious lack of graphic art, so striking
when we compare him with the palaeolith, is fully accounted
for if we may suppose that his whole spiritual energy was
concentrated upon a task hitherto unattempted, the discovery of religion. Artless he was not ; he had at least an
impressive and splendid architecture ; but this was an art
not free, like the palaeolithic, but absorbed into the service
of religion.

The next stage took place within our own racial memory.
Science was invented by the Greeks, with what help from
Egypt and Babylon we need not stay to ask. Setting aside
a similar and roughly contemporary movement of thought

in India, almost everything we know as science to-day begins among the Greeks and achieves at once in their hands a vigorous life of its own. Other races like the Aztecs have repeated quite independently some of the Greek discoveries, but in the form in which they have permanently influenced the world's history they have been due to the Greeks, and this—not their art, splendid as it was—is the real debt which humanity owes to the Greek people.

History is a later invention. In the sense parallel to that in which Euclid and Archimedes were scientists, the ancients had no historians. As the Babylonians and Egyptians seem to have collected observations and made measurements without really achieving the scientific outlook upon astronomy and mathematics, so Thucydides and Tacitus recorded with industry and imagination what they had seen and heard ; but observation and measurement are not science, and memoirs and legends are not history. Observation and measurement become science when they are transmuted by the explicit emergence of the concept, the pure *a priori* act of thought ; and this did not happen till the Greeks achieved it. So memoir and legend become history when they are lifted out of the region of authority by the birth of historical criticism, and this is the discovery of our own modern world, its contribution to the advancement of human knowledge. Critical history is the child of the eighteenth century. It began in the hands of men like Vico and Hume, Gibbon and Lessing, and Herder and Niebuhr, and ripened into the nineteenth century when history stood forth the unmistakable queen of the sciences and biologists like Darwin and Huxley, philosophers like Hegel, theologians like Baur and Newman, and economists like Marx explicitly resolved the problems of their special sciences into historical problems, and all the waters of art, religion, and science went to swell the great river of historical thought. So gigantic has been the effect of this revolution that as yet people hardly appreciate it. They talk of Evolution, of Progress, of the metaphysical reality of Time, as if these were notions of the first importance and grand discoveries of modern science. But they are only half-understood and mythological expressions of the concept of history. And those among us who criticize these notions, who scoff at progress and pour scorn on the idea of evolution, mostly do so because the revolution has somehow escaped their notice, because they cannot see any intrinsic difference between the historical outlook of a Herodotus and a Mommsen, and imagine themselves to be still living in the scientific period of the world's thought.

If history only found its feet a century or two ago, the next phase can hardly yet have begun ; and if this is to be the philosophical phase we can understand the truth of Kant's saying that our own philosophy is at best a poor groping affair, like mathematics before the Greeks : justified rather by what may come of it than by what it has already achieved.

But that is pure speculation. Of schemes like this, which compress human life and history into an abstract formula, we can only say that the best in this kind are but shadows. The worst, however, are no worse, if imagination mend them : only, as Hippolyta sagely added, it must be your imagination, and not theirs. Such formulae are good servants but bad masters ; they may give a valuable clue to a mind active enough to seize it and careful enough of detail to avoid being misled by it when, as all such formulae do, it fails him. Any clever fool can make a symmetrical philosophy, and it takes nothing more than ingenuity to find quincunxes in the heavens above and in the earth beneath. But at present all we want is a clue. We have seen that our forms of experience are not mere species of a genus, because each denies the others ; and because they are not species they have not that indifference with regard to one another which characterizes abstract logical classifications. They must form an order of some kind ; and the empirical order in which they seem to emerge in the life of the individual and of the race is enough to suggest that our discussion cannot go very far wrong if it follows the same order. But what is even more important than the actual order is the suggestion of serial arrangement as such. For a series of terms implies that each term is as it were built upon or derived from its predecessor and therefore does not start *in vacuo*, is not a wholly fresh embodiment of the universal, but is essentially a modification of the term before. Hence even if we only recognized three terms, and made a series by alternating them, *abcabcabc* . . ., there would be no repetition, for the second *a* would be not the mere first *a* again, but *a* modified by having been developed through *b* out of *c* ; the third *a* would be *a* modified by the same process in the second degree ; and so on. Thus, the art of the adolescent is not the fairy-tale art of the child but a new type of art whose character is enriched by all that has happened to the child between, say, the ages of three and thirteen. To trace in detail this return of a form of experience, recognizably itself, and yet modified by an increment which is simply the accumulation of experience, is the task of such a special study as the history of art.

Or, to quote a case which more nearly concerns the plan of our work, we find within the professional scientific attitude of the mature mind a distinction between science, history and philosophy. All these are intellect self-conscious as such ; but science is aesthetic intellect, or intellect exhibiting the capriciousness of art and framing to itself imaginary objects : history is religious intellect, or intellect submitting itself with self-forgetful devotion to the claims of absolute fact : philosophy is intellectual intellect, thinking *à outrance*. And even within philosophy we shall find an aesthetic philosophy, a religious philosophy, and an intellectual philosophy which splits up into scientific philosophy, historical philosophy, and philosophical philosophy.

The reader need not be alarmed. We are not looking for quincunxes, and we have no intention of holding his nose to any dialectical grindstone. This is merely an illustration of the fact that series means concrete novelty, the denial both of abstract repetition and of abstract change. History —and our work is to comment on history—is not a sheer flux of unique and disconnected events, each absolutely new and unprecedented. And, on the other hand, it is not a barren cyclical repetition of the same pattern over and over again, still less a shuffling of rearranged units like repeated throws of dice, every new event an arbitrary selection from a given number of possibilities. It is a process in which method or regularity does not exclude novelty ; for every phase, while it grows out of the preceding phase, sums it up in the immediacy of its own being and thereby sums up implicitly the whole of previous history. Every such summation is a new act, and history consists of this perpetual summation of itself.

This may seem obscure ; its further explanation must wait for the concluding chapter. Here, all we mean by it is to issue a warning that our five forms of experience are not five abstractly self-identical types of event which, by their recurrence in a fixed or changing order, constitute human experience ; but types whose recurrence perpetually modifies them, so that they shade off into one another and give rise to new determinations and therefore new types at every turn.

Then why do we distinguish five, and not any other number ; and why these, instead of alternatives ?

Because, where any preliminary grouping of problems would be arbitrary, we are entitled to consult the reader's convenience and our own by drawing upon existing and traditional philosophies. We are accustomed to group our problems in certain ways, under the headings of art, religion, science, history, and philosophy : there is no harm in it, and it gives us a convenient starting-point. But it is only harmless so long as we recognize that it is provisional. The life of the mind is not the rotation of a machine through a cycle of fixed phases but the flow of a torrent through its mountain-bed, scattering itself in spray as it plunges over a precipice and pausing in the deep transparency of a rock-pool, to issue again in an ever-new series of adventures.

III

ART

§ 1. *Art as pure Imagination*

THAT poetry is in a special sense the spiritual kingdom of the child was first divined by Plato ; and when the theory of art was seriously taken up again by philosophers of the eighteenth century, they reasserted the same notion as the very heart and core of their new speculations on the subject. When Hamann wrote that ' poetry is the mother-tongue of mankind ', and when Vico a generation earlier laid it down that poetry is the natural speech of children and savages, they held in their hands the clue to the solution of all the problems of aesthetic.

They seem to have meant that art is the simplest and most primitive, the least sophisticated, of all possible frames of mind. Hence it is the normal activity of those minds whose experience has been brief and which have as yet learnt little from others. Children and savages are not better artists than grown and civilized men ; on the contrary, art like all other forms of activity improves with practice and does not spring into existence full-grown ; but children and savages are in a special sense natural artists ; art is to them a life in which they are immersed as in a flood of warm water which bears along in its course passive and effortless organisms. A grown and civilized man achieves aesthetic experience by the effort of deliberately shutting out other competing interests ; he refuses to look at a given object historically or scientifically, and will see it aesthetically. Hence, for the civilized man, art has become a somewhat alien thing and difficult of approach ;

he bewails lost romance and thinks of the aesthetic experience as something that died with his dead childhood, or
exalts beauty into a far-away goal to which some day
a difficult uphill road may lead him. But art is difficult
for him not because it is intrinsically difficult, but because
his entire education has been designed to wean him from it ;
it is far away not because it is on the heights of the spiritual
life, but because it is in the depths. Art is the foundation,
the soil, the womb and night of the spirit ; all experience
issues forth from it and rests upon it ; all education begins
with it ; all religion, all science, are as it were specialized
and peculiar modifications of it. Art is the sleep of the soul ;
as a baby does little but sleep, so the infant soul knows
hardly any experience but art ; as a grown man sleeps from
his labours, so the awakened spirit returns into art to find
new strength and inspiration, going down into that as into
the fountain in which Hera renewed her virginity.

The waking life of the soul is the distinction of truth
from falsehood, the assertion of this as real and that as
unreal. This is the logical judgement, the assertion which
claims truth. Now art, in certain of its manifestations,
contains what seem to be assertions. This feature rises to
the surface in the art of literature. A novelist's work
consists, to all appearances, of a string of statements all
laid down precisely as if they were records of historical fact ;
the dramatist's does not differ in any essential ; and even
the lyric poet makes sufficiently definite assertions as to the
state of his own feelings. Similarly the painter represents
people and landscapes in a way which amounts to saying
' this is the thing as I actually saw it ' ; though in some
arts, notably music and pure design, this element of apparent
assertion does not exist.

It is an old observation that the statements apparently

made and implied in literature and the plastic arts are not
necessarily true. It is not true that Catherine Morland's
father was called Richard, for Catherine Morland never
existed ; it is not true that Tess was hanged or that Romeo
drank all the poison, for like reasons. Nor are aesthetic
statements necessarily true even when the persons about
whom they are made are, like Brutus and Cymbeline,
historically real. Hence poetry has been denounced for
a liar ; and yet the statements it makes are not necessarily
false either.

> Bifel that in that seson on a day
> In Southwerk at the Tabard as I lay
> Redy to wenden on my pilgrimage——

these statements may, for all we know, be true or false, just
as Bellini's Mocenigo may be a good likeness or a bad, and
it is not necessary for us to settle the point. The value of
the *Prologue* or the portrait, as a work of art, is unaffected by
it. Southwark and the Tabard, or the Doge, may never have
existed at all, and yet the work of art remain unimpaired.

In answering the question, What is art ? we must make
this our first fixed point. The aesthetic experience cares
nothing for the reality or unreality of its object. It is
neither true nor false of set purpose : it simply ignores the
distinction. There is no such thing as the so-called artistic
illusion, for illusion means believing in the reality of that
which is unreal, and art does not believe in the reality of
anything at all. Its apparent assertions are not real assertions but the very suspension of assertion ; and what is
called illusion is not the saying to ourselves ' this is truth ',
but the not saying to ourselves ' this is fiction '. This non-
assertive, non-logical attitude is imagination in the proper
sense of that word. The word is sometimes used with the
implication that the imagined object is necessarily unreal,

but this implication is illegitimate ; the correct implication is that in imagining an object we are indifferent. to its reality or unreality. If a novelist writes a story, it may happen that the story is true : he may have met with incidents which struck his imagination in such a way as to satisfy it exactly as they stood. Yet the story, so written, is as much a work of imagination in the proper sense as it would have been if, as we say, he had ' made it all up ' ; and the actual work done by him in the two cases is in kind exactly the same. To make your imagination penetrate historical facts is not essentially different from imagining pure fictions. From the artistic point of view it is a mere coincidence that some of the events in *Julius Caesar* or any other work of art should be historical ; just such a coincidence as it would be did it happen that there really was a Catherine Morland whose father was called Richard. The artist incorporates an incident in his work not because it is true but because it is appropriate by aesthetic, that is, imaginative standards. A work of art, like any work of the spirit, must be a complete and coherent whole, systematic through and through, and built upon one consistent principle ; but the principle of its unity is not the same as that of the unity of a philosophical theory or a historical narrative, but is the principle of imagination. A philosophical theory must be capable of being *conceived* as a whole, a historical narrative, of being *narrated* as a whole—narrated, that is, as true—a work of art, of being *imagined* as a whole.

Art, then, is pure imagination. The artist does not judge or assert, he does not think or conceive, he simply imagines. And this is true even of the most rigidly realistic art. The artist never transcribes facts ' as they are '. He only, at most, transcribes them ' as he sees them ', and whenever the artist says *see* he means *imagine*. The realistic theory of art holds that the imagination is more highly stimulated by a careful and close attention to facts ; but when the artist has attended to the facts it is his imagination, not the facts, that he has to follow. Indeed, it is not altogether true to say that art selects, alters, idealizes or adapts facts ; for the artist as such does not first determine the facts and then convert them into art. The raw material out of which he selects and adapts what will serve his purpose is an imaginative, not a factual, raw material. We say that the artist holds up the mirror to nature, or that he transcribes what he has seen in real life ; but this is mere error if it means that the artist bases his work on the ascertaining and remembering of historical facts. ֺThe real life or the nature to which he holds up his mirror is not the world of science or history, but the world as imaginatively apprehended, the world of imagination. Everybody knows that there is one frame of mind in which one regards an object scientifically, and another in which one regards it aesthetically ; the pathologist is as blind to the beauty of the stained section which he is examining as the landscape-painter to the optical conditions of his sunset ; and we pass over from one of these attitudes to the other by a deliberate and familiar act of will. But the aesthetic and the scientific attitudes are not merely different attitudes towards the same object, namely a sunset. The object is different. The scientist ' sees ' in the sunset a concrete embodiment of certain scientific laws ; the artist ' sees ' in it a harmonious pattern of colours. The very word ' see ' is ambiguous ; with the scientist it means primarily to think, with the artist primarily to imagine, and the world of imagination which is the object confronting the artist's mind when he looks at a sunset is not present to the scientist's mind at all. Indeed, the scientist as such is committed to the denial of its existence ; for beauty is the secret of the universe or nothing, and for the scientist it is certainly not the secret of the universe.

Thus the artist's world is not a world of facts or laws, it is a world of imaginations. He is all made of fantasy, and the world in which he is interested is a world made of the stuff of dreams. For him, from his point of view, these dreams are neither real nor unreal ; that is a distinction of which he knows nothing. They are simply dreamt. The artist as such does not know what the word reality means ; that is to say, he does not perform the act which we call assertion or judgement. His apparent statements are not statements, for they state nothing ; they are not expressions, for they express no thought. They do not express his imaginations, for they are his imaginations. What he imagines is simply those fantasies which compose the work of art.

§ 2. *The Work of Art*

But if art is pure imagination, it is not therefore a purely immediate, instinctive and undifferentiated activity such as would be implied by placing its essence in feeling, emotion, or sensation. Art is a concrete activity ; feeling and sensation are abstract elements which can be distinguished within any concrete activity but cannot form the whole or essence of any. The life of art is not a facile explosion of emotional force or the bare receptivity of sense ; it is a life of discipline and endeavour, a struggle to realize one's being in this way and not in that. Hence the aesthetic experience, like all true forms of spiritual activity, polarizes itself into a positive and a negative. As the life of knowledge distinguishes truth and falsehood, as the life of action distinguishes good and evil, so art distinguishes beauty and ugliness.

The logic of these distinctions is the same throughout. In every case the self-determining mind, just because it is self-determining, distinguishes its ideals from its temptations, that which it would be from that which it is trying not to be. For a being that was not self-determining, these distinctions would be meaningless ; for instance, if the mind were a sensitive plate on which the object automatically impressed a correct picture of itself, the very notion of falsehood could not exist. Because truth is an achievement of the mind, and because achievement implies the possibility of failure, truth has an opposite, namely error. If now the life of art were an immediate instead of a self-determined activity, if it were the mere life of emotion or sensation, it would be a thing that either happened or did not happen. When it happened, there would be a revelation of beauty, when it did not happen, there would be nothing. The existence of ugliness, even in the form of an ugliness successfully avoided, is the standing refutation of all emotional and sensationalistic theories of art ; for ugliness is the failure of the aesthetic experience to achieve beauty, and this implies that the aesthetic experience is a deliberate and constructive activity, an ordered and orderly life which is not bare feeling but feeling individualized into a whole, a *work* of art, whose parts are strictly subordinated to the law of the whole.

The aesthetic experience is thus, in its concrete actuality, the creation or apprehension of works of art. The terms creation and apprehension are here synonymous, for the essence of art is that nothing is asserted and everything imagined, so that the question whether the work of art has or has not an existence independent of the apprehension of it is a question which has, for the aesthetic consciousness, no meaning whatever. From the point of view of that consciousness, every work of art is real just so far as it is imagined and no further. Now this process of imagining a whole, or creating a work of art, is, as we have seen, no mere rudderless drifting of images across the mind ; it is a process of unification in which the mind strives to see its world as a whole, the ' world ' being just the work of art which for the time being absorbs the whole gaze of the mind. The various feelings, emotions, sensations, or by whatever other name we call the subsidiary imaginations, are modified and adapted so as to fall into such an imaginable totality, a single coherent imaginary whole in constructing which we tentatively imagine subsidiary parts and either fit them in or reject them, retaining the right to modify the whole according as a new subsidiary part suggests improvements in it. The whole is not first held in the mind as a whole and then filled out in detail ; for if it were ever held in the mind (that is, imagined as a whole), the work would already be complete ; the whole comes into imaginary existence only in the critical process of experimenting with its parts. Nor, indeed, does the mind exist before it carries out this self-determinative task ; the mind is no machine which, set in motion, produces works of art, but it creates itself as the activity of imagination by creating these works of art which are its imaginary objects. Neither the imaginary object nor the imagining subject pre-exists to the concrete process of imagining ; for the very being of the subject is here to imagine ; of the object, to be imagined.

The law of this process, its guiding principle, is beauty. At every turn, the mind accepts one alternative and rejects another for no reason whatever except that the one gives beauty and the other does not. Now art as such has nothing to do with principles or laws ; it cares nothing for such things, for their essence is that they cannot be imagined but only conceived. Hence the dilemma that if beauty is a concept its apprehension must, as Plato saw, belong not to art but to science ; whereas if it is not a concept it cannot rescue art from the immediacy of bare feeling. Either art turns into science or it collapses into the merely natural life of sensation ; in either case its essence is destroyed. The answer to this dilemma is that beauty is not a concept. It is the guise under which concepts in general appear to the aesthetic consciousness. Beauty means structure, organization, seen from the aesthetic. point of view, that is, imagined and not conceived. This is the solution of the old difficulty arising out of the fact that when people try to describe the beauty of a thing they always either describe its shape, colour and so forth, which are not beauty, or else describe its emotional effect on them, which is not beauty either. The first alternative leads to all the formalistic and intellectualistic theories of beauty, the theories of the serpentine line, of symmetry and proportion, of unity in diversity, of natural form or allegorical meaning ; the latter, to all the emotionalist and hedonistic theories. Beauty cannot be truly defined except as the correlative of imagination ; the activity of imagining creates the objective world of art, and creates it according to its own law, that is, creates it as an imagined whole or thing of. beauty. Thus beauty does not exist except from the point of view of the aesthetic experience, and the attempt to fit it into a table of concepts or categories drawn up from the point of view of logical science would be as contradictory as the attempt to insert the will of God into a niche somewhere among the causes of sidereal motion. For religion, God is not one cause but the supreme cause of causes ; so for art, beauty is not one concept but the very soul and secret of the world.

> Beauty is truth, truth beauty ; that is all
> Ye know on earth, and all ye need to know ;

that is the artist's statement of his own faith. To him beauty is what God is to religion, what truth is to science ; it is his ' definition of the Absolute '.

The concrete life of art is the creation of works of art. But this creation is altogether the act of imagination. The paper and ink, the paints and the clay that we handle are not its materials, and the written page and the painted picture are not its result. An artist paints with one motive only : that he may help himself to see, and to see in the sense of to imagine. His picture, when it is painted, has done that, and he is not further interested in it. Art lives not on canvases but in the fancy ; and only those who are strangers to its inner life can suppose that it has any special connexion with the objects stored in galleries and book-shelves. The reason for this error is that persons in whom the aesthetic life is feeble and intermittent require for its exercise the aid of their betters, exactly as a child can be shepherded through a theorem by its teacher or a novice coaxed up a rock passage by his guide. The teacher's words are not mathematics, but a stimulus to mathematics ; and the rope is not climbing, but a moral support to the climber ; yet through their help it is evident that things can be done by the weaker brethren which without such aid they would not have the confidence to attempt.

Thus the work of art in the false sense, the perceptible painting or writing, is valued not at all by its author, but highly by the aesthetic weakling, because it helps him to aesthetic activities which he could not have achieved alone. And it must be added that he habitually exaggerates the actual help which these things give him. If he is the sort of man who could not see for himself the dramatic force of situations like those of Sophocles, the effectiveness of colour-schemes like those of Titian or of modulation schemes like those of Schubert, he will not see much of these things when Sophocles, Titian, and Schubert thrust them under his very nose : he will simply not notice the irony, the contrast of colours and keys ; and those parts of the work of art which he could not in some sort have invented for himself will pass him by unseen. ' How much, as one grows older, one finds in so-and-so,' people say, ' that one never saw before ! ' Yes ; and how much one has not even yet seen ! For one never sees anything in anybody's work but what one brings to it, and it is as true of art as of nature that

> we receive but what we give,
> And in our life alone doth Nature live ;
> Ours is her wedding-garment, ours her shroud.

§ 3. *The Monadism of Art*

In every phase of development the mind is its own place, and it is as true in science and philosophy as in art that we only see what we have eyes to see and only feel what we have learnt to feel. But in full-blown intellectual activity the mind's limitation to the circle of its own arm's length is tempered by the fact that here the mind is knowing a real world ; whatever falls inside the circle is real so far as the mind's thinking is true. Hence, even if the radius of the circle is finite, it may overlap an infinite number of other circles, so that every mind lives in a world which, however narrow, is in principle at least common to all other minds. But in art this is not so. The world of imagination is a private world, a world inhabited solely by its author. The artist, in the moment of aesthetic creation and enjoyment, knows nothing either of a real world, whether natural or artificial, or of minds other than his own. He lives to himself, wholly wrapped up in his own fancies. His entire consciousness is simply the awareness of the work of art which he is creating. Even of himself, as a historical person, he is unaware ; he imagines himself, just as he imagines his world, and his own descriptions of himself may be quite untrue to facts, to the confusion of those who would use them as evidence for his biography. We may call him self-absorbed, but the self in which he is absorbed is an imaginary self. Thus he is not a solipsist or a subject without an object ; his object may be an imaginary object, but it is none the less an object ; he creates at his own good pleasure an imaginary self and an imaginary world.

This utter self-absorption of the artist in the sense above laid down is something of a scandal at a time when social service has become a fetish ; and artists are eager to maintain that their work is essentially the communication of important or beautiful messages to their fellows, hoping thus to prove their utility to a utilitarian age. But this attempt is necessarily a failure ; and every artist who can recollect the actual aesthetic experience knows that in this experience the world of men and things is forgotten, and that any desire to communicate or seek an audience for his thoughts is subsequent and alien to the experience itself. Artists do exhibit their works, and even sell them ; but neither the exhibition nor the sale is an aesthetic act. The artist has no company, not even his own ; and he does not feel lonely. He has all he needs, namely, his world of imagination.

We have spoken of the world of imagination, but it must be remembered that there are as many worlds of imagination as there are works of art. For since a work of art is not asserted as real but only imagined, its existence comes abruptly to an end as soon as we cease to imagine it. The characters in a story which I tell myself only exist for the purposes of the story, and as soon as my story is forgotten they cease to exist and exercise, so to speak, no control over my choice of characters in the next story. Had they been regarded as real characters, I could not thus have ignored them in the next story; for the real must be coherent with itself, and thus history, which aims at narrating real events, can never break off and begin again quite fresh. The next volume of my history must take up the thread of the last. But it argues poverty of imagination if an artist is for ever dwelling on the same theme and developing the fortunes of the same set of characters. When one imagines, one must imagine *something*; it must be a definite and not a self-contradictory imagination, and hence the necessary unity of the work of art. But it does not matter *what* one imagines; and it is just as easy and satisfactory to contradict yesterday's imagination as to continue it. Yet there is a real difference between works of art in what we call their scale or size: and it argues a more powerful mind, a more highly-developed art, to work on a large scale than on a small. Scale, in this sense, is not mere space and time; excellence in art is not bulk or duration; it is relative to the difficulty of the problem which the artist sets himself and the extent to which his whole being and all his resources are called into play in order to solve it. A long and loosely organized work is in this sense a smaller, more trivial, thing than a closely-knit work of shorter length; and this is why going on writing stories about the same people is merely aesthetic indolence. Whether five years are best spent in the concentrated effort of writing an epic or in the intermittent and disjointed writing of a hundred lyrics is a question which cannot be answered by rule.

Every fresh aesthetic act creates a new work of art, though one such act may last for five years at a time. The number of such works is therefore of necessity infinite, nor is it possible to delimit and define their kinds. For though, like anything else, they can be classified, this classification must be continually adapted to keep pace with their free production and cannot control that production, since classification is the work not of imagination but of abstract thought. Such schemes are for science alone ; art is simply uninterested in them.

Every aesthetic act is an individual internally organized by the harmonious fitting-together of subordinate aesthetic acts ; and this being so, it might be fancied that there is a complete or absolute work of art, in which our dramas and symphonies are but scenes and incidental music, a kind of Platonic heaven into which all works of art are gathered up into a coherent and systematic whole. But this cannot be. Works of art always ignore one another and begin each from the beginning : they are windowless monads ; and this is because they are acts of imagination, from which it necessarily follows that they are careless of mutual consistency and interested only in their internal coherence. This is very clearly the case with regard to different performers' ' interpretations ' of a single sonata or play. Such interpretations may be infinitely various ; every one has a right to his own, and one cannot hope to find a master-interpretation, as it were, which will embrace and include all the others. Strictly speaking, there is therefore no such thing as *art as a whole* ; we cannot say that art as a whole gives us an imaginative view of the universe, but we must say that this individual work of art gives us such a view, the view given by any other work of art being incompatible with it. Thus, in spite of the presence in art of mediation, self-determination, and self-criticism, in spite of the presence of the concept in the imaginative form of beauty, art is in one peculiar sense immediate and intuitive. It is essentially *discontinuous*. It breaks off and begins again in a fresh place. It is an infinite series of individual separate works of art, which never coalesce into a whole, and of which each is pitched in a different key from all the others. There is never any reason in art why the aesthetic consciousness should be engaged on *this* work rather than on any other. No doubt the history of art shows a certain continuity and laws of development ; but it shows these to the historian, not to the artist. The artist as such cares nothing for the history of art. He does not necessarily know anything whatever about it, and if he does, he must sedulously forget it before he begins aesthetic work, for there is no more crushing handicap to an artist than a load of scholarship. The work of art is a monad, and monadology is the philosophy of art.

This monadic withdrawing into itself of the aesthetic consciousness, this ignoring of everything factual, even of its own historical nature and situation, is the necessary consequence of its imaginative character. Art in its pure form is therefore unaware even that it is imagination ; the monad does not know that it is windowless ; the artist does not say ' I am only imagining ', for that would be to distinguish imagination from knowledge, and this he does not do. Hence the aesthetic life of children and uneducated people results in what an unintelligent critic calls lying and hallucination. Such people give imaginary accounts of facts about which they are asked questions, they see ghosts and converse with fairies, and all in good faith because they are not awake to the distinction between imagining and knowing, and therefore do not know that they are imagining. The life of such people resembles that of one who should slip continually and unawares from waking to vivid dreaming and back again. To enjoy the aesthetic experience in this primitive form is to live in a waking dream, to be at the mercy of nameless terrors and to find solid ground nowhere beneath one's feet. The fantasies of childhood and savagery, the fairies and the fauns, are pretty toys for the civilized man who has by long education learnt that they are only imaginary ; but for the child and the savage, and even to some extent for the English rustic of to-day, they are the brood of the nightmare and black with the perils of magic.

§ 4. Meaning in Art

The life of reason, therefore, whose first step is the development of the aesthetic consciousness, finds its second step in the conquest and, in some sort, the destruction of that consciousness. In order to see how this is effected we must go back to the beginning and consider to what extent the account hitherto given of art is satisfactory.

The reader must have seen that it was a one-sided account. We have described art as pure imagination ; and the characteristics which we have deduced from that description have certainly given us a truthful picture of art, so far as it went, but a picture which calls for modifications.

Ordinary thought has always attributed to art a power of teaching truths, moral or religious, or philosophical, which could not be otherwise grasped or uttered. That was the general conviction of the ancients, and even Plato, who opposed it in part, embraced it in the sense that he incorporated poetical myths in the body of his own philosophical writing. It was widespread in the middle ages, and predominant in the Renaissance ; and how far it is from being extinct to-day may be seen when we reflect that one of our most eminent philosophers, lately deceased, wrote a book on *Robert Browning as a Philosophical and Religious Teacher*. A theory so widely held and so firmly rooted is not likely to be altogether false ; and the special problem of the philosophy of art to-day is to work out a theory which shall do justice at once to this old 'pedagogic' doctrine and to the newer doctrine, derived from Vico and the eighteenth century, which we have been hitherto expounding. This has not yet been done, for the aesthetic of Hegel, which comes nearest to doing it, has hardly absorbed into itself the full consequences of the eighteenth-century doctrine, which in our time has been powerfully and systematically restated by Croce. The successors of Croce have not yet reconsidered the somewhat peremptory way in which he dismisses the ' pedagogic ' theory as a mere illusion. The fact seems to be that in aesthetic, as in the other philosophical sciences, the ancients maintained, in general and with exceptions, a one-sided view which, after the Renaissance, tended to be replaced by its equally one-sided opposite ; a tendency which culminated in the eighteenth century : and that the special task of modern philosophy is to overcome both exaggerations and to achieve a theory which will do justice to both points of view. The aesthetic of Croce, with its extremely close dependence on Vico, seems to belong to the second of these phases rather than the third, and the very real attempt made by Croce to reach the third phase by identifying ' intuition ' and ' expression ' seems hardly to have succeeded.

The ' vulgar error ' concerning imagination which empiricist psychologies usually embrace is, that imagination can do no more than redistribute or shuffle materials supplied to it by perception. Hence is derived the false theory of art as the more or less distorted reduplication of natural fact. There is sheer confusion in such a doctrine, for it turns on an impossible distinction between the ' materials ' of thought and their ' arrangement ' ; and indeed it is based not on actual study of the imagination but on the *a priori* dogmas of empiricism. Yet, like all persistent errors, it contains an important truth. For imagination never works in the pure vacuum in which, for experimental purposes, we have hitherto placed it. We have spoken as if it could by itself, with no admixture of any alien element, constitute a complete and self-contained life, which we have called the life of art. That it can do so is precisely the error of such as believe in the melancholy creed of art for art's sake, and adopt the philosophy which in a later chapter we shall analyse under the name of aestheticism ; though this in its turn is an error which contains truth.

Our dreams have a certain continuity with our waking life, and imagination never cuts itself wholly adrift from fact. This continuity is often difficult to trace ; completely to trace it is beyond the power even of the most acute psycho-analyst ; nevertheless, no one doubts its existence. And some kind of continuity between an artist's imaginings and his experiences as a member of the world of facts is undeniable. In part, this continuity is positive ; we imagine most successfully (that is, we find beauty in) things that are familiar matter of fact in our non-aesthetic life. So Scott could draw a Border shepherd better than a Crusader, and Mr. Hardy's dramatic power fails him disastrously when he turns from Dorsetshire peasants to fine ladies. But it is also negative ; for this very familiarity breeds contempt, and the glamour of distance is simply the imagination's assertion of its own freedom. Pressed to extremes, this freedom destroys itself, and in regions too remote from fact the imagination expires for very lack of air to breathe. But if this freedom is not asserted at all, we get the mere absence of art and the substitution of photography ; and that is the danger that threatens the ' realistic ' artists who aim at transplanting historical fact bodily into their pictures and plays.

§ 5. *Knowledge as Question and Answer*

Now we have already insisted that the aesthetic experience is imaginative not in the sense that all its objects are fictitious, but in the sense that it treats them indifferently, whether they are fictitious or real ; its attitude, whether towards a real object or a fictitious, is the attitude which neither asserts reality, truly or falsely, nor denies it, but merely imagines. This attitude which makes no assertions, and whose object is therefore as such neither real nor unreal, has been much studied by recent philosophers, under the name of hypothesis, intuition, supposal, representation, and so forth. The credit of recognizing the identity of this attitude with art belongs primarily to Croce. But all these philosophers fall into the error of isolating this attitude and regarding it as a self-contained phase of experience, from which the other phases—notably the attitude of assertion and denial—must be reached by some kind of transition. And this transition is never successfully described. It is in fact an impossible transition. Once the mind has succeeded in attaining a condition in which it neither asserts nor denies but only represents objects to itself intuitively or imaginatively, there is no reason why it should ever pass out of this condition. The ability to assert or deny is an ability which it could never acquire. Hence it is customary to fall back on some meaningless formula to bridge over the unbridgeable gulf between supposal and assertion : to argue that this is effected by the law of the unity of the spirit—a law which has just been openly defied and rendered impotent ; or by the practical necessities of life—necessities which the mind, as described by these philosophers, would simply fail to face ; or by the intervention of the concept—which is merely postulating that the problem has been solved when it has not, for the question is, how can the concept intervene ?

The fact is that imagination never thus exists *in vacuo*, and therefore the problem of how it is to escape from its vacuum is an unreal problem, and insoluble because it is unreal. Supposal and assertion are not two independent chapters in the history of the mind ; they are two opposite and correlative activities which form as it were the systole and diastole of knowledge itself. A crude empiricism imagines that knowledge is composed wholly of assertion : that to know and to assert are identical. But it is only when the knower looks back over his shoulder at the road he has travelled, that he identifies knowledge with assertion. Knowledge as a past fact, as something dead and done with —knowledge by the time it gets into encyclopaedias and text-books—does consist of assertion, and those who treat it as an affair of encyclopaedias and text-books may be forgiven for thinking that it is assertion and nothing else. But those who look upon it as an affair of discovery and exploration have never fallen into that error. People who are acquainted with knowledge at first hand have always known that assertions are only answers to questions. So Plato described true knowledge as ' dialectic ', the interplay of question and answer in the soul's dialogue with itself ; so Bacon pointed out once for all that the scientist's real work was to interrogate nature, to put her, if need be, to the torture as a reluctant witness ; so Kant mildly remarked that the test of an intelligent man was to know what questions to ask ; and the same truth has lately dawned on the astonished gaze of the pragmatists.

Questioning is the cutting edge of knowledge ; assertion is the dead weight behind the edge that gives it driving force. Questions undirected by positive information, random questions, cut nothing ; they fall in the void and yield no knowledge. Information, when it is not ground to a keen edge of inquiry, is not knowledge but mere pedantry, the talent buried in the earth. It ought to be put out at interest, to yield new knowledge and so to purify and correct itself as well as to increase its bulk. Text-books and encyclopaedias are contemptible only when regarded as constituting and exhausting knowledge itself ; as records of the achievement of knowledge, as constituting the body of information which directs our further questionings, their importance is immeasurable. Information may be the body of knowledge, but questioning is its soul.

Supposal and questioning are at bottom the same thing ; or rather, supposal when seen in its proper perspective as an integral element in knowledge turns out to be questioning. The activity of questioning is a puzzle to empiricist theories of knowledge because in it we seem to contemplate an object which does not necessarily exist, and empiricism believes that it is only because an object really exists that it has, so to speak, the force to imprint itself upon our mind or engage our attention. But we never ask a question without to some degree contemplating the non-existent ; for asking a question means envisaging alternatives, and only one at most of these alternatives can really exist. Thus questioning is essentially a suspension of the activity of asserting, and that is how we have defined the aesthetic experience or imagination. But true questioning is a suspension which looks forward to a renewal of this asserting activity, in the shape of the answer. In art, on the other hand, the suspending of assertion seems to be an end in itself, and does not look forward to its own negation, the renewal of assertion. Art, as pure imagination, imagination without assertion, may be paradoxically defined as a question which expects no answer : that is, a supposal.

But a question looks back as well as forward. To ask any question, even the silliest or most irresponsible, we must already possess information. A mind which did nothing but question could not even frame its questions ; the questions which it asked would be mere marks of interrogation, the empty form of questioning, questions which asked nothing. And they would not be even that, for even the empty form of questioning implies the knowledge that there is information to be had. Similarly, in terms of inductive logic, you must know your facts before you can frame your hypothesis ; and this means not only that without knowing the facts you cannot frame a relevant or illuminating hypothesis, but that you cannot frame any hypothesis whatever. Any act must start somewhere, and a pure act of imagination, just because it was completely divorced from fact, would have nowhere to start from and would therefore have no reason for determining itself in any one way rather than in any other. So, even if art is pure imagination, it must spring from a soil of concrete fact ; the artist must really exist in a real world, and his works of art are necessarily a kind of sublimated version of his experience as a real person, however unconscious of this fact he may be. The work of art is an imaginative cutting edge to a mind whose solid backing of factual experience may be forgotten for the moment, but is none the less very real ; or rather, it is not forgotten but distilled into the work of art, present to the mind in this form and no other.

Thus the imaginative activity of art is itself supported and surrounded by a medium of fact ; but the essence of the purely aesthetic frame of mind is that this medium or background is overlooked. The artist necessarily overlooks it, but that does not excuse the philosopher from doing so ; and his attempt to build up a philosophy from a basis of pure imagination is doomed to failure because the basis itself is unsound. Imagination does not exist in the free state, and itself requires a basis of fact. This basis of fact in turn requires a basis of imagination, for no fact can be known until it has been sought by the imaginative act of questioning, and this question itself requires a further basis of fact, and so *ad infinitum*. This is not an infinite regress only because the two moments, question and answer, are not actually separate. Their distinction is an ideal distinction only, and the presupposition of each by the other is only a way of stating their inseparability. The process of knowledge is therefore, strictly speaking, not so much an alternation of question and answer as a perpetual restatement of the question, which is identical with a perpetual revision of the answer. If it is objected that this reduces all the diversity of knowledge to a bare identity in which there is only one judgement judging one truth, our answer —to be given in full later on—will be that this identity contains all diversity within itself.

§ 6. *Art as a form of Error*

Since pure imagination nowhere exists, since all imagination builds on fact and, as question, returns to fact, there is no such thing as an autonomous and self-contained life of art, art for art's sake, aesthetic experience in which every trace of fact is absent. Empirically we all know that art for art's sake is an illusion, that the self-contained life of

art is a mockery. The artist's life is one of singular instability ; it overreaches itself, bursts its own bonds, fails
him at every turn. His fancies are

> cords of all too weak account
> For Earth with heavy griefs so overplussed ;

his palace of art reveals itself a prison, and its furniture
but a pale copy of the living fact :

> And that 's your Venus—whence we turn
> To yonder girl that fords the burn !

Among artists, only the utterly blind and self-complacent
fail to see the impotence of art to solve the problem of life,
talk boastfully of Art as the very crown and pearl of the
spirit, and revile a Plato or a Hegel if, Philistine that he is,
he dares to differ from them. The rest only beg to be
allowed to dream their dream out undisturbed, or else, if
they are made of stronger metal, try to wake up. Again,
far more than religion or philosophy, art is a trick, an
accomplishment, something that tells one strangely little
about the artist as a man. In art, more than anywhere else,
great gifts are unworthily bestowed : even a fine artist may
be intellectually feeble and morally depraved, and so
common is this, that the ' artistic temperament ' is a term
of reproach. All this may be expressed by saying that art
employs a singularly small portion of a man's personality,
so that a man who is competent in art is competent in
a small section only of his entire life. The artist is an artist
only for short times ; he turns artist for a while, like
a werewolf, and for the rest of the time he only carries
marks by which the instructed may recognize him. In his
hour, all is well with him. The spirit is upon him, and
he is wholly absorbed in the divine work of creation. But
his hour passes, and the vision fades into the light of
common day ; the artist becomes once more an ordinary

mortal, the poorer in that he has utterly lost the vision which was all in all to him, and is haunted by that home-sickness for the ideal which every artist knows too well.

The same instability which affects the life of the individual artist reappears in the history of art taken as a whole. To the historian accustomed to studying the growth of scientific or philosophical knowledge, the history of art presents a painful and disquieting spectacle, for it seems normally to proceed not forwards but backwards. In science and philosophy successive workers in the same field produce, if they work ordinarily well, an advance ; and a retrograde movement always implies some breach of continuity. But in art, a school once established normally deteriorates as it goes on. It achieves perfection in its kind with a startling burst of energy, a gesture too quick for the historian's eye to follow. He can never explain such a movement or tell us how exactly it happened. But once it is achieved, there is the melancholy certainty of a decline. The grasped perfection does not educate and purify the taste of posterity ; it debauches it. The story is the same whether we look at Samian pottery or Anglian carving, Elizabethan drama or Venetian painting. So far as there is any observable law in collective art-history it is, like the law of the individual artist's life, the law not of progress but of reaction. Whether in large or in little, the equilibrium of the aesthetic life is permanently unstable.

This instability of the aesthetic life is of its very essence. It cannot be overcome by any effort or any trick. Flogging the uninspired mind to work, or stimulating it with drink and drugs and sensual excitement, can at best produce the semblance of aesthetic experience, at worst, an end of all experience whatever. The wise man relapses contentedly into an ordinary humdrum existence and waits for the moving of the waters. But why should aesthetic experience be thus intermittent and fitful ? It is because the rhythm of question and answer which constitutes the very life of the spirit cannot suffer interruption. The pendulum cannot swing for ever one way. The artist as such wants a life of pure imagination. He cannot get it : it is not to be had. But what he can do is to emphasize in an exaggerated and one-sided way the imaginative attitude which is a necessary part of all life. By forcing this imaginative aspect into prominence he disturbs the balance of his life, and the aspect which he has neglected revenges itself upon him by reasserting itself to the exclusion of the other. But that is a somewhat mythological statement of the facts. It would be more accurate to say that the artist fails to analyse his own experience correctly, and mistakes a distinction between two correlative elements in that experience (imagination and assertion) for a distinction between two distinct types or sections of experience (aesthetic experience, experience of facts). Strictly speaking all experience is aesthetic, because imagination is a factor in every single cognitive act ; and no experience is purely aesthetic, because there is no concrete experience from which the logical act of assertion is wholly absent. All life is art, but no single moment of life is mere art. Now the artist has only one scale of values. He judges everything aesthetically, nothing logically : what he values in any experience is its imagina tive, not its logical, side. Why then does he not see the aesthetic side in all experience, and merely ignore the logical, thus enjoying an uninterrupted flow of aesthetic experience ?

To detect in every experience its aesthetic element means analysing all experience in the light of a philoso-phical conception of aesthetic activity. The artist has no such philosophical conception. If he had, the structure of his experience would present itself to him not as beauty but as the exemplification of the concept. To see anything as beautiful involves seeing it as imagination and nothing but imagination ; and that means failing to see in it the logical elements which it in reality contains. Now because the imaginative apprehension of an object has been thus purchased at the price of suppressing its logical apprehension, the converse will necessarily occur. When the logical element forces itself upon the mind, the aesthetic element will be suppressed, and this is what happens when the aesthetic experience gives way to the non-aesthetic. Unless it happened, the artist could not eat or drink, paint his pictures on solid canvas or post his poems in a real letter-box. If you ask him to take aesthetic pleasure in his bread and cheese or in the colour of the letter-box, you are forgetting that to be an artist at all is to bifurcate one's experience into one part set aside as aesthetic and another part inevitably left over as non-aesthetic. But this bifurcation of experience is an error in philosophical analysis. The artist's life as such is thus irrevocably based upon a philosophical misunderstanding, and is not what it takes itself to be. The essence of art lies in the fact that the artist regards his works as acts of pure imagination ; their *raison d'être* is to *be* acts of pure imagination ; but there is and can be no such thing as an act of pure imagination.

Of everything that a mind in the full sense does, it gives itself an account as it does it ; and this account is inseparably bound up with the doing of the thing. Thus every activity is also a theory of itself and, by implication, of activity in general ; but not necessarily a true theory. For instance, every scientist has some way of telling himself what he is doing, some logical theory as to the nature of science ; but this logical theory may be and often is a quite unsound one. Nor can its defects fail to influence the immediate scientific practice of the man who holds it ; bad fashions in logic have always had detrimental effects on actual science.

Art in every form, from the most rudimentary organization of passing fancies to the most elaborate aesthetic structures, involves a certain philosophical error which, latent at first, becomes more and more definite as the art reaches higher and higher developments. This error is the belief in the separateness and independence of imagination.

At the lower stages, in the child and the savage, this belief is implicit only ; [1] when the mind slips over unawares

---

[1] The distinction between explicit and implicit is so important that it seems desirable here to call attention to it. In any given experience there are certain principles, distinctions, and so forth of which the person whose experience it is cannot but be aware : these I call explicit features of the experience in question. Thus a moral agent, in so far as he is a moral agent, is necessarily aware of the distinction between right and wrong : to forget that distinction is to cease to be in the full and complete sense a moral agent. On the other hand, an observer studying a certain form of experience often finds it impossible to give an account of it without stating certain principles and distinctions which are not actually recognized by the persons whose experience he is studying. Thus an artist constructs his work on principles which are really operative in the construction, but are not explicitly recognized by himself : in art they are implicit, to become explicit only in the criticism of art. Similarly theology makes explicit certain principles which are implicitly, but never explicitly, present in the religious consciousness ; and in general what we call philosophy reveals explicitly the principles which are implicit in what we call everyday experience. To suppose that a principle which is really present in a given experience must be explicitly present in it—to deny implicitness in general—is either to confuse art with art-criticism, religion with theology, correct use of language with grammar, and so forth, or else to deny all connexion between these pairs of activities and (by calling one merely instinctive and the other rational, or the like) to make incompre-

from waking to dreaming and back again, and the distinction between asserting and imagining has not been reflected upon, all life is art and all objects imaginary. But in the developed and mature aesthetic consciousness, when the artist knows that he is imagining and distinguishes his aesthetic from his non-aesthetic experiences, the belief has become explicit and is then an explicit error.

To correct this error is to destroy art as a specific form of activity, to reduce it to the position of an aesthetic element present in all experience but exclusively or predominantly present in none. One might say that in fact no such thing as art exists, but either all experience is art or none is ; but this would have to be corrected by pointing out that the belief in a specific aesthetic experience, though an error, is an error into which people really fall and which, when they fall into it, produces the specific experience called art, an experience which is unstable and irrational precisely because it is the living embodiment of an error.

Plato, than whom few have seen deeper into the mysteries of the human spirit, was intensely conscious of a quarrel between two forms of experience in which he was interested, poetry and philosophy. On such a matter he was too much a poet and too much a philosopher to speak at random. That fault is rather theirs who, in defiance of warnings like his, treat philosophy and art as coexistent and distinct activities between which there can be no conflict. Plato's aesthetic is as great a feat, and deserves as high a place in the history of thought, as his logic, if only because he realized that art is a ' lie ' but a noble and necessary lie,

hensible the transition which is always taking place from the one to the other. But for the detailed justification of the distinction between implicit and explicit we must refer to the entire course of our argument.

the mother of truth, but a mother that must die in giving birth, only to be born again every time a new human being comes into the world.

But if art is essentially a philosophical error, it must be at enmity not only with true philosophy but with itself. For a philosophical error is not merely that which contradicts the truth ; it is much more vitally—for those who do not claim personal infallibility—that which contradicts itself. Does art, then, contradict itself ?

Undoubtedly it does. Art makes for itself two claims. First, that it is the activity of pure imagination ; secondly, that it somehow reveals the truth concerning the ultimate nature of the real world. Now for pure imagination there is no real world ; there is only the imaginary world. Consequently we are tempted to revise the second claim and make it run ' reveals the truth concerning the ultimate nature of the *imaginary* world '. But then the second claim simply repeats the first, and adds nothing to it. This false reduction of the second claim to the first is, unless I am mistaken, the motive of Croce's famous identification of intuition and expression. The paradox of art is that it is both intuitive (pure imagination) and expressive (revelatory of truth) : two characteristics which contradict one another. Croce resolves the contradiction in his own favourite way, by what I may call *pricking* it, so that the opposition vanishes and the terms collapse into an undifferentiated or immediate identity. But because the opposition thus ' collapses into immediacy ', the outcome is merely immediate, that is, it is just intuition over again. Intuition and expression have not been reconciled. Expression has merely been reduced to intuition ; in other words, expression in the true sense has been ignored.

That which is expressed is necessarily a meaning, something distinct from the intuitive vehicle of meaning. This meaning is asserted as a truth. We do not assert what we *say*, for what we say is simply words, but what we *mean* ; the act of meaning something is thus identical with the act of asserting something, and it is this meaning which our words express. But because the words are a purely aesthetic or imaginary object, it makes no difference whether we say that we, or the words, mean that which is meant.

Now significance, meaningfulness, is certainly a characteristic of all art, and in higher and higher degree as we reach art's higher developments. When Socrates asked the poets what their poems meant, they could not tell him, and he noticed with amusement that the bystanders were far more ready with an answer than the writers themselves ; but neither Socrates nor the poets hesitated for a moment to admit that the poems meant something, and something other than what they said. The aesthetic of pure imagination would reply, as Mendelssohn replied in a similar case, ' they mean what they say ' ; and the reply would be a mere evasion, suggesting either that they meant nothing, or that the questioner had failed to see their plain and unambiguous meaning. In Mendelssohn's mouth it probably amounted to a mere refusal to go farther into the question. And this was right ; for the meaning of a work of art cannot be restated in other terms. It is embedded in the work itself and cannot be torn from its imaginative setting and put down in philosophical prose. The meaning itself, the expressed concept, exists in the work only intuitively, under the form of beauty, and the beauty of a beautiful object cannot be separated from the object itself. The beauty simply is the object as aesthetically seen, or imagined.

But this is a contradiction in terms. A concept can only be conceived, not intuited ; to say that a concept exists intuitively, to speak of a meaning fused or identified with its sensuous vehicle, is merely to contradict oneself. And yet this contradiction is the essence of art. Art is valuable, beautiful, just in so far as it is significant or expressive ; but if we ask what it signifies we get no reply, because (in defiance of the definition of significance) what it signifies is just itself. Kant was stating this fact when he said that beauty was purposiveness without purpose ; the beautiful, he meant, had the air of carrying out some purpose, of meaning or intending something, and when you came to ask *what* it intended, you could never say. Rather than copying Kant by defining art as significance without signification, one might say that it signified *something*, but no one could say what. Hence the perpetual attempt to allegorize art, to detect stratum below stratum of occult meaning beneath its painted surface, is as inevitable as it is fruitless. People have always asked of art ' what does it mean ? ' and they will never stop asking. And answers, necessarily more or less capricious and unsatisfying, will always be found. The facile reply that art means nothing but what it says, is the very pedantry of despair, in which critics who begin to weary of criticism may take refuge, but which the uninstructed will reject for the sophistry that it is.

By emptying it of all meaning and reducing it to the pure play of imagination, the attempt is made to place art on a basis from which it cannot be dislodged, as a permanent and autonomous activity of the mind. But this is *propter vitam vivendi perdere causas.* The real value of art is just its purposiveness, its significance.

True, we cannot say what precisely it purposes or signifies. But that is because art is only art and not philosophy. When you know what you mean, you have achieved philosophy ; but when you know that you mean something, and cannot tell what, you have already achieved something : you have achieved art. And the first stage in knowledge is the discovery that you mean something : the stage in which the mind's reach exceeds its grasp, and barely touches a conception as yet undetermined. This stage only exists to be superseded. When we discover what our meaning is, the aesthetic stage in the history of that thought is over and done with. Art must perish as knowledge grows. But it perishes like the phoenix, to rise again from the very ashes of its own body. To speak of the growth of knowledge is to imply that new thoughts, new facts, are perpetually coming to consciousness. Every one of these must begin as the significance of a work of art ; must begin, that is to say, by being that of which we can only say that we know it is there but cannot tell what it is. This purely intuitive knowledge grasps or presages its object solely as beauty ; and thus beauty is the birthplace of truth, and art, as we have said, the womb and night of the spirit.

The value of art as a form of experience is thus its self-transcendence. Art is not attacked and destroyed by philosophy as by an external enemy ; it destroys itself by its own inner contradiction, by defining itself as at once pure intuition and also expression, imagination and thought, significance without definable signification, the intuitive concept. This contradiction is not irreconcilable. On the contrary, its reconciliation is the whole life of thought. The very existence of the mind is a standing synthesis of intuition and conception, immediacy and mediation, the *that* and the *what*. But it is not at the level of art that the synthesis is effected. Art is the cutting edge of the mind, the question as yet unanswered, the antithesis as yet unsynthesized. The fact that such an unsolved problem exists in the reality of experience is a guarantee that other problems have in the past been raised and solved, for every question, as we know, is weighted by a body of information already won ; and therefore the life of art is always more than art : art rises like a flower from a soil which consists of fact. Yet the flower, though it has absorbed the soil into itself, knows nothing of this soil, and art thinks of itself as a pure act of imagination, cut off and disconnected from anything outside itself. This erroneous self-conception is what marks the artist out and gives him his peculiar character. Positively, he has the freedom of the world of imagery and the mysterious power of presenting in a riddle the solution of the world's problem ; negatively, this freedom is paid for by all those weaknesses and miseries which fall to the lot of the soothsayer. His life is torn in two between the ecstasy of a fruition which, though it solve the riddle of the universe, is itself another riddle, and the despair of those dark hours when the universe is not even a riddle but a tissue of meaningless fact, a tale told by an idiot, full of sound and fury, signifying nothing.

§ 7. *The Dialectic of Art*

By analysing art as a conflict of two opposing elements, we have made possible a dynamic view of its life. If these two elements collapse into an undifferentiated identity, the result must follow that art is a thing—one can hardly call it an activity—which is always and everywhere precisely the same, a tap turned on in the mind or a number turning up again and again in the throw of the dice. But if it is a conflict between intuition and expression, it will change its form and modify itself from top to bottom as this conflict works itself out.

Pure imagination, devoid of any trace of assertion, would be a mere chaotic riot of fantasies in which every image, by its mere transitoriness, would be wholly indeterminate, incapable of being called an image at all :

> Too like the lightning, which doth cease to be
> Ere one can say, It lightens.

Not this condition, but something approximating to it by reason of the random and disconnected character, is found in the vague day-dreaming and night-dreaming of the mind whose control over itself is relaxed. This looseness of control is not a thing to surprise us, but quite the contrary : the sanity of rational life is no gift of nature but an immensely difficult achievement of the mind, and an effort from which even those who most securely grasp it willingly rest from time to time. In such repose the mind returns most deeply into what we have called the night and womb of its being.

Even here, in the activity which we may generically call dreaming, there is no lapse to a mere abstract immediacy. Not only are the separate images retained in consciousness long enough to become definite, but there is a certain interconnexion running through them. Though this be madness, yet there is method in it : this method being the element of structure or organization which differentiates even the wildest dream from the abstract and never actualized ideal of a pure sensational flux. This structure, present even in dreams, is the element which, by becoming more and more explicit, determines the difference between a dream and a work of art. It is not true to say that there is *more* structure in the latter than in the former. Psycho-analysis has shown us, even empirically, that there is an unlimited amount ' of structure, so to speak, in every dream : that connexions can be found by the skilled eye between the most apparently discontinuous elements of the most apparently chaotic dream. But it needed not psycho-analysis to show that a dream, merely by being regarded as a dream, that is, as a single whole, was already recognized as possessing its own unity and therefore an implicit law of its structure. Nothing can, however, be more instructive than the way in which psycho-analysis reveals the distinguishing mark of this structure. It is essentially a structure which is, in the terminology of the psycho-analyst himself, *unconscious*. The dreamer himself is unaware of it until, in collaboration with his psycho-analyst, he brings it to light. The mythological way of stating this fact is to say that the structure was ' in the unconscious '. This is frankly nonsense ; but there is no reason why psycho-analysts, so long as they can actually perform miracles, should be grudged the privilege of choosing their own language, even if it is nonsensical, when describing them. It is nonsense because the structure is not in the unconscious but precisely in the dream, for it is the structure of the dream ; and the dream is conscious enough. If it had been unconscious, that recognition of it by the dreamer which is such a striking incident of good psycho-analysis could not happen. The dreamer actually says, when the structure of his dream is explained to him, ' I see that this *was* the way in which I was actually building up my dream.' That is to say, the revelation made by psycho-analysis is not the bringing into consciousness of what was unconscious, but the bringing into explicitness of what was implicit, the noticing of something already actually experienced in a light in which it had not been noticed before. This new light or new aspect of an experience, separated by a false abstraction from the experience of which it is a new aspect, is called ' the unconscious ' ; and the result of this false abstraction is to obscure the fact that the new light in question is nothing but the hitherto overlooked structure of the experience in

question, and to create the false suggestion that it is another
and a ' repressed ' experience lying behind the ' explicit '
experience. Since *ex hypothesi* the repressed experience
is repressed, that is, reduced to the non-existence of un-
consciousness, the psycho-analyst can say whatever he likes
about it and adopt the most arbitrary and unscientific
canons of interpretation with perfect impunity. Thus the
mythology of the ' unconscious ' frustrates the most brilliant
discovery that psychology has ever made, and covers it with
a growth of rank superstition.

The real function of psycho-analysis is to reveal the
implicit logical or structural element in the dream. Now
this structure, as the psycho-analysts have empirically
shown, can be discovered in all dreams ; but what makes
them dreams, or incoherent imaginings, is that the dreamer
is unaware of it. But unaware in the proper sense he
cannot be, for he is aware of the dream and the structure
is just the dream. The point is that his dreaming of the
dream is, so to speak, just a dream-awareness of this
structure itself. The structure is present to him in an
intuitive or immediate form, and the so-called content of
the dream is nothing but the immediacy of its own form.
This may sound abstruse and unfamiliar, but it is a commonplace of art-criticism. We all know that the meaning of
a work of art, which is just its ' form ' or structure, is so
embedded in the work of art itself that to extricate it is
impossible : it is, in poetry, not a meaning behind the
sounds but ' a resonant meaning or a meaning resonance ',
as Mr. A. C. Bradley puts it. The form and the content are
indistinguishably one ; and the content being imaginative,
the form is not explicitly logical but imaginative too.
The form is the beauty, and beauty as we have already seen
is nothing but the concept in its imaginative guise, thought

in the form of intuition. This may be said to be nonsense, but if so it is nonsense to deny which makes nonsense of all art. It is the description of a paradox, and lays an intentional emphasis on its paradoxical nature. The paradox is an actual paradox, not an imaginary one; and its actuality depends on the fact that intuition and thought are not distinct activities but correlative aspects of experience itself.

Intuition and thought are inseparable, being only the immediacy (actuality, positiveness) and mediation (reflection upon itself) of all experience. Now experience as such is not partly intuitive and partly conceptual, it is all intuitive and all conceptual. But the life of art is a life which falsely conceives itself to be merely intuitive. Now this very life must in reality be conceptual as well; and thus its conceptuality is precisely what appears to it as pure intuition. Hence the paradox that the content of the work of art is its own form in an intuitive guise.

When the dreamer undergoes psycho-analysis he discovers not the hidden meaning of his dreams, but the fact that his dreams were intuitive manifestations of concepts. He discovers that the direct experience of dreaming presents as intuition something that is really thought. To discover that one's dreams thus have a structure may result in going on dreaming as before and then, on waking, analysing their structure; or it may result in fusing these two processes in one and actually constructing one's dreams by a conscious process of control, deliberately determining their course according to a principle of relevance. The first alternative splits life up into an alternation of imagination and reflection, which cannot be stable because the reflection is nothing but the discovery that the imagination never was pure imagination but contained a reflective element or

structure implicit within itself. The second alternative is
art in the ordinary sense.

The difference between art and dreaming is that the artist
is aware that his fantasies have a structure, the dreamer is
not. Art is coherent, and this coherence is attained by
a deliberate effort. Dreaming is incoherent and thus
effortless. But the incoherence of dreaming is only apparent
and not real. The dreamer, and this is what makes him
a dreamer, does not know that he is an artist : does not
know that his dreams are actually being constructed
systematically. A dream that is constructed systematically
in an explicit manner is just a work of art.

In the true life of art, then, the presence of structure is
explicit, and a deliberate effort is made to be systematic.
But this structure is still wholly intuitive, wholly embedded
in the work itself, and incapable of being extracted from
its material and set over against it as ' meaning ' distinguished from the ' words '. Art lives, as art, by keeping
the meaning and the words together in an immediate
unity. The abstract identity of form and content is the
keystone of the artistic consciousness, and artists who
reflect on their art are significantly unanimous in em-
phasizing this fact. Significantly, because the points
emphasized in such self-descriptions are always the points
of danger. Adam, taking visitors round the Garden of Eden,
would always have taken them first to the Tree of the
Knowledge of Good and Evil: ' This is the tree whose fruit
we do not eat.' The artist's effort to be systematic already
implies a distinction between the form or system of art and
its content, the imagery systematized. If this distinction
were allowed to develop, it would split up the unity of the
work of art into form and matter, meaning and words,
conceptual element and sensuous element. This would

destroy the work of art as such altogether. The words would lose their unique or poetic significance, and become prose, mere counters indicative of a conceptual meaning outside them : the life with which art vibrates would vanish, and the whole would become a dead mechanism, a body whose soul lay outside it in the region of disembodied spirit.

All art maintains itself in existence by staving off this separation of body from soul. But in the creative process by which a work of art comes into being, the separation is already implicit : the soul always exists to some extent in advance of the body, for it is only because the artist already knows what his picture is aiming at that he can continue it in one way and not in another. This does not mean that he imagines it in advance of physically painting it : that he may or may not do. But he conceives it in advance of imagining it, in the sense that at any given moment in the process of creation he has in his mind a criterion which enables him to distinguish between the right and the wrong way of continuing the process of imagination itself. Otherwise, he is no real artist but only a dreamer. In so far as he is a real artist, his artistic creation is a self-critical creation, and the criticizing moment or concept —the idea of structure or relevance—is always in advance of the criticized moment, the flow of imaginations which it controls.

To be conscious of this control is to have broken with the life of dreams and to have entered upon the life of art in the ordinary sense. The rationality which distinguishes the artist from the dreamer is nothing but the consciousness of control. Not only is the result of the control conscious, so that the work of art when complete is seen as a systematic whole whose every part is relevant to the rest, but the actual control itself is conscious. The dreamer doubtless works in a sense at constructing his dream, but he does not know that he is working at it. The artist knows he is working : he toils at artistic creation, but because what he is toiling at is imagining, he cannot foresee the end of his toil ; if he could, it would be achieved. So he can give no account of the purpose and aim of his labour, and can only compare it with the agony of childbirth, in the sense that each is an instinctive and unreasoning act of creation calling forth the utmost effort of a human being.

When the artist thinks about his own work and recalls the agony of his travail, he sees that it was an agony because it was an attempt to ' embody an ideal ', to carry out a scheme or plan which was implicit before it was explicit. To the mere passive spectator it would seem that a work of art is nothing before it is explicit ; but that is only the result of drifting round picture-galleries, and saying ' that is a pretty picture ' or ' that is an ugly one ' without troubling to analyse the way in which these judgements grow up in the mind. The creative artist cannot well overlook the fact that these judgements have an origin in which they really come into being by passing from implicitness to explicitness.

But what is the aesthetic act in its implicitness ? It can only be the opposite of the aesthetic act in its explicitness : abstract conception as opposed to abstract intuition. Hence the presupposition of the birth of a work of art is the purely abstract concept of relevance as such : aesthetic structure in general. The painter adds another touch to his picture —real or imaginary—because it is ' needed ', it is ' what the picture wants ' ; in other words it is the abstract concept of relevance that is his explicit criterion.

The concrete life of art is thus explicitly both imaginative and conceptual, and has thus overcome the one-sidedness of pure imagination. And because this is so, because the work of art is constructed on a framework of thought, art is not the withdrawal of the soul into a purely imaginative fairyland but is concrete fact. Hence the necessity for physical works of art and for the recognition by the artist of real minds other than his own—including among these his own future and past mind—with which he desires to communicate, teaching them and learning from them. If art were pure intuition there could be no society of artists, no communication, no physical works of art.

But even now there is a discord in the life of the artist. The concept, pure relevance, is not art itself but a principle outside art which controls it. The work of art, as achieved, is not relevant to itself but beautiful, which is a very different thing. For beauty is relevance become intuitive, the concept losing its abstract conceptual character. Art is thus an alternation between concentration on the abstract concept of relevance (the ' fundamental brain-work ' of which Rossetti spoke) and flight to the abstract intuition of beauty. The cleavage between means and end, technique and inspiration, talent and genius, materials and result, is inevitable in the life of art, and only those who idealize that life by looking at it from the outside deny the dualism. The artist knows that he can only get his work of art by passing through a non-aesthetic world which is that of facts, training, daily life, and so forth. The non-aesthetic character of this world means that he regards it as non-intuitive or purely conceptual : it is for him mere machinery, though indispensable machinery. Of course, to call this world of fact mere machinery is as wrong as to call the world of art pure intuition : they are complementary errors and one implies the other. But they are errors both essential to the life of art.

The artist, then, realizes that abstract conceptual machinery is necessary to his art. Now the abstract concept of aesthetic form is bare relevance, and the artist's concentration of thought on this is art-criticism. Criticism is the opposite of art ; it is pure thinking where art is pure imagination, intellect where art is feeling, and so forth. But it is an opposite into which the artist, is forced by the life of art itself. Either the artist is an incoherent dreamer or he is a critic ; and since he cannot be the former he is always the latter. But though every artist is a critic, he succeeds in being an artist by forgetting and denying that he is a critic ; for to be a critic is not to be an artist. The artist who has failed to keep up the pretence of not being a critic is the person who becomes a critic in the ordinary sense of the word, and hence the truth of the common saying, intended as an insult, that a critic is a man who has tried to be an artist and failed. He has failed because of the vigour of his own mind, which could not be content with the self-deception of being an artist. In the same spirit one might describe a poet as a person who has tried to be a dreamer and failed.

The critic's business is to describe the abstract principles of the genesis of art. But these principles are never really abstract : as the principles governing the origin of this and that particular work of art, they are always historical concrete facts. Therefore the critic is right not to be content with the bare minimum of criticism to which the abstractness of his task might seem to condemn him : he is right to be dissatisfied with saying : ' This is successful and that unsuccessful.' To divide works of art as merely beautiful and merely ugly is not to avoid abstraction, it is to commit the last and most barren of all abstractions ; and that is why a teacher of art would never make such a division in criticizing the work of his pupils. He must describe the specific way in which a work has succeeded or failed, and this necessarily gives rise to all those minute classifications of the sublime, comic, tragic, the epic, drama, lyric, the novel, the short story, and so on *ad infinitum*, which to bad critics are the mere dead weight of weapons they are too weak to handle, and a snare to philosophers who try to reduce them to order either by neatly arranging them in tables or by making a clean sweep of the lot, and substituting the one concept of beauty which unites all their faults in itself. For their fault is just their abstractness, and the alleged concept of beauty is nothing but the abstraction of an autonomous and self-contained aesthetic activity.

Art by its own dialectic gives rise, over against itself, to criticism, which is science. If art is abstract intuition, criticism is abstract conception. But when it is realized that criticism is no abstract thinking but concrete philosophy, it follows that art is no abstract imagining but concrete philosophy too. When these abstractions have been removed, art and criticism can be identified ; and then all life will be seen to have an aspect which is aesthetic and an aspect which is logical. The aesthetic aspect, which the life of art mistakes for the whole, is what we have called the mind's cutting edge : the logical aspect is the weight of fact as asserted, which gives the edge power to cut.

In our account of art we have thus tried to give an account of the cutting edge of the mind, the element of pure spontaneity or inquiry which is the true beginning of knowledge. The so-called aesthetic experience is either a name for all experience in so far as this element of spontaneity, questioning or supposal, enters into it, or else it is a name for something that does not exist at all, namely the alleged life of art, a specific type of experience whose existence is asserted by the philosophical error which abstracts the aesthetic from the logical function and erects them into separate experiences. The consistent pursuit of this error is what we call, empirically, the life of art ; and because it is thus based on an error, the life of art is a futile quest and contradicts itself at every turn. If artists actually live and do well, that is just because they are more than artists, and because their practice is better than their theory ; because they have given up the attempt to live according to their hopelessly unpractical ideal and follow, however unconsciously, the principles of a sounder philosophy, resolving in their life the contradictions which their art cannot resolve.

§ 8. *Play*

As thought, in its most rudimentary form, is art, so action in its most rudimentary form is play. The aesthetic consciousness frames to itself an object which is not asserted but only imagined ; that is to say, the distinction between truth and falsehood does not matter to it, and its object is what it is only because it capriciously chooses to have it so. But this is the very definition of play ; which is that form of action in which the will is untroubled by any question as to right and wrong, expedient or inexpedient, and chooses an end which is an end only because it is thus irresponsibly chosen. The end in play is not chosen as right, or chosen as useful, or chosen as correct, conventional, customary ; it is simply chosen. *Hoc volo, sic iubeo ; sit pro ratione voluntas ;* the will is here an irrational will in the sense that it can give no reason for its choice, precisely as the aesthetic consciousness can give no reason for its imaginings.

Yet there is a reason, in both cases alike. The autonomy of the aesthetic spirit is an illusory autonomy, for it is rooted in facts of which it does not give itself an explicit account ; and just as, from an artist's historical position, we can explain the origin of his artistic prepossessions and outlook, so we can give an explanation of the origin and, as it were, the unconscious motive of any game. We can show how the games of young animals and of children anticipate the serious work of life and train them unawares to meet the problems which will face them later ; and in the games of grown men we detect the expression of ancestral instincts which civilized life on its more serious side fails to satisfy. But all such explanations of play are in part mythological and forced, because they ascribe to it motives which the player, by his very character. as a player, does not feel. From its own point of view play is motiveless, immediate, intuitive ; what motive it has is implicit only.

Art and play are the theoretical and practical forms of the aesthetic consciousness. But because the distinction of will and intellect, being a merely abstract or ideal distinction, does not become explicit till we reach the level of scientific thought, art and play can only be distinguished from a scientific, and not from an aesthetic, point of view. From inside the aesthetic consciousness, no distinction between them can be seen. Thus, from the child's point of view, all playing is playing ' at ' something—playing at robbers, at bears, and so forth—which is imaginative or dramatic personification ; and thus the famous identification of art with play, which has so scandalized scientific theorists, is due not to a philosopher but to an artist, Schiller.

Schiller's identification has often been rejected because art is a high and serious thing and play a childish and trivial ; or because art is a thing of the spirit and play a thing of the body, its source the mere exuberance of physical energy, its aim merely physical pleasure. But these antitheses are

totally false.   Serious art is serious and trivial art is trivial ;
children's games are for children and men's games are for
men.   But as children are naturally and instinctively artists,
so they naturally and instinctively play ; and as art for
grown men is something recaptured, a primitive attitude
indulged in moments of withdrawal from the life of fact, so
play is for grown men something to be done as a legitimate
and refreshing escape from ' work '.   Yet the distinction of
play from work does not consist in its being less hard ;
children work astonishingly hard at their games, which do
not on that account cease to be games ; and many a man
works harder on the football field or on the north face of
Scafell than ever he worked in his office.   The refreshment
and relaxation of play are purely spiritual ; they result
from the fact that play is capricious, that in it we choose
our end for no conscious reason whatever.   Hence it is
a complete mistake to suppose that play is the overflow of
mere physical energy and aimed at merely physical pleasure.
It ought, since the work of Plato and Aristotle on the subject,
to be impossible for any one to speak of merely physical
pleasure ; and to use such language in describing the ' feel '
of one's skin after bathing is merely a sign of careless
analysis, however truthfully one may plead ignorance of the
Philebus and the *Ethics* in excuse.   Certainly, one could
not sail a boat in half a gale unless one had a body ; neither,
for that matter, could one paint a picture.   And the pleasure,
which in neither case is unmixed, but is always a struggle
with and a triumph over pain, is in both cases equally
spiritual.

The prejudice against play on this double head is therefore
groundless.   What may legitimately be said in depreciation
of all play is precisely what may be said against art as such :
namely that it is a primitive, innocent and childlike attitude,

one which has not faced the problems of life and seems to transcend them only by evading them. Yet for this very reason play, like art, gives one a foretaste, as it were, of that condition in which the mind will be when it has faced its problems and conquered them. The innocent soul that has not sinned is merely immature and ignorant compared with the sinner who has repented and been saved ; yet innocence is a foretaste of salvation and far liker to salvation than it is to sinning. So art and play have something in them which though not really divine is a likeness of divinity; and God may be pictured as an artist, or as playing, with far more verisimilitude than as a scientist or a business man. Aristotle actually raised the question whether play might not be considered a good definition of God's activity ; and the only reason why it cannot is that the *sit pro ratione voluntas* of play is below the claims of expediency and right, the action of God above them. God's will, the will of absolute mind, chooses its ends simply because it chooses them ; but this choice includes every possible kind of rationality in itself. Thus to describe God as playing is to make a mockery of man, who must not play ; and to degrade God to a level below that of his creatures.

The enjoyment of play is sensuous, precisely as far as, and in the same way in which, that of art is sensuous : where sensuous means intuitive, immediate, innocent of explicit reason. So the pursuit of play is capricious, like that of art ; and individualistic, like that of art. Play in its simplest form is the solitary play of the child, which plays ' peep-bo ' to itself with a cradle-blanket at the age of a few months ; in a more complex phase the player, like the artist, wants an audience ; and later still he wants competitors. Competition, which is sociability seen from the standpoint of individualism, is the form which sociability most naturally

takes in play ; and the same thing reappears in the intellectual individualism of the economic life. When team-play,
the play of a cricket or football match, begins, we have
reached a high point in the development of play and one
at which individualism is beginning to be transcended.

The love of adventure for its own sake, which leads some
men to eat their lunch out of doors and others to die in the
antarctic winds, is justified by no moral or utilitarian
standard, but by an aesthetic standard. It is not because
it is right or because it is useful that we indulge it in ourselves
and commend it in others, but because it is beautiful, *dulce et
decorum* even to the last extremity. That a man who had
studied the poets all his life should die looking at the sunrise
from high up on Monte Rosa is itself a poem ; and the adventure of love is the mother of poetry because it is already
poetry, because the lover's unreasoning choice of his beloved
is an act of play no less than the climbing of a mountain ;
high and serious play, both of them ; play in which life and
health are staked against the joy of the game and the faith
in a training that has schooled one to play well. Of play,
as of art, the justification is its own splendour. After listen-
ing to the tale of the Mount Everest expedition of 1922, told
with modest eloquence and illustrated by an unforgettable
lantern-show, a sharp-faced middle-aged lady was heard
to remark : ' Well, *I* should like to know what 's the use of
it all.' Use ? the use of sunsets and symphonies, of children's games and lovers' kisses, of swimming in starlit water
or finding a new way up the Pillar ? One can only reply,
as a certain midshipman, questioned as to the use of battle-
ships, is said to have replied, that they are ' no damned use
at all '.

But the lady's question is provocative of swear-words just
because it is right and unanswerable. All play, even the

most splendid, is only play. Beyond it and above it stands the world of utility, and above that again the world of duty. Children play because they have not learnt to take up the burden of life, because they are too young to work and weep : their very sorrows are the sorrows of fancy, and of the real sorrows that stand round their cradle they know nothing. And those of every age who permit themselves to play are permitting themselves to forget that there are duties waiting to be done and evils crying out for correction all round them. Nor is it an answer to protest that the bow cannot always be bent, that the overstrained spirit must be allowed some relief from the burden of its responsibilities ; for these responsibilities, properly understood, are nothing but its own highest and freest life, and to face them is to find, not to sacrifice, our happiness.

The true defence of play is the same as the defence of art. Art is the cutting edge of the mind, the perpetual out-reaching of thought into the unknown, the act in which thought eternally sets itself a fresh problem. So play, which is identical with art, is the attitude which looks at the world as an infinite and indeterminate field for activity, a perpetual adventure. All life is an adventure, and the spirit of adventure, wherever it is found, can never be out of place. It is true that life is much more than this ; it is never, even its most irresponsible moments, a mere adventure ; but this it is ; and therefore the spirit of play, the spirit of eternal youth, is the foundation and beginning of all real life.

IV

RELIGION

§ 1. *The Transition from Art to Religion* [1]

THE life of art is an error. But no error can be purely and
simply erroneous ; and the claim of art to be an expression
of profound and ultimate truth is not a false claim. In art
the very secret of the universe is laid bare, and we know
those hidden things for which the scientist and the philosopher are painfully searching. In good art we apprehend

[1] I may perhaps be permitted here to refer to a book called
Religion and Philosophy which I published in 1916, and in which
I tried to give a general account of the nature of the religious
consciousness, tested and illustrated by detailed analyses of the
central doctrines of Christianity. With much of what that book
contains I am still in agreement ; but there are certain principles
which I then overlooked or denied, in the light of which many of its
faults can be corrected. The chief of these principles is the distinction between implicit and explicit. I contended throughout that
religion, theology, and philosophy were identical, and this I should
now not so much withdraw as qualify by pointing out that the
' empirical ' (i.e. real but unexplained) difference between them is
that theology makes explicit what in religion as such is always
implicit, and so with philosophy and theology. This error led me
into a too intellectualistic or abstract attitude towards religion, of
which many critics rightly accused me ; for instance, in the interpretation of religious symbolism I failed to see that for religion itself
the symbol is always an end, never a mere means to the expression
of an abstract concept. Hence I failed to give an account of the
uniqueness of Christ, of miracle, and of worship ; I failed to discover
any real ground for the concrete distinction not only between man
and God, but between man and man ; and I confessed my inability
to deal either with the problem of evil or with the all-important
question of the relation between religion and art. In these and
kindred ways I would offer this chapter as a correction of the book
in question, out of the recognition of whose shortcomings it has in
fact grown. But, as required by the plan of the present book, the
whole subject is far more briefly treated.

the secret of the universe in its truth, in bad art we are
mocked by a lying revelation. Yet, since the work of art is
only our own imagination, there is no way of settling the
disputes concerning the merit of a particular work, though
just because art reveals truth these disputes are inevitable.

But however truly the secret of the world is expressed
under the form of beauty, the expression is always formally
imperfect. It is of the essence of truth that the mind should
be able to say what it is, to state it in explicit terms, subject
it to criticism and attack, and watch it emerge strengthened
from the ordeal.   The secret revealed in art is a secret that
no one can utter, and therefore not truly revealed ; in the
actual aesthetic experience we clasp it to our bosom in an
ecstasy of passion and try to make it inalienably ours :

Nequiquam, quoniam nil inde abradere possunt . . .

At the crowing of the cock it vanishes from our presence
and we are left to face the dawn of another day in the
knowledge that we have lost it.   The soul does not want
a ghostly lover ; she asks for the fate not of Margaret :

Is there any room at your head, Saunders,
Is there any room at your feet ?
Or any room at your side, Saunders,
Where fain, fain I wad sleep ?

but of Janet :

They shaped him in her arms twa
An aske but and a snake ;
But aye she grips and hauds him fast
To be her warldis make.

They shaped him in her arms twa
But and a deer sae wild ;
But aye she grips and hauds him fast,
The father of her child.

The secret of the universe, in its own right nature as
rational truth, is to the soul no weird visitant from beyond

the grave, but husband, father and son at once, a lamp to her feet and a rod and staff to comfort her. Yet, as the old ballad-maker knew, it reveals itself to the soul in this its true shape only after strange and terrible trials of faith. Of these trials, which together make up the dark night of the soul—that dead hour of the night when Janet heard the bridles ring—the failure of art is the first, and, because the first, the most heartrending.

The failure of art is, as we have said, not a complete failure. Substantial truth is revealed to us ; we are not cheated of that ; but it is revealed only in the equivocal form of beauty, submerged, so to speak, in the flood of aesthetic emotion. It is only because truth is revealed in it that the emotion is aesthetic ; but emotional truth, truth in the guise of beauty, is not truth at all in the formal sense. Art asserts nothing ; and truth as such is matter of assertion. To be itself, it demands logical form. Art fails us because it does not assert. It is pregnant with a message that it cannot deliver.

To overcome the failure of art, it is necessary to introduce into it a logical element. Now we know already that art, as pure imagination, is a thing that cannot exist, for any and every experience as such must already contain a logical element. The true way of overcoming art's failure is the discovery of this truth, the discovery that what we have been enjoying all the time is not mere aesthetic experience but aesthetic-logical experience, which means, as we shall see in the sequel, philosophy. What appeared as art turns out to be philosophy, and thus the analysis of experience travels direct from art to philosophy, as we saw in the last chapter.

But in point of fact people become aware of the breakdown of art long before they are able to effect this new analysis of the so-called aesthetic experience. They find that the life of art (that is, the life built up on the erroneous belief that imagination and assertion are distinct and separate activities) does not satisfy them. It fails to satisfy them precisely because of this separation between imagining and asserting ; for this separation is the root of the instability and insecurity which are the bane of the aesthetic life.

When the artist becomes aware of this, when he achieves in some sort the diagnosis of his own disease, even if he does it no less instinctively than a dog eats grass, he must find a remedy. We have already indicated the true remedy ; but that can hardly be discovered without deep reflection and long experience. The simplest remedy, and therefore the one which is likeliest to be adopted in the blind gropings of a soul which as yet knows little of its own nature, is to reunite forcibly the activities which have been divided : to assert what it imagines, that is, to believe in the reality of the figments of its own imagination.

This is the definition of religion, so to speak, from beneath : the purely abstract or formal definition whose purpose is to give the minimum account of the lowest and most rudimentary religious consciousness. It is the mere armature on which our concrete conception of religion is to be built up, and the reader need not trouble to point out its inadequacy as a description of the higher religions. Here and elsewhere, in fact, the reader is earnestly implored to resist the vice of collecting ' definitions ' of this and that and the other, as if any one but a fool imagined that he could compress a thing like art or religion or science into an epigram which could be lifted from its context and, so lifted, continue to make sense. Giving and collecting definitions is not philosophy but a parlour game. The writer's definition of religion (as of art and so forth) is coextensive with this entire book, and will nowhere be found in smaller compass. Nor will it be found in its completeness there ; for no book is wholly self-explanatory, but solicits the co-operation of a reasonably thoughtful and instructed reader.

Religion, relatively to art, is the discovery of reality. The artist is an irresponsible child who feels himself at liberty to say exactly what comes into his head and unsay it again without fear of correction or disapproval. He tells himself what story he likes and then, at the bidding of a whim, ' scatters the vision for ever '. In religion, all this irresponsibility has gone. His vision is for the religious man no toy to make and mar at will ; it is the truth, the very truth itself. The actual object of imagination, which in art obscurely means a truth that cannot be clearly stated, in religion is that truth itself : the secret of the universe is revealed, no longer merely shadowed forth in parables but made manifest in visible form ; and this revelation makes explicit for the first time the distinction between reality and unreality, truth and falsehood.

§ 2. *The Growth of Religion*

In our study of art we found it necessary to distinguish between various grades of aesthetic experience : first, the unreflective fantasy of the child who does not ask himself whether stories are true or false, whose life is therefore an undistinguished and confused web of fancies and facts ; and secondly, the deliberate aesthetic act of the educated man for whom this confused web has settled down into its component parts, so that he passes from fact to fancy, and back again, in full consciousness of what he is doing. In the first phase the distinction between fact and fancy is implicit ; in the second, it is explicit. Thus, it is impossible to give a true account [1] of the experience of a person who sees

---

[1] Yet, of course, the truth of this account is not ultimate, because it is tainted by the fallacious way in which the distinction is conceived.

fairies without saying 'Now he is perceiving, now he is imagining'; but the person himself does not make this distinction, and the observer must make it for him. But an artist in the ordinary sense does make this distinction, at any rate in the moments of transition from aesthetic to non-aesthetic experience and vice versa. Hence the principle of aesthetic experience is implicit in the child and the unsophisticated seer of ghosts and fairies, explicit in the artist; indeed that is what makes him *par excellence* an artist; he has made a discovery about himself which raises his aesthetic life to a wholly new level.

This distinction is repeated in religion. There is a primitive grade of religious experience in which all fantasies tend to be asserted as real. We have spoken of the *seer* of ghosts and fairies as an example of rudimentary art; the *believer in* ghosts and fairies is the parallel example of rudimentary religion. In this primitive stage it is not easy to distinguish the two. Even the artist, with all his reflective self-consciousness, can hardly give you a satisfactory answer to the question whether he believes in Hamlet or only ' sees ' him without believing in him. The point at which a child begins to ask whether stories are true, and passes through the crisis of learning to disbelieve in fairies, is by no means an early point in its development; and when it arrives, it indicates the emergence of religion from art, of the primitive religious consciousness from the primitive aesthetic consciousness which is its soil and its source; till then the question whether a given fantasy was real or unreal had simply not occurred to the mind; that is, art had not yet given birth to religion. For ultimately, religion cannot mean the assertion of all fantasies as indiscriminately real. That is impossible, because they are in open conflict one with another. The assertion of some as real involves the denial of others, and religion is this polarized activity of assertion-denial as applied to the world of fantasies.

Primitive religion does not yet explicitly realize the full nature of this activity. For it ' all things are full of gods ' ; that is, it begins by trying to assert all its fantasies indiscriminately, and peoples the world not only with gods, heroes, fairies, nymphs and so forth, but with other and less anthropomorphic imaginings, strange energies, impersonal but beneficent or dangerous, the power of the spell and the charm, the mysterious significance of the hearth or the merestone, the creative forces that lurk in the organs of sex or the world of springing plants. Such are the gods of primitive religion, for all primitive religion is polytheistic, in whatever shape it conceives its gods. It is idle, in this primitive phase of the religious consciousness, to seek for distinctions between gods and ghosts, between spell and prayer, between the divine and the diabolical. Religion and magic are here fused in their primitive unity ; for magic is but the shadow of religion, becoming sharper and blacker as religion takes on a more and more definite shape and substance in the self-consciousness of the developing mind.

Just as art solidifies out of the chaos of infantile imaginings into the order and clarity of developed aesthetic form, so out of this primitive welter of gods the religious mind by its own inner dialectic rises to the higher religion. The mainspring of this dialectic is the recognition of the true nature of assertion. Pure fancy is monadic, tolerant : it cares for nothing beside its momentary object, and does not even trouble to find out whether anything incompatible with this object is being fancied elsewhere. But assertion is the transcending of this monadism, for to make any given assertion is to commit oneself to the denial of whatever contradicts it. Now religion is essentially assertion, belief. To believe this is to deny that. Therefore religion by its very nature is pledged to selectiveness, to a discrimination between the utterances of the spirit, to a dualism between true vision and false vision. At first, when religion in its most primitive phase is as yet ignorant of its own nature, and asserts without understanding what assertion means, it thinks it can assert every fantasy that arises in the mind ; and in this phase anything may be an object of worship. Here it is only the attitude of worship that distinguishes religion from art ; in the indiscriminateness of their fancy they are identical. But when the religious mind discovers that to assert one fantasy means denying another, primitive religion and its easy polytheism are doomed. The historical steps by which this dialectic has worked itself out in human history are not here our business ; we are concerned only to point out the nature of the principle which has been at work.

The effect of this principle is to produce for the first time a world or cosmos of imagination. Art has no cosmology, it gives us no view of the universe ; every distinct work of art gives us a little cosmology of its own, and no ingenuity will combine all these into a single whole. But religion is essentially cosmological, though its cosmology is always an imaginative cosmology. Any given religious experience can be fitted by this cosmology into the scheme of the whole, and labelled as an ascent into the third heaven, a temptation of the devil, and so forth. Hence religion is social, as art never can be. The sociability of artists is a paradoxical and precarious thing, and ceases the instant they begin their actual artistic work. But the sociability of religion is part of its fundamental nature. The life of religion is always the life of a church. This is because religion achieves an explicit logical structure. It is assertion, and in its higher forms knows that it is assertion, though even in its most primitive

forms its implicit logic produces the instinctive and unreflective sociability of primitive cultus. Now assertion or
the logical function of the mind is the recognition of reality
as such, and reality is that which is real for all minds. If
a number of minds are engaged in imagining, they have no
common ground, for each man's imaginations are his own.
But if they are engaged in asserting, they at once become
a society, for each asserts what he believes to be not his own
but common property, objective reality. And even when
their assertions are different, they are not merely different,
like different works of art, but contradictory ; and contradiction, even in its extreme forms of persecution and war,
is a function of sociability.

It is the explicitly rational character of religion that
necessitates religious controversy and persecution, for these
are only corollaries of its cosmological and social nature.
To deprecate them and ask religion to refrain from them is
to demand that it shall cease to be religion ; and the demand
is generally made by those shallow minds which hate the
profundity and seriousness of the higher religions and wish
to play at believing all the creeds in existence. This religious
aestheticism, or degradation of religion to the level of play,
for which a creed is a mere pretty picture to be taken up and
put down at will, is only one of the enemies which religion
to-day encounters, and a despicable enemy at that. There
are others, more formidable because they are the children
of religion itself.

The development of religion, when it proceeds healthily
according to the law of its own dialectic, results in the ideal
of a single supreme God worshipped by a single universal
church. Within this God all the obscure ghosts and demons
of primitive polytheism find their account ; within this
church the most diverse impulses of savage superstition are

absorbed and transmuted. This transmutation of a primitive formless chaos into an ordered system of belief and ritual is the work, never quite beginning and never quite ending, of the religious spirit in its self-critical development, a work carried out simply by using the logical weapons of assertion and denial. A given element of primitive religion is split up by analysis into elements of which one can be placed on the side of affirmation as an attribute of God, a sacrament, a rite, and so forth, while the other is placed on the side of denial as an attribute of the devil or a form of witchcraft, magic, or blasphemy.

For, just as the aesthetic consciousness in its self-organization distinguishes the positive ideal of beauty from the negative ideal of ugliness, so the religious consciousness polarizes its own self-development into the acts and beliefs which it asserts and those which it denies. And over against God with his hierarchy of angels and saints the very nature of religion requires that there should be spirits of evil culminating in the devil ; over against the church there must be an antichurch of idolaters or devil-worshippers whose practices are not religious in the proper sense but magical, that is, not non-religious but anti-religious. The dreadful history of witchcraft is no cruel freak of the world-spirit ; it is a necessary manifestation of the religious consciousness, and every religious age, every religious revival, will always produce similar fruits.

§ 3. *Religion and its Object*

The secret of the universe, which to art only appears in the equivocal form of beauty, is revealed to religion in the definite and clear-cut form of God. That which art cannot express except in its immediate intuitive shape, can by religion be stated in words in the form of a creed. This is because the assertive or logical element in religion has checked the unregulated flow of images which characterized art, and fixed one image to the exclusion of others ; or rather, this one image absorbs all others into itself, either positively as parts of itself or negatively as elements excluded from itself, but on that very account implied by it as its own shadow.

Now God, as essentially describable in terms of a creed, is a unity, but not a mere abstract unity. Had he been such a unity, he would not have been describable, for he would have been merely himself, as a work of art is merely itself, and therefore only expressible by saying that he is what he is ; this being in fact the only way in which a work of art can be described. Thus a religion which makes of its God a mere abstract unity does violence to its own nature as religion, and falls back from religion into art. This seems to be what has happened in the case of Mohammedanism ; and the result, namely the Mohammedan negation of art, confirms this; for that religion, being itself already characterized by an unresolved residuum of art, regards any further concession to art as at once unnecessary and dangerous.

The existence of a creed is thus bound up with the conception of God as no mere abstract unity, but a unity which contains in itself its own differentiation. Whenever this conception of God tends to be lost, as is sometimes the case in mystical religion, God tends to appear as the unutterable or indescribable, that is to say the value of the creed, which is the sign and guarantee of the rationality of religion, tends to be denied.

God, we are told by theologians, is the ultimate reality, conceived as spirit ; spirit omnipotent, omniscient, creative, transcending all sense or immediacy, yet immanent in his church. But this language, well enough in theology, is very far from natural to religion ; and it is of the utmost importance to avoid premature identifications of religion and theology. From the simple and unsophisticated point of view of the religious consciousness, it is not the spirituality nor the immanence of God that is important, nor even his power or goodness, but his holiness, the necessity of falling down before him in adoration. This sense of the holiness of God is the explicit differentia of the religious experience ; though doubtless there is much that is implicit in that experience, to be discovered there by theological or philosophical reflection, beside that or rather behind it.

This sense of holiness or attitude of worship is so far the centre and nucleus of religion that any account of the religious consciousness depends for its success on the way in which it deals with this feature. It is a feature generally recognized by modern students of religion. We are sometimes told that the essence of religion is a certain feeling for the divine, and that any object which excites this feeling, or (which would seem to be the same thing) possesses this quality of divinity, is a proper object for the religious consciousness. Sometimes, more explicitly, we are told that the feeling in question is the feeling of ' the uncanny ', which seems to be a word chosen in order to embrace both poles of the religious principle : the positively holy and the negatively holy, the divine and the diabolical. But the writers to whom we have alluded make no attempt to give a real account of this feeling, whatever they call it. They simply state it as a curious fact that religion is empirically characterized by this feeling. Yet if it is a universal characteristic of religion, it must be bound up with its essential nature, and capable of being deduced from it.

Holiness is to religion what beauty is to art. It is the specific form in which truth appears to that type of con-

sciousness. As religion, therefore, is a dialectical development of art, so holiness is a dialectical development of
beauty. Now religion is art asserting its object. The object
of art is the beautiful, and therefore the holy is the beautiful
asserted as real. All the characteristics of holiness and of
God as holy are found to revolve round this centre. The
holy is, generically, object of aesthetic contemplation, and
as such beautiful ; and this is true of all the objects of
religion. Further, holiness, like beauty, polarizes itself into
the positively holy (God) and the negatively holy, that which
we are forbidden to find holy or worship, the devil and all
his works. But specifically, holiness is asserted as real,
and therefore God is regarded as not our own invention,
not a fancy or work of art, but a reality, indeed the only
and ultimate reality. Hence that rapture and admiration
which we enjoy in the contemplation of a work of art is in
the case of God fused with the conviction that we here come
face to face with something other than ourselves and our
imaginings, something infinitely real, the ground and source
of our own being. It is this fusion which constitutes the
sense of holiness, and forms the basis and motive of worship.
Neither the real nor the beautiful is as such the proper object
of adoration : it is only the aesthetic attitude towards
ultimate reality, or conversely the elevation of beauty into
a metaphysical principle, that constitutes worship. Thus
the enemy of religion is idolatry, or the attempt to worship
an object which, however exquisite to the artist's eye, cannot
claim to be the ultimate reality. The sin of the idolater is
to worship his own works of art known to be such. This is
not true religion, because true religion worships the real
God, no mere figment of the imagination. But it is easy to
slip into idolatry just because the aesthetic attitude and the
religious attitude are so closely akin. The difference is

simply that in religion we believe in the reality of our object while in art we do not ; and hence in religion the mind becomes aware that it is in danger of illusion.

God and religion are thus correlative ; and to doubt the reality of God is to deny the validity and legitimacy of religion. There are no religions without a god or gods : what have passed by that name have been either philosophies, or religions whose gods have escaped the eye of the observer, or a kind of mechanical contrivance put on the market by a deluded or fraudulent inventor.

The life of religion is worship, and because religion is fundamentally social this means social worship. This worship is, naturally, at bottom an exercise of the aesthetic consciousness. All acts of worship, whether they take the form of singing, dancing, speech, or the like, are first and foremost aesthetic acts. Prayer and the ritual of the mass are developments of artistic speech and the gestures of dancing, and bear unmistakable traces of their origin. But worship is no more mere art than holiness is mere beauty. It is a dialectical development of art, and a development of this kind involves the surrender or transmutation of much that characterized the earlier stages of the development. Religion in general parts with that freedom and irresponsibility which are the mark of the spirit's infancy in art, and this gives the clue to the development which art must undergo before it becomes worship. Worship is art whose object is conceived as a reality. This implies that the artist when he becomes a worshipper is no longer free to fancy anything he likes, just because it is beautiful. He must in all his worship glorify God, that is to say he must make his aesthetic acts illustrate the creed of his religion. His subject is given : he is no more free to choose it than to choose his creed. And again, though this really comes to

the same thing, his art must be a corporate art, not one that
satisfies his own standards simply, but one that suits the
special needs of his fellow-worshippers. The musician
gravely misunderstands his place in the church if he offers
to overhaul our hymn-books and replace all the ' bad music '
by good. He may be a perfectly competent judge of music,
but music and religious music are not the same thing. And
this applies equally to those forms of quasi-religious art
which express the common aspirations of a nation, a school,
or a political party. Songs and poems of this patriotic type
are almost always very bad indeed by the standards of art ;
but to condemn them for that reason would mean overlooking the whole of the dialectical development which
separates art from religion.

§ 4. *Symbol and Meaning in Religion*

Hitherto we have been describing, in the briefest possible
summary, the more superficial aspects of the religious
consciousness. But we have not yet attempted to understand the inner meaning of its life.

The key to the comprehension of religion is a principle
which in religion itself exists only implicitly. This principle
is the distinction between symbol and meaning.

Religion is a structure of sensuous or imaginary elements,
like art, and—for that matter—like every other form of
consciousness. These elements in religion take the form
partly of mythological pictures and narratives, partly of
acts of worship ; these two being the objective and subjective sides of the same reality. The ritual of a particular
festival and its mythology are intimately bound up together,
so intimately that it has been possible to argue now that the
mythology is the source of the ritual, now that the ritual
is the source of the mythology. In point of fact they are

inseparable and come into existence together, sacred act and sacred story ; and they attain their highest and most rational form when the sacred story reveals itself as a creed and the sacred act as the solemn recitation of that creed. This combination of an act with an account of the act given by the acting mind to itself, or—to put it the other way round—the combination of a certain idea with actions appropriate to that idea, is not peculiar to religion, though under the name of ritual it is especially characteristic of religion.

Now these acts and stories, with all their developments, form the body of religion, and its soul lies beyond them in their meaning. They are thus symbolic in character. Their value and purpose lie not in what they are but in what they signify. They are but the ' outward and visible signs ' of an ' inward and spiritual grace ', and are related to this ' grace ' as word to meaning. We said just now that this principle was only implicit in religion, yet we have quoted a statement of it from the English Catechism. This statement, when closely examined, will be found to miss the real point ; and therefore our first remark holds good. We are told that the ' inward and spiritual grace ' is ' the body and blood of Christ, which are verily and indeed taken and received by the faithful in the Lord's Supper '. But in the natural and literal sense of these words, they are simply not true. Whatever view of the Eucharist we take, it is heretical to assert that the communicant partakes of the body and blood of Christ naturally and literally. The sacred body and blood are present only by a miracle, and this implies that, in spite of the ' verily and indeed ', the statement that the body and blood of Christ are received by the faithful is not a complete statement. It is not merely that the bread means the body of Christ ; the body of

Christ in its turn means something which is not explicitly stated.

To take a simpler case, we tell little children that God is their other father up in the sky. These words are the outward sign of a certain imaginative act (to analyse the case as the Catechism analyses the Lord's Supper), and this imaginative act reveals to the child a more or less elderly person in a tweed suit living somewhere out of sight over-head. But is this the *meaning* of the child's religion? certainly not; it is the mere imagery of it. The imaginative picture of God is a symbol, whose value lies not in what it is but in what it means. And this, which is so plainly true of the pictures of God which we encourage children to form, is equally true of all those imaginative pictures of God which constitute the body—as opposed to the soul—of any religious belief.

Now when we are teaching a child about God, we do not, if we are gifted with ordinary intelligence, say: 'Of course, God isn't *really* your heavenly father, because he isn't literally your father and he isn't literally in the sky: you must interpret these symbols in a spiritual sense.' We know that this kind of qualification would prevent the child from getting anything at all out of our teaching, good or bad, except a certain contempt for the whole subject. Whereas if we boldly say to the child what we know to be literally untrue, that it has a loving and watchful father in the sky, what actually happens is that the child will develop simul-taneously two lines of thought. First, it will speculate as to how God ever came there, how he gets his dinner, and so forth ('I expect he has an aeroplane,' and the like). Secondly, it will, perhaps rather to our surprise, start interpreting the symbolism in a spiritual sense on its own account; connect this heavenly father with its own moral life, with the beauty of nature, with family affection, and other spiritual elements in its experience. These two trains of thought, the superstitious and the rational respectively, the literal and spiritual interpretations of the symbol, develop in a child's mind side by side with no appearance of conflict ; or at least, with only minor and occasional conflicts. What the child never does is to say clearly to itself that the literal or superstitious element is mere fiction, and the spiritual or rational element truth. The truth grows up in a scaffolding of fiction within the child's mind ; deprive it of the scaffolding and it will never grow, or at best, like an apple-tree that has not been properly supported by a dead stake in its youth, will grow crooked and mis-shapen, and fail to strike its roots firmly home.

All religion conforms to this type. It is all, from top to bottom, a seed growing secretly, surrounded by an integument which is not itself the living germ but only its vehicle. It is thought growing up in the husk of language, and as yet unconscious that language and thought are different things. The distinction between what we say and what we mean, between a symbol or word and its meaning, is a distinction in the light of which alone it is possible to understand religion ; but it is a distinction hidden from religion itself. It is implicit in religion, and becomes explicit only when we pass from religion to science. In science, language is transparent and we pierce through it, throw it on one side, in reaching the thought it conveys : in religion, language is opaque, fused with its own meaning into an undifferentiated unity which cannot be separated into two levels. Lose the symbol, and in religion you lose the meaning as well, whereas in science you merely take another symbol, which will serve your purpose equally.

The distinction between symbol and meaning is implicit

in religion, and this is perhaps the most fundamental thing
about religion in general as distinct from other forms of
experience. All religious terms, phrases, acts, are symbolic ;
but if they were explicitly recognized to be symbolic they
would be recognized to be exchangeable with others. If
churchgoing was an explicit symbol, we should know what
it symbolized—the unity of human society as informed by
the divine spirit, or whatever it may be—and we should be
able to find the same meaning exemplified in other acts,
like waiting to be served in a shop or travelling in a third-
class carriage. These other acts would then become symbolic of the same meaning, and would be substitutes for
churchgoing. If a boy learns a certain geometrical truth,
he is taught to symbolize it in terms of a particular triangle.
But if he is unable to separate it from this triangle and to
see it equally well in another, we say that he does not yet
understand it. So a truth which is only grasped under the
symbol of a particular act or phrase and cannot be freely
symbolized in other acts or phrases is as yet imperfectly
grasped.

   If, with these arguments in mind, we say : ' To-day I will
glorify God by weeding my garden or playing tennis instead
of going to church,' and if we defend ourselves by quoting
Scripture to the effect that God is everywhere and is not
confined within the four walls of a church, our parish
priest will reply that God has appointed his own means of
grace, which to neglect is to neglect God ; that the attempt
to sanctify the whole of life can only lead to the sanctifying
of none ; and that in point of fact our real motives for
staying away from church are irreligion, indolence, and
spiritual pride. This will be his reply if he is a religious
man and knows his business ; for we have been trespassing
on the implicitness of the religious symbol and so breaking

away from the religious attitude. This is in itself a legitimate act, and a priest will not despise it, though he may disapprove of it. But if it shelters itself under the cloak of religion, it becomes hypocritical and the object of a just contempt. It is irreligion arguing in the name of religion.

But the strange thing is that this very attitude, irreligion appearing in the guise of religion, is typical of religion itself in its highest manifestations. The great saints really do find God everywhere, really do prove their proposition about any triangle that is presented to them, really do transfuse with religion the whole of life. This is at once the perfection and the death of the religious consciousness. For in grasping the inmost meaning of ritual and worship it deprives these special activities of their special sanctity and of their very reason for existing ; the whole body of religion is destroyed by the awakening of its soul. But the awakened soul, in this very moment of triumph, has destroyed itself with its own body : it has lost all its familiar landmarks and plunged into that abyss of mysticism in which God himself is nothing. Mysticism is the crown of religion and its deadliest enemy ; the great mystics are at once saints and heresiarchs.

These consequences flow from the fact that the distinction between symbol and meaning is implicit in religion. Because the distinction is there, is not merely absent, the religious word or act is charged with significance ; it is felt to be burdened with all the weight of an unspoken message, and this sense of oppressive meaningfulness is the true source of holiness and worship. For these are the character of the mysterious and of our attitude towards it. We do not understand or see the truth, but only the symbol which bodies it forth ; and because this symbol does contain the truth we regard it as infinitely precious. Yet the distinction between symbol and meaning is not explicit, and hence, because the truth and its symbolic vehicle are fused together, the importance really attaching to the truth is transferred to its symbol, and we cling to the symbol, the outward act or image or formula, instead of trying to get behind it, slough it off and reach the truth it conveys.

Thus for the religious consciousness the symbol is sacred. Feeling religious in bed is no substitute for attending the Eucharist ; and a philosopher would not be regarded as a Christian for subscribing to a statement which he declared to be a mere paraphrase of the Apostles' Creed in philosophical terms.   Indeed, the moment he began talking about the Absolute Spirit, all pious people would unhesitatingly write him down an atheist.

But because the symbolic principle is implicit in religion, it follows that religion itself is in constant danger of explicitly discovering it, and this at the very moment when religion attains its highest and purest form.   Ordinary religion maintains its equilibrium, so far as it does so, because of its low potential.   It is not religious enough to upset its own religiosity.   But an intensely religious person, one who takes seriously the highest and deepest elements of his own faith, is bound to come into conflict with religion itself. Very religious people always shock slightly religious people by their blasphemous attitude to religion ; and it was precisely for blasphemy that Jesus was crucified.   But here we touch on a subject to be dealt with in section 6.

To distinguish a symbol from its meaning is to put oneself in the way of explaining or translating the symbol. Now it is matter of common observation that religion never explains itself.   It states itself in the form of ritual and imagery, and if the catechumen were to ask, ' What does this language mean ? ' he would get no answer, except further imagery of the same kind. In point of fact he does not ask the question. He picks up the meaning as best he can, all embedded as it is in the imagery. Anthropologists who have long forgotten, if they ever knew, what religion really is, inquire of savages what they mean by their ritual and get no answer, and jump to the conclusion that they mean nothing. Such a *salto mortale* only proves that there are no limits to the possibilities of misunderstanding; for one would have supposed no frame of mind to be more familiar than that in which one repeats an act or phrase in the conviction that one has expressed one's meaning literally when, in point of fact, one has only uttered a metaphor. This is the normal way in which primitive and unsophisticated thought expresses itself. It neither explains nor asks for an explanation. To ask for explanations is the mark of extreme sophistication; in other words, it is the mark of the life of explicit thought. Thus a professor, asked by a member of the Salvation Army whether he was saved, replied 'Do you mean σεσωσμένος, σωθείς or σωζόμενος?' and conversely the great Dr. Johnson, great in his simplicity of heart, revisiting Pembroke College in his old age, once expressed a doubt to the then Master as to whether he might not be damned. 'What, sir,' said the scientific intellect in the person of gentle Dr. Adams, 'do you mean by damned?' But Dr. Johnson was not to be beguiled. 'Sent to hell, sir,' he replied, 'and punished everlastingly.'

Art is untranslatable, religion cannot translate itself. Art cannot be translated because it has no meaning except the wholly implicit meaning submerged, in the form of beauty, in the flood of imagery. Religion cannot translate itself not because it has no meaning, for it has a very definite meaning, to elicit which is the progressive task of theology and philosophy; but because, although it has a meaning

I

and knows that it has a meaning, it thinks that it has expressed this meaning already. And so it has, but only metaphorically ; and this metaphorical self-expression, this fusion of symbol and meaning, requires translation just because it thinks it does not require it. For literal language is only language recognizedly metaphorical, and what we call metaphorical language is language failing to realize that it is only metaphor. Religion utters formulae of worship and prayer in which it thinks it is saying what it means. But what is said is never, in religion or elsewhere, what is meant : the language never is the meaning. This truth religion has not discovered, and it thinks that its symbolic imagery, blood and fire, sin and redemption, prayer, grace, immortality, even God, is the literal statement of its thought, whereas it is in reality a texture of metaphor through and through.

Hence arises a perpetual misunderstanding. Taken literally, the statements made by religion are often false, or at least doubtful. But religion is committed to asserting them as true. Just as some incidents in Shakespeare's histories are historically true, so some incidents in the Bible are historically true. But—and religion by its very nature cannot see this—neither in the one case nor in the other has this historical truth anything to do with aesthetic or religious value. It is not important in the interests of religion to prove by historical research that the world was really made in seven solar days, or that Jesus was really born of a virgin. But it is intensely important to discover what people have meant by asserting that these things were so. To say they meant nothing except to assert an historical fact is to destroy the whole of religion at a blow. It is to deny the soul of religion in order to have the amusement of quarrelling over its body. The assertion of such facts as the existence of a person called God, this person's intention of judging the world at some future date, and so forth, is not religion : religion exists only in meaning the right thing by these assertions. But whereas the bare assertions, without the meaning, would be not religion but art, the bare meaning severed from the assertions would be not religion but philosophy.

Something of this kind is symbolized by religion itself in the concept of faith. One aspect of the great paradox of religion is the fact that religion claims truth but refuses to argue. Rational truth—and all truth is rational—is essentially that which can justify itself under criticism and in discussion. But religion always withdraws itself from the sphere of discussion, leaving that sphere to its ally theology, and claims (or at least, permits theology to claim on its behalf) that religious truth is grasped by faith and not by ' reason ' or the argumentative frame of mind. But this claim is a self-contradiction, and critics of religion not altogether unjustly accuse it of trying to ' have it both ways ', of claiming knowledge, which means rationality, as long as the claim can be conveniently maintained, thus inviting criticisms which it then refuses to face, and retiring into a shelter of agnosticism. Such a religious agnosticism is worthy of honour and respect when it takes the form of the mind's self-abasement before divine mysteries in the face of which all our creeds are but childish prattle and all our worship a superstitious mummery ; when, that is to say, it represents the recognition by religion of its own inability to solve its own problems. But when it is flaunted by a complacent religiosity as an excuse for believing anything it likes, in defiance of the protests made by the scientific and historical consciousness, it deserves nothing but the contempt which, happily, it as a rule excites.

Faith is described by the writer to the Hebrews as
πραγμάτων ἔλεγχος οὐ βλεπομένων, an outreaching of the mind
beyond that which it immediately possesses. Now in a
sense this is simply a generic description of experience as
a whole. Experience as such is self-transcendence, and

> a man's reach must exceed his grasp,
> Or what 's a heaven for ?

where ' heaven ' simply means the transcendent, the goal
as yet unattained. The definition quoted, therefore, is of
interest primarily as showing that the writer, like the other
great writers of the early Church,[1] recognized the self-
transcending character of religion, the essentially self-
destructive dialectic of the highest religious life. But faith
is the specific form of the religious reason. It is that knowledge of ultimate truth which, *owing to its intuitive or
imaginative form,* cannot justify itself under criticism.
This qualification is important, for other modes of knowledge—science, history—fail to justify themselves under
criticism, as we shall see, and yet are not forms of faith.
To overlook this is a common source of confusion and
sophistry. Religious apologetic, seizing upon the truth that
science depends in the last resort upon unjustifiable assumptions, accuses science of being in the same boat with religion,
the boat of faith. Nothing could be less true or better
calculated to confuse the whole issue. Faith is essentially
intuitive and not assumptive. God is the object of faith,
not an hypothesis : Euclidean space is an hypothesis, not
an object of faith.

[1] I refer to such passages as 1 Cor. xiii. 12, which I have ventured
to take as the motto of this book ; Rom. viii. 18–25 ; Rev. xxi. 22,
on which I have commented below ; and all the passages dealing
with the Parousia, which I interpret as, at any rate in part, a symbolic
presentation of the same thought. In St. Paul the thought breaks
the bonds of the Parousia symbolism and becomes explicit.

Faith is thus the mind's attitude towards a symbol which expresses a truth not explicitly distinguished from the symbol. Hence the truth is something 'not seen', for the symbol, so to speak, occults it, it is hidden behind the symbol, which is opaque to thought and yet is felt to be charged with the significance of the hidden truth. By being so charged, it acquires an intense emotional value, for it 'reveals' the truth, that is, presents it in an intuitive or imaginative form, not a form that can be justified by criticism. We cannot argue about the truths of religion just because they are thus occulted by their own symbols ; and it is this hiddenness, this darkness of the glass, that gives religion all its negative characteristics.

The positive characteristics of religion are its illumination, its freedom, its power of saving the soul ; in a word, its priceless gift of ultimate truth. Its negative characteristics are that it lives only by faith and not by sight, that God is not known but only worshipped, 'reached' but not 'grasped' by the mind, that it cannot justify itself to reason or rise wholly above the level of superstition, and that therefore in the long run and in spite of all its best efforts it falls back into feeling, emotion—love, awe, and so forth—and therefore, like art, is an intermittent and unstable experience. The division of life into sacred and profane, Sundays and weekdays, is a permanent and necessary feature of religion, though the highest and most positive religion always fights against it and tries to sanctify the whole of life. For this division is the logical consequence of the negative side of religion, that side which makes it a matter of *mere* faith. This negative side reduces religion to feeling, and therefore affects it with the necessary impermanence and instability of feeling.

Its negative side condemns religion to leave something

outside itself, to have an opposite standing over against itself unreconciled. This opposite appears now in the form of body as opposed to soul, now in the form of the devil as opposed to God, now in the form of secular life as opposed to sacred, or the priest as opposed to the layman, but fundamentally and most deeply in the form of man as opposed to God. These oppositions are the fruit of religion's intuitive nature ; as feeling is necessarily intermittent, so the intuitive form of truth erects into two concrete and distinct images truths which are really not distinct but complementary aspects of the same truth. Because religion is rational, the specific task of religion is to overcome these dualisms, and to this subject we shall return in the sixth section of the present chapter.

§ 5. *Convention*

The truths expressed by religion are expressed in symbols whose distinction from the truths they symbolize is not explicitly recognized. In terms of conduct, this means that the moral principles inculcated by religion are exemplified through certain actions which are regarded as possessing in their own right the sanctity which really attaches to the principles they exemplify. Hence, where morality says ' act on certain principles ', religion says ' do certain actions ' Religious morality is thus a morality of commandments, a formalistic morality, one in which the spirit in which an act is done cannot be separated from the act itself. This is illustrated by the fact already analysed, that religion requires us to go to church not because hating God in church is preferable to loving him anywhere else, but because religion identifies the service of God with the outward act, namely churchgoing, which symbolizes it :

an identification against which the highest religion, as we have seen, struggles but struggles in vain.

To consider the same fact from the other end : religion is art asserting its object. The object remains essentially an image, but it is now regarded as real. Therefore religious morality is aesthetic morality asserting as real an end which is still essentially an imaginary or capricious end, an end chosen in play. This assertion of its end as real makes religion social ; therefore the end is now a common end, no longer the individualistic end of play ; but essentially the end is still the same, an end chosen not because it is useful or morally obligatory but just because it is chosen.

Thus from both ends we reach the same conclusion, that the morality of religion is conventional morality. This is the type of action in which the agent does a given thing not because he chooses it, but because his society chooses it. But the reason why he does it is nothing more than this. If he reflects that his society may injure him on his refusing to follow its example, his action becomes utilitarian ; if he persuades himself that his society has a moral claim upon him for conformity, it becomes an act of duty. But conventional action is wholly free from these ulterior motives. A man dressing for dinner does not normally reflect on the consequences of dining in knickerbockers or ask himself whether he ought to defy the conventions. He does not raise these questions at all. He dresses simply because it is ' the thing ' ; and this is the essence of conventional action.

The reader may protest that all religion is in reality a war against conventionality and the assertion of the spirit as against the letter. But to say that is to confuse religion with a special form of religion ; excusably, because that form is the highest and truest form ; but yet a confusion.

Religion is a world which embraces the highest and most spiritual Christianity, not to mention other forms of higher religion, on the one hand, and the lowest and crudest heathenism and superstition on the other ; and in our account of religion we are trying to start from a point of view which embraces all these varieties of experience in a single concept. To condemn this attempt as unduly ambitious is absurd, for we all use the word religion in this broad sense, and thus, unless we are using words quite at random, actually possess just such a concept. Now the conventionality or formalism of the lower religions is obvious enough. It is only when we reach the higher religions that we make the discovery that God is a spirit, and that the spirit of our acts is in his eyes more important than their conventional orderliness. The higher religions always fight against conventionality ; but the enemy against which they are fighting is their own conventionality, that formalism which they inherit from the lower religions and which they cannot wholly expel from themselves except at the cost of ceasing to be in any recognizable sense religions and becoming philosophies.

The modern world, with its strong tendency to detach itself from religion, makes a habit of decrying conventional morality. And this is in the main right enough ; for conventional conduct is on a lower level than duty or even utility ; it is unreasoning and tainted with something of the primitiveness of play. But it has a very real importance and value. It is pointed out in *Tom Brown's School Days*, not without a certain air of pompous self-satisfaction on the part of a society which had invented the noble game of Rugby football, that football is a finer game than fives because in fives you play for yourself whereas in football you play for your side. The end aimed at by a football team

is an end capriciously chosen, but here caprice ends : each
of the fifteen members makes that end his own and acts in
concert with the others for its attainment. His action
ceases in this manner to be mere play and becomes convention, thereby rising to a higher level of rationality,
for in reply to the question, ' Why do you do this ? ' instead
of the nugatory answer of pure play, ' Because I do,' he
can now answer, ' Because the others do.'   But this loyalty
to a common purpose is only rational in a low degree,
because it is circular :   A does so because B and C do,
B because A and C do, C because A and B do ; and there is
no reason why A, B, C all do it, and therefore no reason why
any of them do it except collective caprice.

To reduce conventional action to collective caprice is to
analyse it correctly according to the letter, but to miss its
spirit.   It is in fact identical with reducing religion to
collective fantasy, which is the aim of that ' rationalism '
of which we shall have some hard things to say later on.
The letter of the most loyal convention is collective caprice,
precisely as the letter of the most harmonious married life
is *égoïsme à deux* : for marriage is the conventional aspect
of that same activity whose aesthetic or play-aspect is
falling in love ; but their spirit is loyalty to the ideal of
a common good.   No good is really common which is the
good of one group as against another ; but such a com-
petitive good symbolizes something beyond itself, namely
the harmonious life of an organic whole which includes
all reality.   Such a perfect whole may be an unattained
and unattainable ideal ; at the level of mere convention
it must be ; yet it is an ideal, and our social institutions
have value just so far as they point towards it, as our
religious symbols have value in so far as they body forth
a reality as yet unattainable by plain thinking.

Because of this symbolic value of convention, the popular revolt against conventions, the commonplace cry that one ought to ignore them and live one's own life, is mere silliness. The people who join in that cry argue that because convention is only collective caprice, they see no reason why on its account they should surrender their own individual caprice. From the ethics of convention they wish to return to the ethics of play. This is a backward step, at bottom identical with that of the people who want to make up a religion for themselves by just choosing what they please to believe. It is a step from a position which is partly, though not wholly, rational, in the direction of one less rational. It is a movement away from sanity and towards idiocy. And it admits of four answers. One is: 'Very well: if you won't play with other people, they won't play with you.' This is the retort courteous from within the limits of conventional ethics. The second is: 'If you annoy people in this way they can and will crush you.' This is the countercheck quarrelsome or verdict on appeal to the higher court of expediency. The third is: 'Other people have a claim on you, which you are a cad to ignore.' This is the verdict of duty or lie circumstantial. The fourth is the one we have already given: 'You are making a fool of yourself; that is, doing your best to become an idiot by your own act.' This is the verdict of philosophy or the lie direct.

§ 6. *The Task of Religion*

We have already described the path by which religion comes into being and reaches maturity. That maturity consists of the ideal of a universal Church worshipping a universal God. But if and when this ideal is achieved, religion has not thereby come safe into harbour and resolved

itself into the heavenly hymn of popular eschatology.[1]
It has come face to face with its ultimate task.

This task is the synthesis of opposites, the breaking-down
of the mid-wall of partition between man and God, the
subject and the object of the religious consciousness. There
are other oppositions at stake, for as we have just seen
they break out in religion on every hand ; but this is the
key to all the others. As Christian theology rightly sees,
the reconciliation of man to God draws the devil's teeth
without more ado ; that is to say, the contradiction between
God and the devil solves itself automatically, and so with
all the other contradictions.

The Christian solution of this great problem represents
the high-water mark of religious development, and it is
difficult to see that religion in its essential form can ever
achieve anything higher and more ultimately or absolutely
satisfying than the twin conceptions of the Incarnation
and the Atonement. In these conceptions the task of
religion is accomplished and its problem solved. Man is by
them redeemed in very truth from his sins, that is to say
from the alienation between him and God. And in these
conceptions the worship which all religion gives to God
is rightly and necessarily extended to the Son of Man in
whose holy and sinless person the redemption of all mankind
is effected, in whom ' God made himself man that he might
make us God '.

The starting-point of this task is the starting-point of all

---

[1] An eschatology not, I would remark, warranted by the highest
authorities. The hymn of Rev. iv is a prologue to the great judgement, and of the New Jerusalem we are explicitly told (Rev. xxi. 22)
that there is no temple therein, that is to say, no act of worship. The
self-transcendence of religion has never been more strikingly asserted
than in this plain statement that there will be no religion in heaven.

religion. This is the assertion of God as holy, with its implication, that the worshipper is unholy. Unholiness is sin, which is not a moral idea but a religious idea, though no doubt it is the symbol under which moral problems are attacked by the religious consciousness. This antithesis or severance between the subject and object of the religious consciousness is a new thing. In art it does not exist. Not that the artist is a stranger to self-consciousness. Self-consciousness is coextensive with consciousness in general. But the artist's self-consciousness, like his consciousness in general, is specifically imaginative and not assertive. Just as in dramatic art the artist invents objective personages whose existence he does not assert as real, and whose troubles and trials need not therefore shake the foundations of his entire life, so in lyrical art he invents an imaginary self and unlocks a heart which is, in point of fact, not his real heart but only an imaginary one. The griefs and joys of the lyrical poet are not necessarily historical facts, any more than the griefs and joys of other *dramatis personae*. If therefore the artist feels dissatisfied with himself—and the greatest of all artists looked upon himself and cursed his fate,

> Desiring this man's art and that man's scope,
> With what I most enjoy contented least——

it is no more than a passing mood ; it is overcome even in the act of giving it aesthetic utterance, and is thus only asserted to be denied. But in religion this self is asserted as real, and at the same time as other than the true reality God. Hence the self is by the very presuppositions of the religious consciousness alienated from God and in a state of sin. This is the so-called Fall of Man, or original sin. Here again, there is no question for philosophy as to whether there was an historical fall, and Darwinism has no quarrel with Genesis. The fall of man is his awakening to the religious frame of mind, and the doctrine of original sin is his recognition, in this frame of mind, of the *fait accompli*, the severance of man as such from God.

The short and easy way of dealing with these conceptions is simply to deny them, to point out, what is perfectly true, that the severance of subject from object is no philosophical truth but an error incidental to ' picture-thinking ', to the imaginative form of knowledge. To one who really conceives, instead of imagining, the subject-object relation, it is evident without more ado that this is a relation of correlatives in which each requires the other for its own existence. But to make this point is to pass at a leap beyond the sphere of imaginative knowledge and to short-circuit the whole train of development from the beginning of religion to the end of philosophy. There is no objection to doing this; quite the contrary; if any one can do it, he will save himself a great deal of trouble. But he cannot do it at all unless he is gifted with an extraordinary degree of acuteness and elasticity of mind. In practice, people do not adopt these heroic remedies. They answer, if any one suggests them, ' Need we really scrap the whole machine for the sake of this flaw ? can't we get over it, within the terms of our presuppositions, by a little adjustment ? ' So the adjustment begins, and the length to which it may proceed is infinite ; and then suddenly the manipulator turns round to find that his machine has become a wholly different thing. The mind, if one may suggest a portmanteau-proverb, *non facit saltum praeter necessitatem*.[1]

The religious consciousness, then, accepts original sin as its starting-point, and in a sense the whole of religion

[1] The point at which they realize the necessity for a leap is, of course, just what distinguishes minds according to their insight or intelligence.

represents a progressive attempt at self-purification, the sanctifying or deifying of man. Hence the supreme blasphemy is to claim an immediate or natural identity of man with God, to make oneself equal to God ; for that is to deny the whole meaning and value of religion by asserting that one possesses by nature what in religion we are trying to obtain by grace. But this attempt at union with God is futile as long as religion is in its naïve polytheistic state, for the object is here in a state of flux, god succeeding god, and a real union is only possible with that which is itself one. Thus the problem of reconciling man with God first begins to be seriously attacked by the monotheistic religions, and can only be solved by a religion which has achieved a thorough and, so to speak, ingrained monotheism. In such a religion the tension between God's holiness and our sin becomes unbearable, and we are faced with the alternative of either shirking it—declining to recognize it, and occupying our minds with those details of legalistic ritual which are the symptom not of a trivial religion but of one too profound and serious for its devotees to live up to—or else finding a solution for it.

The solution can only come from the side of God, for we in our fallen state are powerless. It must, that is, be an act of unmerited grace. God must give himself to us. Now the gift is to consist precisely of the abolition of the gulf which separates man from God : God and man, once separate, are to be fused in a new unity, God becoming incarnate as man, and man becoming by redemption and adoption the child of God. But by becoming incarnate, God does not become sinful ; for sin is precisely the separation of man from God, and the negation of this is the negation of sin. He takes the burden of sin upon himself ; that is, he himself, and no other, faces the situation of the existence of sin and triumphs over it. But this very triumph is achieved only by his own sinlessness. And this result is foreordained before the beginning of the world : it was an integral part of God's plan, that is to say, the inevitable dialectical result of the very presuppositions of the religious consciousness, though its inevitability can only be seen by us *ex post facto*, because there was never any guarantee that the religious consciousness of a given race would have the vigour and steadfastness to work out its salvation aright.

This solution of the problem of religion was actually achieved, as was indeed necessary, by and within religion itself, unaided by philosophy or science. But the very religion which had produced it repudiated it, and repudiated it specifically as blasphemy or irreligion. The solution of the religious problem came to its own, and its own received it not. And this, again, had to be. It was as necessary that Christ should be rejected as that he should rise again on the third day. For his message was the death-warrant of the religious consciousness itself, and all that was strongest and most vital in the religious consciousness rose up against it to destroy it. The religious consciousness in its explicit form is simply the opposition between man and God, an opposition perpetually resolved in the actuality of worship and perpetually renewed as the intermittent act of worship ceases. The Christian gospel announced the ending of that opposition once for all, not by the repetition of acts of worship, by the blood of bulls and goats, but by the very act of God which was at the same time the death of God. The one atoning sacrifice of Christ swept away temple and priests, ritual and oblation and prayer and praise, and left nothing but a sense that the end of all things was at hand and a new world about to appear in which the first things should have passed away. In the death-grapple between religion as a specific form of experience and the Christian gospel which by solving its insoluble problem annihilated it, it was necessary that the representatives of the Christian gospel should be put down by force ; but it was equally necessary that their message should prevail, just because it was the truth, in a world which at bottom desired the truth.

If the reader is tempted to reply that the view here set forth makes Christianity not a religion at all, and thus stultifies the implied definition either of Christianity or of religion, he must be reminded that Christianity has here been defined not as something different from religion in general but as the solution of the problem whose existence constitutes religion in general. To find this solution is the work of the religious consciousness, not of any other form of consciousness ; and the solution, being correlative to its own problem, only continues to exist as long as the problem continues to exist. The very existence of the religious problem in any phase, however primitive, implies some kind of dim and instinctive solution of it. Hence even the darkest heathenism is, as Christians have always said, an implicit, blind or caricatured Christianity. On the other hand, the origin of explicit Christianity marked, not the disappearance of religion, but the discovery by religion of the answer to its own questions. Now a question whose answer is given logically ceases to be asked ; and that implies the end of religion on the coming of Christianity, and that in its turn implies the end of Christianity also. But what is true in the logic of explicit reason is not true in the logic of implicit reason, reason in its intuitive form. Here the problem and its solution present themselves, not in the form of logical question and answer, but in the imaginative form of an enacted drama or sacred story. Logically analysed, the whole point of this drama is the overcoming of its own initial error ; but in religion, logical analysis is only implicit ; it solves problems, it gives knowledge, it reveals truth, but without knowing what it is doing. Hence religion can only satisfy itself that its problem is really solved by restating both it and its solution in their imaginative form : the cosmic mystery-play of the fall and the atonement. Thus Christianity, which is implicitly the death of religion, is explicitly the one true and perfect religion, the only religion which gives the soul peace and satisfaction by solving the specifically religious problem.

This brings us to a question with which we cannot now refuse to deal—the place of religion in the modern world.

Religion is a hybrid of the literal and spiritual, of superstition and truth. Far more than art, it conveys to man real knowledge of himself and of the world ; for whereas the message of art is wholly obscured by its imaginative presentation, in religion the message takes definite, though as yet only mythical, shape. But religion is not the highest or final form of truth, even though the truth which it reveals is substantially the highest and final truth. Its message is formally imperfect, tainted by the displacement of assertion from the truth to the symbol, so that religion can never say what it means. This inability to express its own meaning is grasped by religion itself in the form of the conviction of sin, of alienation from its own ideal.

The philosophical error of asserting the reality of an image instead of asserting the reality of the truth which that image means may not be a necessary error, in the sense of a phase through which by some law of nature every mind must pass, but it is an error into which it would appear that every human mind actually does fall. Mankind, it has been said, is incurably religious. Not incurably, perhaps, for Christianity is there to witness the contrary ;

rather endemically. Superstitions of all kinds break out on all hands even at this enlightened stage of the world's history ; and there is no reason to think that they will soon become extinct. Now superstition of every type is the fuel on which Christianity feeds ; for Christianity would seem to be the only agent by which the human mind has ever yet succeeded in liberating itself from superstition. The direct passage from superstition to philosophy has been tried, and it is a passage so choked with wrecks that a wise man will hardly venture to attempt it. Christianity, the *via purgativa* of the religious mind, will become out of date for any given person or society only when in the mind of that person or society superstition has vanished for good and all. At that rate there are not many persons, and certainly not any societies, that can afford to despise the teachings of Christianity.

§ 7. *The Transition from Religion to the life of Thought*

No more pitiable manifestation of thought exists than that kind of anti-religious polemic which is known as ' atheism ' or, as if *per antonomasiam*, ' rationalism '. Its method is to take any assertion made by religion, to assume that it means what it says, and then to show, which is always easy, that so interpreted it is false or at least doubtful. Great triumphs have been won over religion by showing that the world cannot have been made in seven days, that Eve was probably not made out of one of Adam's ribs, that the age attributed to Methuselah and other patriarchs is certainly exaggerated, and that no known species of fish can have swallowed Jonah and cast him up three days later. It has also been forcibly argued that there must be one God or three, and that you can't have it both ways ; that the fictitious transference of our sins to Christ is a legal quibble quite unworthy of a righteous Judge ; and that if God were really both powerful and good he would have made short work of tuberculosis and the Borgia family. Just at present this type of thought is chiefly concerned with the birth, miracles, and resurrection of our Lord, and we may leave it there.

The interest of this ' rationalistic ' thought, for us, is the question of its origin. No one confutes Swift on the ground that Lilliputians are physiologically impossible,[1] and on the other hand no one accuses Cecil Rhodes of lying on the ground that even if he had owned an apple-cart, Dr. Jameson during his raid was far too busy to upset it. In the former case every one realizes that Swift was only fancying, and not asserting, the Lilliputians ; in the latter, it is clear that the upset apple-cart was only a metaphor. But religion is neither art nor explicit metaphor ; it is implicit metaphor, metaphorical assertion mistaking itself for literal assertion. The early Christians, when they said the end of the world was coming, genuinely thought that they meant what they said, and the rationalists of the day were doubtless taken in by this and consequently, when the end of the world did not come, condemned Christianity as a fraud. In point of fact, the expected Parousia was only the imaginative symbol of a spiritual event which really did take place ; so that what the early Christians implicitly meant by it was true, though what they said was false. Similarly the Christianity of a century ago said, and thought it literally meant, that the world was created in seven days. It has now learnt not only that, so understood, the assertion was untrue, but

---

[1] Though there is the story of the sea-captain who closed *Gulliver's Travels* with the remark that he didn't believe a word of it.

also that it was never really meant to be so understood, but was always a symbol of something else.

Religion, in short, as by now we have abundantly seen, always mistakes what it says for what it means. And rationalism, so to speak, runs about after it pointing out that what it says is untrue. The mistake of rationalism is to think that by doing this it is refuting religion; but that is a mistake first made by religion, and rationalism only errs through accepting the account given by religion of itself. Rationalism would be justified in doing this if it claimed a place within religion; but in fact it claims a place in philosophy, and if it is to deserve this place it must not naïvely accept religion at its own valuation but study it afresh and work out a new theory of it. It is this elementary misunderstanding that makes rationalism so contemptible a thing. If the rationalist had any intelligence he would see that his attacks on religion are too easy to be sound, and that there must be a catch somewhere.

This 'catch' is the root of theology. The task of theology is to convert the implicit thought of religion into explicit thought, by disentangling the symbol from its meaning and making clear the merely metaphorical character of religious imagery. Theology is thus the answer to rationalism. But just because it makes terms with rationalism, because it so far agrees with the rationalist as to admit that the symbol is not literally true, theology is always looked upon with some suspicion by religion itself. The rise of theology is inevitable, for otherwise religion lies helpless under the guns of the most idiotic rationalist; and yet theology is to religion a wolf in sheep's clothing. The theologian has crossed the line which separates religion from philosophy, and he is only tolerated by religion as long as, wolf though he is, he conscientiously plays the sheep-dog. There is no help for this ; he must be tolerated ; for rationalism is no external enemy whose attacks will perhaps never be repeated, it is at bottom a manifestation of the religious attitude itself. We saw that religion, as intuitive and therefore a matter of feeling, was necessarily unstable and intermittent. Every religious man has his irreligious moments, and in these irreligious moments he is either a rationalist or a theologian. Either the bread and wine are, in these moments, for him just bread and wine, or else he has schooled himself to regard them as symbols : that is, he has turned theologian. Hence religion, by its own inner dialectic as an intuitive form of consciousness, creates within itself first rationalism and then the antidote to rationalism, theology.

But theology is the negation of religion. To distinguish between the symbol and what it means is by definition to pass outside religion, to recognize that religion by itself is not sufficient to ensure the permanent peace of the soul, and to condemn religion as a confusion of thought. The task of theology is to carry on its analytic work while rebutting the inevitable accusation of irreligion. The actual life of theology (is there any theologian who does not know this ?) is a life of compromise. It is taken up enthusiastically, in the belief that there are in religion just a few unexplained metaphors—Jonah's whale and the seven days of creation and so forth—and that by expounding these we can clear all difficulties from before the feet of honest doubt. But metaphors multiply as the theologian looks at them. He finds that they infect the whole length and breadth of religion, and then, if his eye is sufficiently penetrating, he begins to see them in depth as well : when he has expounded one metaphor, he finds that the terms in which he has expounded it are themselves metaphorical. But he is committed to the defence of religion, and therefore he must take religion's word for the point at which she finds his analysis intolerable. Jonah's whale and the seven days of creation, very well ; but what about the resurrection and the virgin birth ? It is easy to condemn as inconsistent those who cry ' hands off ' at this point. But perhaps they have right on their side. For—this is what the enthusiastic young theologian does not know—theology, if it is to remain theology, must stop somewhere. The young theologian thinks that religion has a kernel of literal truth which, if only his bishop will let him go on digging, he will in time bring to light. But religion, as Goethe said of nature, has neither kernel nor husk ;[1] and those who are bent on peeling it will some day exemplify the parable of the onion.

The ultimate logical conclusion of theology is the explanation of the entire mass of religious imagery in terms of the concept of God. The concept of God is the nucleus of literal truth which theology assumes religion to possess. In the last conceivable resort, the theologian might explain every single clause of the creeds as metaphorical except ' I believe in God ' : that is the literal fact of which all the following clauses are, so to speak, metaphorical illustrations and expansions. I do not say that any theologian now advocates such a position, but it is obviously the conclusion to which much of our theology is tending, and therefore it closely concerns us to investigate it.

---

[1] ' Thought growing up in the *husk* of language,' we said on p. 125 ; but there is no inconsistency. To distinguish the language from the thought, the husk from the germ, is, as we have throughout maintained, possible ; but it is the destruction of religion and the affirmation of science. In this very destruction the spirit and truth of religion are not quenched ; they live on, and at a higher level ; but it is a level at which the theologian is certainly not consciously aiming—a level at which the chalice becomes a crucible and the church a laboratory.

The assumption is that God is a concept, an object of thought, the ultimate reality of philosophical analysis. Now is this identification of God with the absolute legitimate? All theology assumes that it is; but it cannot be. God is the holy one, the worshipped, the object of faith. The absolute is reality, the demonstrated, the object of reason. No one can worship the absolute, and no one can prove the existence of God. It is true that people have tried to do both these things, but they have uniformly failed. The proofs of the existence of God form a long and glorious chapter in the history of human thought, but they have always ended by proving something that is not the existence of God. The attempt to worship the absolute has been a not uninteresting chapter in the history of religion, and it has always ended in the worship of something that is not the absolute. The simple religious consciousness is here our best guide. It knows that God is revealed not to the intellect but to the heart, which means not the 'practical reason' or the 'emotional faculty', but simply the religious consciousness. God is not known, he is adored. We cannot think him, we can only love and fear him. The simple religious consciousness knows that when philosophers call their ultimate reality by the name of God they are taking that name in vain and pretending to be what they are not. They are, in fact, as insincere as is a religion which talks of the Supreme Being.

God and the absolute are not identical but irretrievably distinct. And yet they are identical in this sense: God is the imaginative or intuitive form in which the absolute reveals itself to the religious consciousness. We are accustomed to recognize that the gods of the heathen are but mythological and perverted presentations of the true God; we know well that the father up in the sky of whom we

talk to children is likewise at bottom a mythological figment.
But we do not sufficiently realize that all religion, up to its
very highest manifestations, is mythological too, and that
mythology is finally extruded from religion only when
religion itself perishes and gives place to philosophy. God
as such is the mythological symbol under which religion
cognizes the absolute : he is not a concept but the symbol
of a concept. However hard we try to purify our idea of
God from mythological elements, the very intuitiveness of
our attitude towards that idea mythologizes it once more.

' I believe in God ' is therefore a religious statement,
never a philosophical statement. It is a statement which
challenges the philosophical reply ' What do you mean by
God ? ' and when that question is asked nothing but a
deliberate stopping of the wheels of thought will arrest
the conversion of theology into philosophy. No attempt to
save theology, under the name of philosophical theism, can
resist this process

In point of fact, we have long ago left religion behind.
Theology is a manifestation not of the religious spirit but
of the scientific spirit, and to that we must now turn. In
taking this step, we leave the world of imagination and
enter upon the world of thought. The world of imagination
is thought implicit ; the world of thought, so called, is
thought explicit. In art and religion thought is present,
but it is deceived as to its own nature. In art it is so far
deceived as to be ignorant of its very existence, and to
suppose itself mere imagination : yet even in that error it
is thought, for nothing but thought can err. Thus art is the
last possible degree of the implicitness of thought. In
religion thought knows that it exists ; religion asserts and
knows that it asserts. But though here thought knows that it
exists, it is so far ignorant of its own nature that it mistakes

imagining for thinking, and asserts the reality of what is really only symbol. Hence the truth is in religion only intuitively known, not logically known, and its real nature as truth—as concept, as object of thought—is concealed. Religion, like art, is a philosophical error. It is specifically the error of mythologizing reality, of taking language literally instead of metaphorically. But in spite of this formal error, religion is an infinitely precious achievement of the mind and an unfailing revelation of truth. It is the giver of freedom and salvation, because it liberates the soul from the life of imagination, of semblance and unreality, and leads from the things that are seen and temporal to the things that are unseen and eternal. And in that passage the visible world, the world of semblance, is redeemed and made the fit temple of the spirit ; for in the very negation of this imaginary world as the supreme reality, it is invested with its true positive value as the vehicle of the supreme reality, the Word of the Spirit.

V

SCIENCE

§ 1. *The Life of Thought*

ART and religion, to the superficial observer, are forms
not of thought but of language. Art, it has been said, is
simply language itself, language in its pure form apart from
any meaning. Mythology has been called a disease of
language, a development from language in its purity to
language claiming a function which it does not rightly
possess, the function of thought ; and thus declaring itself
in a morbid condition. Both these descriptions we should
reject if taken as serious definitions of art and religion, for
they are descriptions of the surface instead of the solid,
definitions of the letter substituted for definitions of the
spirit. Art is not pure language, but thought failing to
recognize that it is thought, mistaking itself for imagination. Religion is not a morbid growth of language but
a dialectical development of art, art realizing that it is not
bare imagination but assertion, and then proceeding to
misinterpret its own assertions and to suppose itself to be
asserting the image or word when it is really asserting the
meaning of the word. In a special sense both art and
religion are thus linguistic functions, forms of expression
rather than forms of thought ; for though, properly understood, they exist only to express thought, yet the thought
in them is concealed rather than expressed by their language,
the language becomes opaque and presents itself as if it
were the real aim and end of the activity. And thus in
a sense it is true to say that the artistic consciousness is

one struggling to master the bare technique of expression, playing scales on the instrument of speech as a preliminary to using it as a means for the expression of a determinate thought ; and in the same sense it is true to say that religion is the error of mistaking these scales for music, mistaking speech for thought. Art and religion are both phases in the history of a mind preceding its attainment of complete mastery over the means of expression : they are the experience of one who is still learning language and has not yet fully learnt it. Hence his attention is concentrated on the language and not on the meaning ; the language appears to him, falsely, as an end in itself, and he does not realize that while he is practising himself in the use of speech he is all the time learning to think. The total absorption in the technique of expression is art ; the first consciousness of the claim of thought, misinterpreted by identifying thought with its own expression, language with reality, is religion.

Art and religion may thus be taken together as two phases in the development of language, first the phase of language practised as an end in itself, mere meaningless expression, and secondly the phase of language recognized as a vehicle of thought, but of a thought confusedly identified with its own vehicle. When once it has been realized that the function of language is to be transparent to thought and to express a meaning which is other than itself, language falls into its proper subordinate position with respect to thought and attention is taken off the letter and concentrated on the spirit, the thought or meaning. When this happens art and religion cease to exist as self-contained and autonomous forms of experience, and give way to a life no longer of expression but of thought. In this life of thought expression is not left behind. On the contrary, the life of thought is a life of thought as expressing itself, embodying itself in language ; and this linguistic embodiment, so far as it is expressive, is in a sense art, and so far as it is metaphorical, in a sense religion. But the artistic and religious elements in the life of thought are not felt as existing for their own sake ; they are sunk in the thought they express, and even tend to be overlooked and their very existence denied.

This denial of the existence of sensuous or linguistic elements in the life of thought would be an error, but it is an error due to the fact that the elements thus denied are subordinated to thought, a mere means to thought as an end. To deny the existence of intellectual elements in the life of art and religion is a parallel error, but an error of the opposite kind. Here, too, in the life of sense or imagination, thought is really the end and imagination only the means by which we express it ; but here it is the end, not the means, that tends to be overlooked and denied. To call art and religion mere phases in the development of language is to commit this error, to forget that what is really developing is not bare expression but expressed *thought* ; and similarly if we described science and history as mere phases in the development of thought we should be forgetting that what here develops is not thought in the abstract but *expressed* thought. The transition from religion to science is therefore strictly not a transition from language to thought but a transition from one form of thought to another. But to the person who is effecting the transition this fact is invisible, and it can only be seen from the point of view of philosophical reflection. To the person himself it seems that he has passed for the first time into the region of thought, that a pre-intellectual or infra-intellectual state of mind has been left behind, and that now, for the first time, he is taking up a rational attitude towards the world. The truth of the matter is that his previous attitude was rational also, but he did not know it ; his new attitude is peculiar not in being rational but in being consciously rational.

This rationality consists in the freedom of thought from its own expression, the distinction between thought and language. In every form of experience this distinction exists, but by art and religion it is not recognized to exist. It exists *in* them, but not *for* them ; its existence in them can only be discovered by an examination undertaken from an external point of view, namely, that of philosophy. Science for the first time recognizes this distinction from within, that is, recognizes that it is itself making it. Hence thought, which in its own nature always was free, discovers its freedom first in science. Language henceforth falls into its place as the mere servant of thought, and science treats it despotically, making it mean just what it likes ; and with this consciousness of its own mastery over language, thought attains its majority, and the life of the spirit may henceforth be described as, in a special sense, the life of thought. Henceforth the whole effort of the mind is deliberately concentrated on the problem of meaning, and the question of what is said is sunk in the question of what is meant. This is the literal, as opposed to the metaphorical, use of language. As we have already seen, language never is its own meaning, and is therefore always symbolic or metaphorical ; but when this fact is as yet undiscovered by the user of language we say that he is using it ' metaphorically ', and when he realizes that words are mere symbols and distinguishes what they are from what they mean, then by facing and accepting the metaphorical character of all language he has overcome it and is henceforth using language ' literally '. This revolution in the use of language is the birth of science.

§ 2. *Science as the assertion of the Abstract Concept*

The attempt of thought to understand the world began by erecting a screen or veil of imagery between itself and its object, thus frustrating its own purpose. The veil, which in art is a fleeting impermanent tissue of fancies, in religion becomes a solid screen of dogma and ritual, attempting in its permanence and universality not merely to represent but to be the real world. But this permanence and universality are not native to the imagination, not effortless achievements or even secure possessions. They are arbitrarily and forcibly imposed by the religious consciousness upon an object all unsuited, with its essentially aesthetic character, to receive them. Religion insists that its object shall be permanent, though in fact it is always fleeting, and shall be universally accepted, though this universality is never attained. The claim cannot be enforced, because religion seeks reality where it cannot be found, namely, in imagery. But if its enforcement were not attempted, religion with all its immense stores of truth and wisdom would disappear and sink back to the level of art.

There is only one way out of the position in which religion finds itself. That way is the recognition, which in the case of theology we have already analysed, that imagery is nothing but imagery, not thought but the symbol of thought. When this is seen, the veil of imagery, hitherto opaque, becomes transparent, and the thinker sees through it to the object which it symbolizes. The transparency of the symbol does not mean its abolition. Thought never outgrows the need of language, never learns to live without that immediacy or intuitiveness which marks the aesthetic consciousness. To lose that would be to lose its own cutting edge.

The life of thought is that consciousness which has freed itself not from language but from the opacity of language. The thinker has mastered words and bent them to his purpose ; he has pierced through language to that which it means, the concept or object of thought.

The concept is not something outside the world of sensuous appearance : it is the very structure or order of that world itself. The arrangement and the material arranged are only distinguished by an abstract and arbitrary distinction within an indivisible whole. The universal is only real as exemplified in the particular, the particular as informed by the universal. The symbol is what it is because of its meaning, the meaning is only what that symbol means. Hence the meaning or concept or universal is not a separate object of consciousness, other than the world of sense ; not something seen through a veil of sense, but the structure of that veil itself.

This is the point of view of concrete thought ; and ultimately we shall find ourselves forced to adopt it. But to a mind struggling to free itself from the religious attitude, such a point of view seems excessively remote and unnatural. In religion the mind is accustomed to regard the unity of God as standing in perfectly self-contained independence over against the plurality of empirical facts ; the one and the many, the universal and its particulars, are thrown outside one another and regarded not as correlative aspects of a single concrete whole but as independent concrete beings. This is a consequence of the imaginative nature of religion, which inevitably ' personifies abstractions ', or presents ideal distinctions in the guise of concrete objects. Now in abandoning religion and turning to science the mind ceases to personify abstractions, but it thinks this is enough : it does not go so far in self-reformation as to stop abstracting them. To abstract is to consider separately things that are inseparable : to think of the universal, for instance, without reflecting that it is merely the universal of its particulars, and to assume that one can isolate it in thought and study it in this isolation. This assumption is an error. One cannot abstract without falsifying. To think apart of things that are together is to think of them as they are not, and to plead that this initial severance makes no essential difference to their inner nature is only to erect falsification into a principle. But this is a lesson which can only be learnt by bitter experience.

The specific character of science, its abstractness, is due not to reflection on the alternatives and the conscious adoption of abstract thought as preferable to concrete, but to an inheritance from religion. The concept, as it emerges from its chrysalis state into explicit life, carries with it a relic of its intuitive character in the shape of a bias towards abstractness. This bias is allowed unconsciously to control its development, and this is why the most primitive form of explicit thought is not concrete thought but abstract, not history but science.

Because the abstractness of science is a perpetuation of the abstractness of religion, science most naturally arises out of a religion which has not overcome this abstractness, that is to say, out of a non-Christian religion. Hence European science has its roots in the religion of pagan antiquity, as we shall see later. Science in the modern world is science Christianized, science fed by a religious consciousness in which the primary abstractness of religion has been cancelled by the notions of incarnation and atonement. This gives the distinction between the *a priori* science of the Greeks and the empirical science of the modern or Christian world. But religion, even in the form of Christianity, never really transcends its abstractness, because this abstractness is nothing more than the intuitive or imaginative character of religion. It only cancels this abstractness by adding to itself a new series of images whose purpose is to warn us against the inevitable abstract interpretation of the old ; but these new images (redemption, grace, &c.) are only images again and therefore liable to the same fault. The aim of science is to avoid this fault : Greek science aims at avoiding the specific fault of Greek religion, modern science at avoiding that of Christianity, namely, its liability to misinterpretation in a sense which makes God an arbitrary tyrant, whose very gifts are an insult to a free man.

The history of European science begins with the breakdown of a religious view of the world in the mind of ancient Greece, and the concepts of Greek science appear as a kind of depersonalized gods. The early Greek scientists were trying to replace a world of religious imagery with a world of intelligible concepts. These concepts, like the gods they superseded, were suspended above the sensible world in a heaven of their own ; for, precisely because the dualism of the religious consciousness was not overcome, the secret of science was found in the absolute distinction between the universal and its particulars, the world of thought and the world of sense.

The world of sense, whose component objects were regarded [1] as the particulars of the universals constituting the world of thought, was mere appearance ; neither real

---

[1] The conceptions expounded in this paragraph are not consistently maintained by all Greek philosophers at all times, and the reader need not suppose me ignorant of variations and departures from them ; I am trying to give an account of what seems to me the typical and fundamental Greek view.

nor unreal ; not illusion, but appearance in the sense of being neither asserted nor denied, ' opined ' as Plato has it. Reality was found in the world of universals, and unreality in the world of what one may call counter-universals, the empty potentialities of determination which are only the negative aspect of the universals themselves. The universals were abstract. Whether they were said to ' exist ' in severance from their particulars or to be only thinkable in that severance, it was agreed that they were indifferent to their own exemplification in this particular or that, and differentiated only in their specifications, these specifications being always universals again, never particulars. Individual distinctions between the particulars did not flow from the nature of the universal, but—since they necessarily had a ground of some kind—they were ultimately referred to the counter-universals. The polarized world of abstract concepts—polarized into asserted universals and negated counter-universals—was thus lifted bodily clear of the sensuous world of appearance, and this very dualism is a relic of an unresolved intuitive or religious view of the world, as we have seen. Indeed the constant description of the soul's grasp of the universals as ' intuition ', ' gazing ', and so forth, betrays the imaginative character of the entire conception.

Because any given universal was, in its abstractness, indifferent to the variations of its own particulars, these particulars organized themselves in the form of a class. Classification is the key-note of the scientific spirit ; but classification is nothing but the abstractness of the scientific concept. For a class as such is a collection of individuals without any mutual cohesion or organization except their common membership of the class. They have no reference to each other, but only to the universal ; and each one refers to the universal in precisely the same way as every other. As soon as they refer to the universal in different ways, or, what is the same thing, as soon as they develop a system of mutual relations between themselves, they cease to be a mere class and become an organized and articulated system ; and the universal ceases to be an abstract universal (class-concept) and becomes a concrete universal, or one to which the differences between its particulars are relevant. Thus classification is the most rudimentary conceivable kind of order ; and if structure in general is the object of thought in general, science as the explicit apprehension of class-structure is the most abstract and primitive kind of explicit thought that can exist.

The Greeks who worked out the theory of the classificatory universal did not, of course, deliberately proceed by abstraction from individual facts. Implicitly no doubt they did so ; they could not do otherwise ; but their own theory of the matter was that these universals could be apprehended by themselves, in all their abstractness, irrespective of their exemplification in facts. Indeed, it is significant that Greek philosophy has no word for ' fact ' or ' individual ', distinct from its term for the abstract particular. To describe Socrates, for instance, as using the inductive method of modern science is a glaring anachronism, and as a description of the dialectical basis of science it is false in the same way in which the doctrine that the artist copies historical facts is false. Artist and scientist alike are working at levels of thought below that at which fact in its concreteness is recognized at all.

§ 3. *A priori or Deductive Science*

Science is the affirmation of the abstract or classificatory concept as real. Now because this concept is abstract, its nature is to be apprehended by abstract thought, thought deprived of any aid from sensation. Sensuous experience is therefore unnecessary to the scientist, and all he has to do is to think. If the metaphysic of science is that of the world of forms, the methodology of science is that of pure thought.

This is the simplest and historically the first form of the scientific consciousness, as it was worked out by the early Greek philosophers and described by Plato. In a sense, the development of scientific thought does not begin here ; for there is an important truth in the common observation that primitive systems of magic and religion are rudimentary forms of science. Together with much that is altogether fanciful and irrational, such institutions as that of *tabu* constantly enforce principles which are in substance scientific. But we are here dealing with the origin, not of principles which can be called scientific in substance, but of science as a definite and self-conscious form of experience. It is the very essence of a dialectical development that each phase in it should contain the next implicitly, and it is this implicit presence of elements which are, as it were, submerged in the immediacy of a particular phase, that necessitates the collapse of that phase. Every phase of experience is implicit in its predecessor, and therefore it is not surprising that science should be implicit in religion ; but the scientific content ·in *tabu* and the like is felt not as science but as religion.

Science in its purest and most unsophisticated form, as the mere assertion of the abstract concept, is *a priori* or deductive. It is built up by simply drawing out the implications of a given concept. But because the scientist's knowledge of concepts cannot be derived from sensuous experience, the concepts which form the objects of science must be known independently of all such experience. And when we ask what concepts can be thus known, remembering that the concept is always the abstract class-universal, it becomes clear that because any difference between one class and another class is empirical, the only really *a priori* or pure concept is the concept of a class as such, the concept of classification or abstraction. From this point of view the subject-matter of science will consist of nothing but the implications of classification : that is, the indeterminate plurality of the members of a class—indeterminate because the abstract class-concept is perfectly indifferent to the number of instances in which it is exemplified—each member being simply another instance of the universal. This indeterminate plurality of units is precisely the numerical series. Each unit is distinguished from the rest simply as being another : that is, by its ordinal number ; and the common nature of units in general is simply that they are that of which there is an indeterminate multiplicity. This indeterminate multiplicity is the mathematical infinite, which is therefore another name for the perfect abstractness of the mathematical universal. Since all content has been exhausted from this universal, nothing is left to determine either the nature or the interrelations of its particulars, which therefore become a mere plurality of abstract units.

Mathematics is thus the one and only *a priori* science. It has nothing to do with space or time or quantity, which are elements of concrete experience : it is simply the theory of order, where order means classificatory order, structure in its most abstract possible form. The numerical series is the residuum of that abstraction which sets thought and sensation over against one another in false isolation ; it is the false mutual transcendence of the one and the many. The self-contained solidity of each unit in the numerical series, which makes it possible to shuffle and manipulate them without affecting their inner nature, is nothing but this false transcendence : it is the corollary of the self-contained character which it is the error of science to attribute to pure thought. Once we have, by that relic of religious transcendence which infects all science, divorced the world of thought from the world of sensation, the mutual externality of these two worlds reproduces itself *ad infinitum* within science itself, and gives rise to that logic of external relations which is just the mark of science's failure to free itself altogether from the domination of a religious habit of mind. Hence the inevitable failure of the claim still sometimes made, that pure mathematics must be the ultimate arbiter of metaphysical truth.

The purely *a priori* or deductive ideal of science at this stage has further results beside the genesis of mathematics. Because the concept contains all its possible implications within itself, waiting merely to be extracted by thought, science consists only in turning this way and that a concept which is always immutable and self-identical. Hence all science is not merely mathematical but mechanistic or deterministic. Scientific determinism is, like mathematics, a product of the abstractness of the scientific consciousness. Mathematics implies the ideal reduction of what are really unique individual facts to mere units ; mechanism implies the ignoring of the omnipresent individuality of the real and the imposition upon it of an abstract law which determines every case indifferently from the outside. If mathematics means the false mutual transcendence of the one and the many, mechanical determination means the false transcendence of the condition with regard to the conditioned.

A further product of the same process is materialism. Matter is not that which we sensate, the visible, tangible, and so forth, but that which in its indifferent self-identity underlies all immediate objects of sense. Matter is in fact, as Berkeley once for all pointed out, simply the abstract concept, the substantiality or reality of objects conceived as transcendent with regard to the objects themselves.

It is sometimes fancied that modern physics, with its tendency to resolve ' gross matter ' into energy, events, or determinations of space-time, is in process of overcoming materialism by its own dialectic. This is not so. The essence of materialism, its assertion of an indifferently self-identical substrate behind the variety of empirical fact, is unchanged whether this substrate is called matter, energy, or space-time. Materialism is a logical phenomenon, it is the indifference of the abstract universal to its own particulars ; and all the popular and philosophical objections to it rest upon this fact and are unaffected by the ' dematerialization of matter '. In fact the old-fashioned gross matter was a mark of incomplete materialism, for its grossness was just a relic of sensible qualities not yet extruded from the pure concept.

Mathematics, mechanism, and materialism are the three marks of all science, a triad of which none can be separated from the others, since in fact they all follow from the original act by which the scientific consciousness comes into being, namely, the assertion of the abstract concept. They are all, it may be said, products of the classificatory frame of mind, corollaries from the fact that in this frame of mind the universal and the particular are arbitrarily separated and the universal asserted in its barren and rigid self-identity. It is this barrenness and this rigidity which confer their character upon the doctrines of scientific materialism.

Hence it is idle to imagine that materialism is justified in some sciences and not in others. It is idle to protest that science ought to surrender its materialistic prejudices when it finds itself face to face with a non-material object such as the soul. No object is material, in the metaphysical sense of the word, except so far as scientific thinking conceives it so ; for materiality means abstractness, subjection to the formulae of mechanical determination and mathematical calculation, and these formulae are never imposed upon any object whatever except by an arbitrary act which falsifies the object's nature. This only appears paradoxical when we fail to see the gulf which separates the common-sense materiality of a table, its sensible qualities, from its metaphysical materiality, the abstract conceptual substrate of those qualities. It is this substrate whose transcendent or abstract existence is asserted by materialism. Hence we cannot distinguish objects like tables which are really 'material' from objects in whose presence science must unlearn its materialistic habits of thought. Materialism is no more the truth in physics than in psychology, and no less. It is the truth about any object, just in so far as this object is by abstraction reducible to terms of pure mathematics ; and no object is so reducible except by consciously or unconsciously shutting our eyes to everything which differentiates it from anything else. This conscious or unconscious act of abstraction is the very being of the scientific consciousness ; and it is therefore no matter for pained surprise when science shows a bias towards determinism, behaviourism, and materialism generally.

It will be noticed that though we called pure mathematics the only *a priori* science we have been speaking as if other sciences might come into existence. As long as science is rigidly *a priori* this cannot happen. It can only happen in two ways, which are at bottom identical : first, if concepts containing some empirical element are admitted into science ; secondly, if science is allowed to indulge in hypothesis. In the first case we might obtain Euclidean geometry regarded as a systematic account of actual empirical space ; in the second case we might get the same science regarded as a pure deduction from the wholly *a priori* hypothesis that Euclidean space existed. But in the first case science would not be pure, and in the second case it would not be true, for it would merely work out the implications of hypotheses, not those of concepts asserted as constituting the real world. And by definition science was to be knowledge by pure thought of the real world. This, then, can only exist in the form of pure mathematics, or the theory of classes which have no members. For it must be borne in mind that the abstract concept is nothing but the abstract structure of the sensible world, and therefore if the concept alone is real the world whose structure it is will be mere appearance and not reality, and therefore the concept will be a class whose members are not real.

Reality on this view turns out to be a null class ; and this conclusion represents the breakdown of science in its first form, the form which the Greeks struggled to give it. The self-identity of the concept, in abstraction from the difference of the sensible world, collapses into nothingness and leaves us with the empty form of a thought which thinks nothing. If modern mathematical science is not threatened by the same fate, that is because it belongs to a far higher stage in scientific development than the movement which we have been following hitherto.

§ 4. *Utility or Abstract Ethics*

When the mind becomes conscious of itself as thought it simultaneously becomes conscious of itself as action. Thought and action, truth and freedom (' ye shall know the truth, and the truth shall make you free ') are inseparable, and are in fact correlative aspects of an indivisible reality.

Hence they became simultaneously explicit in the mind's process of self-discovery. Till then, they have both been implicit only, and in that implicitness they have not been distinguished. Religion is no less pregnant with moral truths than with metaphysical ; but the moral consciousness is in religion intuitive, a mere ' moral sense or unreasoning emotional spring of action, for here the moral ideal is in-extricably fused with the concept of a supreme objective reality, and thus knowledge and action, truth and duty, are represented in their undistinguished identity as the love and fear of God. Play and convention are not, from the point of view of art and religion, distinguishable from those activities themselves ; they are not even distinguishable elements of them, but immediately identical with them in their entirety ; and it was only, so to speak, prospectively, to prepare the way for the present section, that we discussed them separately.

The distinction between intellect and will is an ideal distinction, as is that of the universal and the particular. But science, which discovers both these distinctions, treats them both in the same way, by converting them erroneously into concrete distinctions, treating as separate terms which are only distinguishable. Terms such as inside and outside, back and front, beginning and end, are distinguishable and indeed distinct, but not separate ; the specific error of science would be exemplified in regard to these terms if we tried to conceive an inside that had no outside, and so on. The separation of knowledge from conduct is thus a result of scientific abstraction, and it is therefore under the heading of science that we first find a special doctrine of the will.

The will, like any other concept, is by science abstractly conceived. It is a self-identical principle to which its own varying manifestations are indifferent. The characteristic question of the scientific mind is ' What is there in or behind all these varying instances which is one and invariable ? ' Now this question, applied to human action, can have only one result. Action as such is purposive, and anything purposed is an end. Hence to be means to an end is the invariable characteristic of all action. If we approached ethics from a concrete point of view we should see that every action stood in a unique relation to a unique end, and that the separation of means and end was a mere artifice of thought : that in any given instance the means and the end were inextricably bound up together. But such artificial separations are the essence of scientific method. That method, therefore, applied to the study of conduct, necessarily gives the result that all actions, no matter what, aim at something other than themselves, which may be called their end or good. Action is not the good, it is means to the good ; and hence action as such is not good but useful.

The ethics of the scientific consciousness is always utilitarian, using that word in its broadest sense. This is not because such utilitarianism is a true account of action, for it is true only in the very restricted sense in which its twin brother materialism is true ; it is because, just as materialism abstracts from concrete objects their objectivity and calls this abstraction matter, so utilitarianism abstracts from concrete actions their purposiveness and calls it utility.

It affords an interesting light on the passage from religion to science if we remember that theological ethics is notoriously a form of utilitarianism, and that in fact modern utilitarianism is largely a theological product. Now religious ethics is never utilitarian. Action, for the religious man, is not a calculation of means to end, and it is quite true that ' high heaven rejects ' such calculation. To accuse religion of a self-seeking morality is fundamentally to misunderstand

the religious mind and to throw in one's lot with ' rationalism ' But theology, by distinguishing the religious symbol
from its own meaning, opens the door to the parallel, and
indeed identical, distinction between the religious act and
its end ; and the means and end once disentangled and set
over against one another, there is no avoiding utilitarianism.
Hence theology is bound to rationalize religion by attributing
to it a self-seeking of which explicitly it is altogether innocent.

Utilitarianism, like materialism, is not untrue ; it is only
the irreducible minimum of truth. Its error lies not in what
it asserts but in what it denies ; but it asserts so little and
denies so much that the error in it is a great deal more
conspicuous than the truth. The error is simply its abstractness, its separation of elements which are really only distinct.
The result of this is that action appears to utilitarianism
as a mere indifferent colourless medium, any act being
analysed in exactly the same terms as any other act, and
all differences between them ignored. This ignoring of
differences is perfectly possible and in a sense perfectly
legitimate ; but it brings us into a world of abstractions and
barren formulae where all actual reality is lost to sight.
Utilitarianism, the calculus of conduct, is the most abstract
and dialectically primitive of all possible kinds of ethical
theory. The will is by it conceived as the bare abstraction of will in general, precisely as mathematics conceives
organization or structure as the bare abstraction of order in
general.

The utilitarian view of action, since its essence is to be
abstract, results not only in the false abstraction of the will
from the intellect, but in the inevitable consequence of this
false abstraction, the arbitrary distinction of men of thought
from men of action. The man of thought, in such a scheme
of things, is the scientist ; for in this context thought means

abstract thought, which is science. The man of action is similarly the man of abstract action, action regarded from the utilitarian point of view : that is to say, the man of industry and commerce, or in general the business man. The full and detailed description of the business man, regarded as capitalist on the one hand, and wage-earner on the other, or, in the abstract synthesis of socialism, capitalist and wage-earner in one, as worker in a nationalized productive machine, is the work of the science of economics, which is in the long run identical with utilitarian ethics. Economics is not a true description of one kind of action but an abstract, arbitrary, and therefore erroneous description of all action ; and the ' economic man ' whom it describes is not, in these days, denied to be a fictitious entity. None the less, business men exist. Capitalists and wage-earners are as much an element in actual society as artists and priests ; and their existence is to be explained on the same principle. In each case an error as to the true nature and meaning of life reacts on that life itself and produces not indeed a reality corresponding to the error—which would in that case cease to be an error—but a reality of a one-sided kind, showing within itself various strains and symptoms of faulty equilibrium resulting from the error.

It is easy, in fact it is a commonplace, to point out such morbid symptoms in the fabric of an ' acquisitive society ' based on the concept of utility. The fundamental distinction of means and end implies that in such a society every one regards every one else as a means to his own ends : if the employee is regarded as a living tool, the employer is regarded as a living machine for the payment of wages, and the conflict of interests is an inevitable result. Interests conflict, not by the malignity or stupidity of the persons concerned, but by their own inherent nature : interests indeed might be defined as the field of conflict, for the notion of interest, as distinct from duty, is simply the notion of abstract ' individuals ', the individuals of individualism, each setting itself against the others. Even when we speak of a common interest, this is always the interest of a group—nation, class, race, union—setting itself against other such groups.

A second conflict is that of the business man and the scientist, the world of utility and the world of knowledge, the practical ideal and the speculative ideal. The scientist is not a business man, and his aim is not to make useful discoveries but to make discoveries ; and yet it is realized that industry and commerce are not only dependent upon these discoveries but are their necessary outcome, and also to a certain extent their necessary condition, in so far as the pure scientist is supported and subsidized [1] by the profits of business. Science and business are mutually dependent ; but though they are tied together by this mutual dependence, their ideals are in permanent conflict. A nation of traders is generally a nation of scientists ; but the two elements disagree.

The third conflict is between business and the state. This is a conflict of a different kind : not between a pair of opposites which belong to the same dialectical phase of experience, but between one phase and the next. The state is an historical, not a scientific, conception—a concrete, not an abstract, universal—and its deduction is to be found in the next chapter. Business is essentially a matter of private enterprise, individualistic, based on the principle of *laisser faire*. It knows nothing of the concept of duty or law : its duty is expediency, its law the law of self-preservation. Hence the notion of state regulation is as necessarily alien

[1] For science, unlike any other form of knowledge, is expensive, and cannot be pursued except by the rich.

to that of business as the notion of scientific thought to religion. But in the one case, as in the other, the more primitive notion generates the more advanced by its own dialectical movement. Business men cannot in practice treat each other as enemies and nothing but enemies : their very existence implies a mutual understanding, a mutual agreement *nec laedere nec violari* in certain more or less determinate ways. Thus a system of law and order is implicit in the business world itself ; and when this becomes explicit it takes the form, as we have suggested, of the theory of the ' social contract '.

The contractual theory of society is the ethical or political analogue of inductive logic. As the abstractive work of science is by inductive logicians based on the notion of an ultimate primary abstraction, the law of universal causation or pure notion of abstraction as such, so the work of business, which is contractual through and through, is by this theory based on a primary contract, the contract to make and observe contracts. Both theories are true in the sense that they really express, in a mythical form, the true nature of the abstractive consciousness ; both are false through their failure to realize that the abstract rests, not upon a further abstraction, but upon the concrete. Science really, as we shall see with increasing clearness, rests upon the concrete truth of observed fact ; and business in the same way rests upon the concrete truth of duty or law, a claim which overrides the claim of expediency and compels the business man to forgo profits which, from the economic point of view, are legitimate and reasonable. The recognition of such a claim, under the form of the so-called social contract, heralds the breakdown of the economic view of life and the emergence of the political or historical view, just as inductive logic heralds the breakdown of the purely scientific view of thought and the emergence of explicitly historical or concrete thinking.

In order to concentrate the ethical and political fruits of the scientific consciousness into a single section we have anticipated the rise of empirical or inductive science : to this we must now return.

§ 5. *Empirical or Inductive Science*

Pure deductive science breaks down because its object turns out to be a chimera, a structure which is the structure of nothing, a law with no instances. This breakdown is in part historical, in part ideal only. It is ideal in the sense that no science has ever been wholly the analysis of pure *a priori* concepts. Science has explicitly claimed to be that, and in so far as it was what it claimed to be, its breakdown was a foregone conclusion ; even in the infancy of science Plato saw that the ideal of thought as purely *a priori* implied that the thinker had known everything from all eternity, that is, he saw that science had to be presupposed as already complete before it could begin. But these difficulties, like many others, *solvuntur ambulando*. Science actually advanced and prospered in the hands of the Greeks, and defied the gloomy auguries which might have been drawn from the account given of it by its devotees. This was simply because the account was false.

But in part the breakdown was historical. At the close of the middle ages the scientific mind of Europe reached the definite and positive conclusion that scientific practice was being vitiated by an unsound theory, and this theory was simply the *a priori* or deductive ideal. Scientific research was felt to be at a dead end, blocked by an impassable wall of dogma. This was not religious dogma but scientific dogma, the dogma of *a priori* method. No doubt theology, itself

an example of *a priori* science, played its part in the main-
tenance of that dogma, but this was not because it was
specifically theology but because it was generically science
on the deductive model.

The great scientists of the Renaissance fought a battle
which ought never to be necessary again, the battle for the
recognition of facts. Observation and experiment, they
maintained, were the true sources of scientific knowledge,
and *a priori* reasoning was inherently barren. They achieved
in this way what may be called the coming-of-age of the
scientific consciousness, a real revolution in thought.

It is sometimes imagined that there are two kinds of
science, *a priori* or deductive, and empirical or inductive ;
that mathematics belongs to the former type, and the
sciences of nature to the latter. This is a distortion of the
truth. The great scientists who laid the foundations of
the empirical method were not enemies of mathematics ; and
the subsequent progress of science has not left mathematics
on one side. These men were mathematicians before everything, and the advance of mathematics since their day has
been one of the most brilliant triumphs in the history of
thought. It is the purely abstract or deductive ideal of
science which, as we saw, gave birth to mathematics ; but
it gives nothing more. In the atmosphere of pure deduction,
mathematics cannot live a moment. It *is* pure deduction,
but it can only have concrete reality as the deductive
element in a totality of science which supplements and
reinforces it with an inductive or empirical element. Mathematics is the skeleton of the body of science ; its flesh and
blood—the very digestive organs which build up the skeleton
—are empirical.

Greek science was not in point of fact purely mathematical.
It was, in its biological, astronomical, and humanistic

interests, richly empirical. But it was only implicitly empirical, and failed to recognize the empirical side of its own character. Hence, when it inquired concerning the origin of the concepts which it studied, it mistakenly replied that it obtained them *a priori*, from a source untouched by sensuous experience. The error of this account is obvious if we look at the actual scientific achievements of the Greeks. Plato thought that he was in the *Republic* developing the wholly *a priori* concept of society, but no one can fail to see that he was really commenting on his profound experience of Greek political life. It was only in his theory of science, never in his actual scientific work, that he shut his eyes to the world of facts.

Thus the battle against ' Aristotle ' which marked the Renaissance was an effort to make explicit that empirical study of fact which in Greek thought was always implicit : always present but never recognized. The result was on the theoretical side the substitution of inductive logic for deductive ; on the practical side, an immense expansion and consolidation of scientific thought, which, because freed from the false ideal of pure deduction, could now for the first time realize its true nature as based on the empirical study of fact.

But the novelty of this movement must not be exaggerated. Science remains science still. The emergence into explicitness of its empirical character does not make a new thing of it. Inductive logic does not really supersede deductive ; it stands over against it as at once a friend and an enemy. Observation and experiment do not supersede *a priori* deduction ; rather they are said to underlie and be presupposed by it, every deductive process resting on a previous induction. Thus the theory arose of which Mill is the great representative, that science proceeds by an alternating rhythmical process of which induction is the first moment and deduction the second. This theory breaks down on discovering that induction itself rests on a principle, variously described as the uniformity of nature, the law of universal causation, and so forth, which, just because induction rests upon it, induction is powerless to establish. Thus the whole of induction falls to the ground because it is found to assume that of which it is ostensibly in search.

This principle of uniformity, which induction assumes, is also the principle which deduction assumes, namely the existence of abstract concepts in general ; for uniformity is nothing but the abstractness of the concept, its indifference to the variations of its own instances. Thus induction does not overcome the fundamental abstractness of deduction but simply reasserts it, and this fundamental assertion in which both agree is nothing but the definition of the scientific consciousness. Both deductive and inductive logic are therefore developed out of the definition of science as such. But the abstractness of science, which posits the transcendence of the universal to the particular as its first principle, leaves science face to face with the question of the hen and the egg. If the universal and the particular are separate, which comes first ? Do we proceed in this direction or in that ? Such a question has no answer, for the separation is not real and there is consequently no process in either direction. For this very reason, no good ground can be given for asserting the priority of either process to the other. Therefore science is bound to maintain both at once, and to do what it can towards sandwiching the deductive and inductive accounts of itself in slices as thin as possible but never actually fused together. If this fusion took place, which is the only possible solution of the problem of logic, science would cease to exist, for the distinction between induction and deduction would have vanished, and this would imply the denial of any distinction between the process from particular to universal and that from universal to particular, and this again would involve the discovery that the universal and the particular are not separate things, but only distinct elements of a whole which even in thought is not divisible. This recognition is the death of science as such, because science is the assertion of the abstract concept. Whether this concept is called, with Plato, a form and asserted to exist by itself in a non-sensuous world of its own, or whether, as by medieval logicians, it is called a universal and the precise manner of its existence is matter of debate, or whether it is called a law of nature, and asserted to be nothing but the manner in which the world of fact is organized, makes no difference. All the schools of thought to which I have alluded agree in the abstractness of the concept, that is, its pure self-identity over against the variations of its instances ; and this is the hall-mark of science. But the differences of view to which I refer have great importance within the history of science, as representing the gradual recognition by science itself of the abstractness of its own procedure. When this abstractness becomes explicit, it is transcended : a conscious abstraction is not a real abstraction, for it implies the recognition of a concrete truth underlying the abstraction itself. The discovery of the abstractness of science is, as we shall see, the birth of history.

§ 6. *Science as Supposal*

The modern world has with a curious unanimity changed its mind as to the nature of science almost within living memory.

In the middle of the nineteenth century it was believed

that science was the discovery of the laws of nature ; that is to say, the determination of the structure actually subsisting in the world of facts. A generation ago, or more, this opinion began to collapse ; not owing to the attacks of persons hostile to the pursuit of science, if such persons existed, but owing to the reflection upon their own work of scientists themselves, who began to form the belief that their scientific labours were directed to the attainment not of truth but of something else. On the whole, this movement received little or no encouragement from professional philosophers, who were inclined to suggest that these scientists should mind their own business instead of dabbling in subjects of which they were ignorant ; but even the philosophers showed the cloven hoof in the form of a disposition to attack the sciences of formal logic and psychology. But this attack, though certainly directed to showing that logic and psychology were not true, made no attempt to describe them except, negatively, as errors ; and the interest of the new movement of thought among the scientists lay in the fact that it aimed at giving a positive description of science.

The results of this movement are well known to every one, as indeed they deserve to be. On the one hand we have a school which maintains that the object of science is not the real but the possible, or that science is essentially hypothesis ; and on the other hand we have, in all its variations and ramifications, the doctrine that science is not true but useful.

The whole point of this critical movement—by far the most important intellectual movement of the last half-century—is lost if it is taken for a revival of abstract scepticism. It is not a revolt against thought as such but against the specific form which thought presents as science, and this we know by now to be the abstract concept. Nothing can be a more damning sign of philosophical obtuseness than to regard it as an attack on the validity of knowledge in general. It is an attempt to show, not that knowledge in general is impossible, but that science is not knowledge.

In the form of scientific pragmatism or the economic theory of the concept it need not delay us. This theory is true, but it contains a tautology born of misunderstanding. Science is useful, there is no denying it; but what is utility? We have already seen that utility is action looked at through the spectacles of the scientific consciousness. It is only the fundamental abstractness of science that gives rise to the very notion of utility; and therefore, though science can truly be described as that point of view from which all action, and therefore all thought, is utility, this is no better as a definition than the statement that moles are what make mole-hills. Such definitions are not to be despised, but they do not go far enough.

On the other hand, one may go farther and fare worse. If one first adopts the economic theory of the concept and then forgets that one has been analysing the abstract concept of science, and jumps to the conclusion that the analysis applies to knowledge in general, one becomes a pragmatist. Yet even in this disaster all is not lost, for the very babblings of pragmatism have a kind of method in them, resulting from a confused attempt to overcome the dualism of thought and action.

The movement under discussion reaches a more important, because less tautological, position when it describes science as hypothesis. This view, in fact, seems to be what is really meant by those who describe science as the useful; and it is explicitly maintained by a very large number of eminent people. It is, roughly, as follows.

Science asserts, not the actual truth, but what would be true if something were true which is laid down as an hypothesis. It asserts, never that S is P, but that if there were an S it would be P. Its procedure therefore consists, first, in making an assumption, secondly in deducing the consequences of that assumption. Throughout this process it never makes an assertion, in the sense of a categorical judgement, at all. Its judgements are hypothetical from beginning to end. The geometrician, for instance, has no need to answer the question ' Are there any triangles ? ' It is enough for him, till he turns metaphysician, to say what would happen if there were. He need not even ask the question ' Does Euclidean space exist ? ' but is free to discuss the purely hypothetical implications of that or any other kind of space. Science is a pure tissue of implications, none of which are asserted as facts. The scientist may frame any hypothesis he likes ; the freedom of untrammelled supposal is his ; he must merely suppose something, and then work out the consequences—all equally matter of supposal, never of assertion—which it entails.

This theory of science as fundamentally an act of supposal or hypothesis is not new : it was held by Plato ; and we do not propose to reject it. On the contrary, we regard it as expressing an important truth about the scientific consciousness. But it contains implications which did not indeed altogether escape Plato, but are sometimes overlooked by its modern supporters. A tissue of hypotheses cannot be a self-contained and autonomous organism, for hypothesis as such refers beyond itself, and is relative to something which is not hypothetical but categorical.

Science therefore, as non-assertive hypothesis, can only exist upon a background which is not hypothetical, not therefore scientific, but assertive. We recognize this empirically when we say that some fact or other must *suggest* the hypothesis from which we begin. There need not be any triangles, but there must be things which set us thinking about triangles, which remind us, as Plato says, of triangularity. But our principle does not depend on these empirical facts. If any one is so ignorant as to think that he can frame hypotheses having no relation whatever to his actual experience, so oblivious of the principles laid down by the Renaissance scientists as to suppose that observation and experiment, study of concrete fact, are not necessary preliminaries of even the most abstract mathematical hypotheses, he may be reminded that any hypothesis presupposes at least one fact, namely our own freedom and competence to frame hypotheses in general. You cannot simply suppose that you are free to suppose ; you must assert that you are both free to suppose, and actually supposing. The Euclidean geometrician supposes the existence of Euclidean space, but he does not suppose that he supposes it ; he knows that he supposes it ; his own act of forming an hypothesis is for him an historical fact. This act of framing hypotheses is simply the self-determination of the mind in the form of the scientific consciousness ; and therefore the mind which so determines itself is, in that self-determination, not acting scientifically, that is, framing hypotheses, but categorically asserting a concrete fact.

This is recognized clearly enough by those current theories of science which base it upon mathematical logic. A scientific statement is never asserted as true without qualification, but only as true subject to the given hypothesis. But all scientific statements whatever have a common methodology, of which an account is given by formal logic. The statements made by formal logic are true of every possible object, no matter what it is, that is to say, irrespective of any given hypothesis. And formal logic as the theory of abstraction is identical with mathematics, so that mathematics also is true without qualification of the entire world, actual and possible. Thus logic or mathematics, which is the basis and presupposition of all scientific hypotheses, is not itself hypothetical but a true account of the real structure of reality.

Thus mathematical or formal logic emerges in response to the demand for a non-hypothetical basis for the hypotheses of empirical science. And because science as such is hypothetical, mathematical logic, which is categorically true of every possible object, is supra-scientific or philosophical, and mathematics is declared to be the solution of the problems of philosophy.

But we know already that this is an illusion. Mathematics is nothing but the assertion of the abstract concept, and it can give us no account of the presuppositions of this assertion. Mathematical logic is only the shadow of science itself. It is the truth, but the truth about nothing : it is the description of the structure of a null class. Hence, though the hypotheses of empirical science must have some kind of categorical basis, they cannot find this in mathematics, which is the very distilled essence of hypothesis itself. The abstract cannot rest upon the more abstract, but only on the concrete.

This concrete basis of all scientific abstraction is something which science itself never grasps, namely individual or historical fact. The triumph of the Renaissance scientists lay in bringing this implicit presupposition to light, in discovering that science was an abstraction from the concrete reality of history. Empirical science recognizes itself as being what all science really is, a compressed and simplified account of facts, and fact itself therefore permanently eludes the grasp of science, as is indeed taught by the logical doctrine that the individual is indefinable. 'Scientific fact' is a phrase which aptly illustrates this; for scientific fact is a fact purged of its crude and scientifically scandalous concreteness, isolated from its historical setting and reduced to the status of a mere instance of a rule. It is a fact which has been turned from an individual into a particular. The facts with which empirical science concerns itself are facts thus de-individualized, de-factualized, and this is what distinguishes the sense in which even the most empirical science uses the word 'fact' from the sense it bears in history.

Science is explicitly supposal. But supposal itself, as we saw when discussing art, is identical with questioning, which is the cutting edge of the mind, an activity not self-contained or independent, but implying behind it a body of information or assertion. This body science possesses in the form of history. It is only, as every scientist knows, the actual possession of an ordered body of facts that enables him to frame those hypotheses which are the essence of the scientific life, and these facts, as actually ascertained by observation and experiment, are matter of history. But it is the facts that are true; the scientific simplification of them into instances of laws, abstract particulars of abstract concepts, is not true but arbitrary, useful no doubt, but useful precisely because it is not asserted as true but merely entertained in the form of a question.

Science is the question whose answer is history. To ask that question implies that history is already in existence; and thus we get a process of history—science—history. But history on its first appearance is implicit; it is not known for what it is, and is indeed despised as the mere world of empirical or sensuous reality. It is only when it has been distilled into terms of science and then restored to itself in the form of concepts or laws that it is recognized for what it really is.

The scientific attitude, then, is one of two things. Either it is the mere name for a questioning attitude which forms the cutting edge of history, or else it is the name of a whole activity which is a false abstraction, a philosophical error. The scientist thinks he is working at a world of pure concepts. He is not ; such a world is a metaphysical monstrosity, and the methods by which he says he works at it are logical absurdities. He is really working at the determination and elucidation of historical facts, and if he calls himself a scientist instead of an historian that is only because he is in error as to the nature of his work. Of course that error, like all such errors, reacts on the work itself, and goes some way to destroying its value and substituting for the intelligent determination of historical fact the arbitrary shuffling of fictitious entities ; but this transformation is at most partial, and at bottom the scientist is always, in spite of himself, an historian and engaged in the study of actual fact.

That he is so engaged he can hardly help, sooner or later, discovering. And this discovery, begun at the Renaissance, seems now to be coming to a head. The great scientific discoveries of the nineteenth century are peculiarly instructive in this respect. During that period a large number of sciences openly restated their problems in terms of history, and by that very act achieved answers to them far surpassing in depth all earlier achievements. Now that astronomy has realized that its proper task is to explore the history of the stellar universe, now that geology and geography have united to study the history of the earth, now that biology has realized that the problem of species is the problem of the origin of species, the time is surely at hand when science will feel the need of absorbing itself bodily in history, re-shaping its problems throughout in historical terms, and resolving scientific method into historical method. This process is unmistakably going on round us, and nothing but the downfall of civilization can stop it.

§ 7. *Science as the Intuitive Form of Thought*

The paradox of science may be expressed by calling it intuitive thought. Intuition is the questioning, immediate side of experience : thought is the asserting, explanatory side. Science is explicit to itself as thought, but it turns out on inquiry to be identical with the questioning activity ; that is, it realizes the contradiction of a type of thought which is not thought precisely because it is thought's opposite, intuition.

Here again, as on p. 95, we must bear in mind that the division of experience into intuition and thought, as we find that division in the forefront of all philosophy from Plato to Kant, is a fiction. Intuition and thought are not two separate activities which are somehow united in the body of human experience. Experience is an indivisible whole in which two sides can always be distinguished : an immediate, intuitive or questioning side, which is hypostatized by abstract psychology into the faculty of sensation, and a mediating, reflective, logical or assertive side, which is called thought. Thought is the one, sensation the many. What characterizes the intuitive or sensuous side of experience is just its manyness or perpetual difference from itself, flux, novelty or creation. What characterizes the logical or reflective side is its self-identity, permanence, unity. Now we have already seen that science consists in the separation of these two distinct elements, and the attribution of reality to thought while denying it to sensation. But division as such is the characteristic of sensation as opposed to thought : thought unifies what sensation divides. Therefore any given thing which is made the field of an unreconciled division is thereby placed under the head of sensation, for the characteristic unity of thought has been denied to it. If experience as a whole is now divided into two separate parts, thought and sense, it becomes by this very definition wholly sensuous, and each part of it is a sensuous, not an intelligible, object.

Thus the attempt of science to achieve pure thought frustrates itself, because the very cleavage of thought from sense de-rationalizes thought and turns it into a sensuous object. It is called thought still, but it is intuition.

This argument is more familiar, though more superficial, when stated in terms of logic. The universal has its very life and being in its particulars, of whose multiplicity it is the unity. If now it is disentangled from those particulars and set apart by itself, it becomes not their universal but another particular object, thus losing precisely its intelligibility (universality) and becoming an object of mere intuition, a thing that we no longer think but only imagine.

It is this falling-back upon intuition that constitutes the irrationality, the arbitrariness, of all science. The assumptions made by science cannot be justified under criticism ; their only justification is the frankly irrational *fiat* of the scientist's will. The concept is for him an abstraction, that is to say hypostatized into a thing, reified ; hence it cannot be explained or thought, it can only be intuited, and this intuitive attitude towards a concept is what is meant by assumption in science. To ask the scientist to justify his assumptions is to treat science as if it were wholly rational, to forget that it is essentially thought falling back into the immediacy of intuition. This immediacy is not identical with the immediacy of religious vision ; it is not faith ; for the religious immediacy is the genuine immediacy of imagination ; the immediacy of science is the false immediacy of thought, which is trying not to be immediate, so that its immediacy is the mark of its failure. Science feels that it ought to be able to justify its assumptions ; religion never feels that it ought to be able to prove the existence of God. That is the feeling of theology, which is not religion but science.

The immediacy into which science collapses marks its failure to achieve the infinity of thought. Science has a great deal to say about the infinite, but what is by science called the infinite is precisely the finite. It is called the infinite because that is what it is meant to be ; it is meant to be the object of thought, and the object of thought is as such the infinite. But when the object of thought is set side by side with and separated from the object of sensation, this very separation delimits it, makes it finite, because it places something else outside it. That which is other than the finite can only be a second finite, however loudly it is called the infinite. And in point of fact what science calls infinity is nothing but indefiniteness, ambiguity in definition.

In its intuitive character, science shows certain affinities with the life of intuition *par excellence*, namely art. This is recognized by those who speak of the scientific imagination ; and the way in which science merely supposes instead of asserting its concepts is parallel to the way in which art merely supposes its imagery, instead of, like religion, asserting it as real.

Now the characteristic outcome of supposal is pluralism. We saw that, just because the work of art is merely supposed, the world of art was a pluralistic or monadic world, consisting of an indefinite number of works of art all ostensibly independent of one another and having no such structure as would make them into a single coherent world. This individualism of art, this absence of social or historical structure, is in point of fact tempered by the existence, even in art, of implicit thought ; but this implicit thought, though it enables the observer to see some general plan in art-history as a whole, remains hidden from the artist as such. Science shares the pluralism of art. Scientists are notoriously careless of the history of their own sciences, and this is inevitable and the strict consequence of the scientific point of view. Science always believes that it has just discovered the ultimate truth and that all past ages have been sunk in a fog of ignorance and superstition. It has no sense of its solidarity with and debt to its own past and other forms of consciousness. And further, it is as impossible to classify sciences and reduce them to a single ordered cosmos of thought as it is to do the same with works of art.

The attempt has been made over and over again to reduce all the sciences to such an ordered whole. It seems obvious that there must be a table or hierarchy of sciences in which each has its proper place ; and so there would, if science were the rational activity it believes itself to be. If there really were a Platonic world of pure concepts, in which every concept was dovetailed into the rest, each having a science to expound its nature, then there would be a corresponding world of sciences. But, as Plato himself saw to his dismay, there are concepts of mud and filth and anything one likes to name, and these can never fit into a place in the world of absolute being. The concepts of science are abstract and therefore arbitrary, and because any one may make any abstraction he likes, there cannot possibly be a system or world of the sciences.

But because the immediacy of science is the immediacy not of imagination—immediacy embraced and welcomed as such—but the immediacy of thought, an immediacy felt to be discreditable, an arbitrariness that cannot acquiesce in itself, it follows that science cannot, like art, accept this result with complacency. Science is trying to be thought, and thought is unity or system, and science cannot give up the attempt to co-ordinate itself without giving up the claim to be thought. Hence the production of schemes for the classification of sciences is bound to continue as long as science continues to resist its own absorption in history. For, it is plausibly argued, the abstract concept organizes the world of particulars. But how is the world of concepts organized ? Presumably it too has an organization, and the discovery of this organization is the task of the science which studies the classification of the sciences. But in point of fact the members of a class are not universals but particulars : there cannot be a class of classes, a universal of universals, because it would be one of its own members, being itself an example of a class. Hence even to discuss the problem of the classification of the sciences is to fall into the pit of hypostatization, or rather to reveal the fact that one is already wallowing in that pit. Every science, while it is being pursued, involves the belief that its concept is the one and only concept in existence. To pursue one science means at least forgetting, and in the last resort denying, all the others, with the solitary exception of mathematics, which forms the indispensable skeleton of all scientific work because it expresses nothing but the abstract nature of science in general. But the content in which this mathematical form is embodied in this or that science is ' contingent ' and cannot be reduced to system, just because the form is by definition an abstract universal or one to which the variations of its own particulars are irrelevant.

But though the world of science as a whole, the world in which every science has a place of its own, is a world which science itself can never grasp, there is such a world. The concrete unity of all works of art is not itself a work of art, but the history of art ; and the artist as such is not concerned with this history. In the same way, the unity of all the sciences is not itself a scientific unity, a conceptual scheme, but an historical unity. The history of science can show how the various sciences have grown up one out of another, and can make intelligible their inter-relations. Here again, history solves the question which science asks but cannot answer : the unity of history at once annuls and makes intelligible the pluralism of science.

It is easy, in comparison with the wealth and profundity of religion, to despise science for its abstractness, its air of playing futile games with the small change of thought, its innocent certainty of its own success in plumbing the secrets of the universe. Comparing itself with science, religion is not often tempted to exchange vocations. It feels as an aged and illiterate peasant, rich in the varied knowledge of the countryside and rooted in the soil of an immemorial tradition, feels towards a saucy town lad fresh from the board school. The treasures of religion are so vast and their power over mankind so incalculable that to exchange them for science would seem a worse bargain than Glaucus's exchange of armour. But the movement from religion to science is not really a downward movement, and the reverse movement is not really a gain. The wealth of religion is a pearl of great price hidden in a field ; it is wheat growing among tares. You cannot have the glory and comfort of religion without its superstition, its magic, its brutal hatreds and slavish fears. In the highest and sternest religions these elements are kept in check, but no more. They are always present at the back of the mind, always ready to break out and devastate human life. Religion is always looking forward to the day when it shall be set free from this body of death which, as its own shadow, it perpetually carries with it. That freedom is nothing but the self-revelation of thought, the discovery by the mind of its own nature as a thinking mind.

However abstract and barren may be the first-fruits of this discovery, the discovery itself is an incalculable advance in the history of man. As art and religion lift man above the level of the beasts, science lifts the civilized man above the level of the savage. The material utility of science, its service in feeding and clothing and sheltering us, carrying us from place to place and providing us with comforts, is the least part of its importance. Its real gift is simply the end of dreaming and the promise of a waking life. It sweeps aside with a ruthless hand all mythology, all symbols that are heavy with unrealized meanings and dark with the terrors of dreamland, and bids the mind face the world's mystery armed with nothing but its five senses and the sling of its wit. What that means, no one knows who has not long and carefully weighed the debt which he owes to the scientific consciousness. But when that is done, he will hardly shrink from praising the founders of science for the gift of spiritual freedom even in the words of the ancient poet :

Felix qui potuit rerum cognoscere causas,
Atque metus omnes et inexorabile fatum
Subiecit pedibus, strepitumque Acherontis avari.

§ 8. *Understanding and Reason*

The history of European philosophy from Greece to the eighteenth century is the history of the self-consciousness of the scientific spirit. The logic, the metaphysics, the psychology of this great movement are first and foremost an analysis of the scientific consciousness, which includes as no small part of itself the theological consciousness. But what is for our purpose more important, these studies have actually been carried out from the point of view of the scientific consciousness itself ; they are properly not philosophies but ' philosophical sciences ', a contradiction in terms which signifies that they are fundamentally science, but science turned upon itself, *scientia scientiarum*, the scientific theory of science. Formal logic, whether in its scholastic or mathematical form, is not only reflection upon thought in the special sense of scientific thought, but in the special sense of scientific reflection ; and this is the fact which divides formal logic from that dialectical logic whose point of view is the point of view not of science but of philosophy, and whose object is not the abstract thought of science but the concrete thought of history and philosophy. Hence all the embarrassments by which science is beset equally affect that so-called philosophy which is only science of the second degree.

To this we shall return in a later chapter. At present we are concerned to point out that the revolt against formal logic and psychology and metaphysics, and the revolt against science, are the same thing ; and that this revolt is summed up in the antithesis of understanding and reason.

Understanding is abstract thought, the ' faculty of concepts ', thought spontaneously originating concepts or categories out of itself with no assistance from the world of fact. This is the Kantian and true account of understanding. The two false accounts are the Platonic, which claims that these concepts are self-subsistent entities, free universals, and the Baconian, which claims that they are the actual structure of the world of fact and discovered by the mind embedded in that world. Both these accounts break down by overlooking the fact that because in either case the concept, to be found, must be sought, therefore the act of seeking it is the assertion of its existence, an assertion proceeding from no source at all except the arbitrary act of the mind. The Platonist or the Baconian imagines his forms to be realities because he overlooks the original act of abstraction by which he has severed the universal from its particulars. It is not the universal in its true actuality, the universal living in its particulars, that is the object of understanding, but the universal torn apart from its particulars and converted into a closed and abstract formula. Of this abstract formula as such, the original act of abstraction is the irresponsible and arbitrary creator.

Reason is concrete thought, thought which does not arbitrarily create to itself, by abstraction, any object it pleases for the sake of ease in thinking it, but sets out to study facts as they are, and to conceive a universal which is truly the universal of its own particulars. Hence reason thinks the concrete universal, not the bare self-identity of science which leaves all difference outside itself, but the identity to which difference is organic and essential. Understanding hypostatizes the concept into an object of intuition by itself, outside its own particulars ; and this object is nothing real, but simply the fruit of an error. Reason finds the concept in the particulars, forming with them an inseparable unity.

The characteristic of reason is the unity of universal and

particular, or in general the unity of opposites. The concrete reality of any one opposite is its union with the other ; not a bare indistinguishable identity but a union in which the two sides can be distinguished but not separated. The identity, in the sense of an indistinguishable identity, of opposites is not the principle of reason but a disease, endemic and mortal, of understanding. From the violent and arbitrary separation of two opposites, the assertion that A shall be only A and not-A only not-A, it necessarily results that A, now falsely asserted as a self-subsistent concrete reality, generates a not-A within itself and the not-A conversely generates an A. Thus each of the terms, A and not-A, produces its own opposite, and when that has happened they cannot be any longer distinguished. This is the *coincidentia oppositorum* which always dogs the footsteps of abstract or scientific thinking. Matter and mind, affirmation and negation, good and evil, truth and falsehood, universal and particular, are no sooner resolutely separated than they turn into each other. Hold up a stick, and distinguish its top and bottom : there you have a concrete synthesis of opposites in an individual whole. Take a knife and cut it in two in the middle, into a top half and a bottom half. You have now separated the opposites. But the instant the separation is complete, the top half has its own bottom and the bottom half its own top. The top half is no longer simply a top and the bottom half no longer simply a bottom ; each is at once a top and a bottom, and therefore, considered in terms of top and bottom, each is indistinguishable from the other. Your opposites have now coincided. Abstract thought fends off the *coincidentia oppositorum* by deliberately ignoring the bottom of the top half and the top of the bottom half, and in defiance of facts simply (that is, abstractly and falsely) calling the one half

all top and the other half all bottom. Thus ' the universal '
as such is a particular universal, and ' the particular ' as
such is nothing but the universal of particularity ; but
formal logic conceals this fact and makes its very living by
the pretence that it has not hypostatized (particularized)
the universal.

The antithesis of understanding and reason, or abstract
and concrete thinking, is the antithesis of science and
history. There is a certain temptation to regard understanding and reason as coexistent ' faculties of the mind '
or activities which can be alternately pursued without self-
contradiction ; and a psychology which prides itself on not
speaking of faculties adopts the same point of view when
it devotes separate treatments to scientific and historical
experience and fits them both into its theory of experience
as a whole.

But the separation of understanding from reason is itself
an act of understanding, which reason is bound to repudiate ;
it is just another example of that passion for separating
which is the peculiar vice of scientific thought. Separate
understanding from reason, and you very soon find yourself
landed in a *coincidentia oppositorum* in which you cannot
tell one from the other. Reason, concrete thinking, repu-
diates the abstraction and recognizes understanding as
identical with itself, in the sense of being one necessary
element in itself. Understanding as such, the scientific
consciousness, is committed by its original error to denying
its own identity with history ; but history is just the freedom of thought from that error, and therefore history sees
itself as science and yet more than science, sees itself as
a concrete whole of which science is one end, one pole or
moment.

From no point of view, therefore, can science and history

be regarded as coexistent and equally rational or defensible manifestations of thought. From the strictly scientific point of view science is the only form of thought, and history does not exist at all. From the historical point of view science does indeed exist, but only as an element within the body of history itself, as a mere weapon or tool of historical thinking. The quarrel between history and science is whether generalization is a means to knowledge or knowledge itself. In this quarrel philosophy is so far neutral that the issue can and must be fought out on the ground of science and history, which will both refuse, and rightly, to have it settled by a third party ; but in one sense philosophy cannot be neutral, because the very existence of philosophy depends on history's winning the battle. Just as the defeat of science by religion would enthrone an obscurantism in which thought was deposed by faith and philosophy therefore destroyed unborn, so the defeat of history by science would condemn thought to the arbitrary irrationality of the abstract concept, and philosophy— rational knowledge—would be pronounced in advance an impossibility. For the greatest discovery that thought has made since the time of Plato is that the way to philosophy from science lies through history. This discovery, which is the key-note of the Christian attitude towards the problem of knowledge, was implicit from the first in the Christian gospel as a philosophy of history, and has been becoming progressively explicit ever since Descartes, in his *cogito ergo sum*, laid down that historical fact was the absolute object of knowledge.

The discussions concerning understanding and reason, their distinction and relative nature, which play so large a part in the philosophy of a century ago and more, represent the climax in this process ; for they express an attempt, often concealed in the mythological imagery of a faculty-psychology, to distinguish the scientific from the historical form of experience and to grasp the relation between them as one of no mere difference, but as a dialectical distinction in which one tries to be what the other is, one implies what the other expresses, one questions where the other answers, one overlooks what the other recognizes ; and of which therefore the more primitive is absorbed without residue in the more advanced.

VI

HISTORY

§ 1. *History as the Assertion of Fact*

WHEN a mind that is in error discovers that it is in error, the error is conquered and truth is implicitly reached. The error of science is its abstractness ; and therefore the discovery by science of its own abstractness is the correction of that abstractness and the revelation of the concrete object. We saw that in its first or *a priori* phase science did not know that it was abstract ; it believed itself to be the apprehension of a real object in which, so to speak, its own abstractness was already embodied, so that the abstractness in question belonged not to thought but to its object. But this separately existing universal, as an abstract entity, was seen to be a contradiction in terms, and science recognized itself as the author of its own abstraction, imposing its abstractness upon a world which was in reality a world of concrete facts.

This discovery, foreshadowed by Plato when he spoke of the hypotheses on which the sciences depend, and by Aristotle when he spoke of science as proceeding by abstraction, remained for centuries a half-realized truth, never firmly faced or clearly stated. Neither Plato nor Aristotle, still less their successors, recognized its consequences. In the middle ages it was the mainspring of the debate between nominalism and realism ; but its first real fruit was, as we have seen, the experimental method of the Renaissance scientists. Experiment means the recognition of fact, and experimental science means the assertion of fact, even if only mutilated fact, as the true presupposition of scientific thought.

When the Renaissance scientists reflected on their own work and saw into its presuppositions, they realized what the ancients never realized, that the hypotheses or abstractions of science rested on the knowledge of fact. In their discussions of scientific method they made this very clear ; but the profoundest statement of it, and therefore the most misunderstood, was that of Descartes. All science, said Descartes, rests upon the one indubitable certainty that I think and that therefore I exist. Now the thought and existence of which Descartes spoke were not abstractions—anything thinking anything, or anything somehow getting itself thought about—as those wiseacres believe who offer to emend his formula to *cogitatur ergo est*, or *cogitare ergo esse* or the like. Descartes meant what he said ; and what he said was that the concrete historical fact, the fact of my actual present awareness, was the root of science. He was only going one step beyond Bacon, for whom the root of science was natural fact : Descartes, more profoundly, saw that before natural fact can be of any use to the scientist he must observe it, and that the fact of his observing it is the fact that really matters. Science presupposes history and can never go behind history : that is the discovery of which Descartes' formula is the deepest and most fruitful expression.

This discovery implicitly resolves science into history. I say implicitly, because at first it is regarded only as a revolution within science itself. Empirical science, science recognizing its debt to facts, does not at once cease to be science and become history. Before that happens, empirical science must pass through a complete dialectic of its own, in which the conflict between its own abstractness and the concreteness of the facts upon which it rests is resolved. The origin of history at the Renaissance is therefore only an implicit origin. Fact is discovered, but its nature is distorted to bring it into harmony with the abstractness of science. The empirical scientist respects fact, but it is a peculiar kind of fact that he respects ; it is fact not as it grows, tangled up in the undergrowth of the everyday world, but fact passed through the sieve of his own abstract methods, fact refined and expurgated, the fact of the laboratory. Hence, though the Renaissance scientists did discover the world of facts and to that extent overcame the abstractness of science, the first result of their discovery was, as we have seen, not real history but ' natural history ', a pseudo-history in which historical fact itself became abstract and artificial ; the mere abstract instance of abstract law ; particular, not individual.

But this fault corrected itself in time. Once it was recognized that science owed a debt to history, once it was recognized that no scientist could afford, except in joke, to say *tant pis pour les faits*, the deeper and deeper recognition of the extent of this debt followed as a natural consequence, and the triumphs which have attended the history of science since the Renaissance have gone hand in hand with the progressive shifting of its burdens on to the shoulder of history.

The form of thought which we call specifically history came to its maturity in the course of this process. History in the special sense of the word came into being in the eighteenth century and shot up to a gigantic stature in the nineteenth. It is an absolutely new movement in the life of mankind. In the sense in which Gibbon and Mommsen were historians, there was no such thing as an historian before the eighteenth century. There were *rerum gestarum scriptores*, annalists and compilers of memoirs ; but the gulf between a Thucydides and a Gibbon is not a mere difference of degree between the historian of a short period and the historian of a long. It is the difference between the recorder of those facts which happen to be directly visible from his own empirical situation in history, and the thinker who, defying the empirical limitations of time and place, claims for himself, in principle, the power to recount the whole infinite history of the universe ; restricting himself to this part of it or that not because he happens to be planted there, but because it is his own good pleasure so to restrict himself. Even the slenderest monograph written from this point of view outweighs, as an achievement of the spirit, the whole output of the *rerum gestarum scriptores* ; its writer may be a narrow and pedantic specialist, but he has nailed his colours to the mast as a spectator of all time and all existence.

But even behind the activity of the annalist there is an ultimate form of historical thought which is the most rudimentary of all. This is perception. The concept of perception, like that of a fact, is modern ; the Greeks had no name for it, or rather they called it by a name which showed a misconception of its nature, namely, sensation. Sensation is the false or abstract account of perception. In perception we are immediately aware of our object, which is a concrete and therefore historical fact : perception and history are thus identical. But the immediacy of perception does not exclude mediation, it is not abstract immediacy (sensation) but implicitly contains an element of mediation (thought). When we say that we perceive something, we mean thereby to assert that we are not thinking ; but this assertion is an error, and the analysis of perception reveals inevitably the presence of thought. A group of officers, at manœuvres on a misty day, perceives a moving body on a hill, and some of the officers immediately identify it as a body of troops ; perceive it, they would say, to be such a body. A more skilled and careful observer, watching the movements of its individuals, correctly identifies it as a flock of sheep.[1] Both identifications are described as perceptions, and so they are ; to argue that they are erroneously thought to be perceptions would be to escape Scylla by falling into Charybdis, for it would be an admission that something exists which though not purely immediate (as perception is claimed to be) is mistaken for something purely immediate ; that is, it admits what we wish here to assert, the existence of implicit mediation. Perception is explicitly immediate, but it always contains within itself mediation (thought, ' interpretation of sense-data ', ' inference from the immediately given ', or whatever one likes to call it) and is therefore never abstract immediacy. This fact is denied by those who speak of thought as based upon the ' immediately given in perception ', but their denial of it, though self-contradictory—for *given* is only an obscure paraphrase for *asserted* (by thought) as real—is so far correct that the thought contained in perception is not explicit to the perceiving mind as thought. There is no such thing as the sense-datum of psychological mythology ; what is so described is either a false abstraction or the object of perception, historical fact.

History is thus, as a specific form of experience, identical with perception. But this may seem paradoxical, because perception appears to be the very humblest and most ordinary of cognitive activities, and we are claiming for history a very high and important place in the life of the mind, a place above science, far above religion, immensely above art, whereas perception is something that precedes

[1] Baden-Powell, *Aids to Scouting*.

and underlies all these and is in fact the very bread and water of our spiritual diet.

We must accept the paradox, but with reservations. Our dialectical series of forms of experience moves in a sense forward, in a sense backward. We do not begin with the lowest and simplest reality and make this develop into higher and more complex forms. To attempt the logical evolution of the complex out of the simple, the higher forms out of the lower, is exactly the error of the ' synthetic philosophy ' of Herbert Spencer, which owes its being to a failure to understand the nature of a dialectical process. A dialectical series means a series of terms, each one of which is an erroneous description of the next. In a dialectical series A B C, the truth is C ; B is a distorted account of it, and A is a distorted account of B. Now if C represents the true nature of a mind, B is a mistake—partial of course ; no mistake is a mere mistake—which C makes about itself. This mistake will recoil on C's own nature, for a mind which makes mistakes about its own nature will find its conduct, which is its nature, affected by these mistakes. Its nature will not be so far altered as to coincide with the false conception, but it will be disturbed by that conception.[1] Thus we get B, what the mind now thinks it is, and C_1, what it actually is. The next downward step will be to fail even to get the notion B coherent, to distort and degrade it into A. This still further lapse from truth in the self-knowledge of the mind C is now an error of the second degree, and therefore reacts in the second degree on the conduct and nature of the mind. It no longer therefore behaves as C_1 but as

---

[1] A person may think he is a poached egg ; that will not make him one : but it will affect his conduct, and for the worse. So a person may think he is pure imagination : he can't be pure imagination, for there is no such thing : but he can and will be an artist.

B_1, which is equivalent to C_2. In a sense we may say that it still is C, though it does not know it ; but because its self-ignorance affects its conduct, to call it C is misleading, for it does not behave like C but like C_2.

In such a condition the only sound way of describing the mind is to state the case in full, thus : Implicitly it is C. But it is trying to conceive itself as B, although really there is no such thing as B ; and even this error it has further confused, so that it now thinks of itself as A. Its true nature C, overlaid by the successive misconceptions B and A, comes out in the form C_2. It is, if we like so to distinguish, explicitly A, actually C_2, at bottom or ultimately C. If C is the historical experience, and A pure imagination, a mind which calls itself an artist will still be historical at bottom, but this historical nature will be so affected by the description of itself as aesthetic, that even to the dispassionate observer it does not appear as pure or unqualified history. When such a mind discovers its own true nature the distortion in that nature due to error will disappear.

It follows that a mind which is ignorant of its true nature does not in the fullest sense possess this nature. The true nature of the mind does not exist ready-made somewhere in the depths of the mind, waiting to be discovered. Till it is discovered it does not exist ; but yet it does exist in a confused and distorted form, since the errors made about it are only partial errors, and the dialectical task of bringing it into existence or coming to know it (the two are the same) is simply the clearing up of these confusions, which appear as inconsistencies, conflicts between what, at a given stage, the mind finds itself to be and what it feels it ought to be.

Hence all art, religion, and science rest on perception or history, as the earlier terms of any dialectical series on the later. But the extraordinary powers of history, the kind of intellectual feats that can be performed by a Grote or a Gibbon, though they are an essential part of the historical life, are actually acquired by this life only when it recognizes itself as historical. The less clearly it so recognizes itself, the more these powers are obscured and lost. Nor is this a mere matter of degree. The terms of a dialectical series are not related to one another in terms of degree,[1] but by the assertion in each term of something which in the previous term was wrongly denied.

Now the historical consciousness asserts concrete fact. The scientific consciousness denies the concreteness of this fact, and therefore in its hands the fact becomes the mere abstract instance of an abstract principle. This in history is called ' elevating ' (or strictly, degrading) ' history to the rank of a science '. Fact, in this type of historical error, is supposed to be ' mere ' fact (particular, not individual) and to require supplement from outside in the form of the so-called laws of history. The discovery of these is the work of sociology, economics, and kindred sciences. These sciences, so long as they are incorporated within the body of history itself, are useful to it and aid its progress, as do archaeology, numismatics, and other historical sciences ; but if they are conceived as ends to which history is the means— engines to which historical fact is so much fuel—they represent a downward movement in the path of thought, an attempt, which may easily be successful, to put back the clock of progress, and a recommendation by the tailless fox for a general decaudation of his brethren.

[1] The reader will see from this sentence, without further discussion, my attitude to the doctrine of ' degrees of truth ' ; but while I should entirely reject the category of degree in such a connexion, I cannot too heartily support the destructive criticisms which have been put forward in the name of that doctrine.

For the religious consciousness, fact appears as simply the manifestation of the will of God. Thus religious history, like scientific history, denies the concreteness of the fact and subordinates it to an abstract transcendent cause, now conceived not as an object of thought or law, but as an object of imagination or Supreme Being. History now appears as the operation of the divine providence, the miraculous working-out of a foreordained plan which is not the plan of any human agent, a drama whose author and spectator sits aloof while his puppets blindly strut and fume their little hour till he has done with them.

The aesthetic consciousness regards history not as a divine drama but as a drama pure and simple. Asked for fact, it gives fable, and honestly does not know that it is lying. It would be invidious to give examples of these three false forms of history; but they are common enough.

Now the false forms of any given reality betray their falseness by the presence in them of unreconciled oppositions. Scientific history finds its opposite in ' the contingent ', a derogatory name invented by it to describe those facts which it cannot force into its abstract schemes. Such facts are recalcitrant to thought simply because thought is here abstract. For history there is no contingent ; no fact is turned away from the historian's door. Religious history finds its opposite in ' nature ', or whatever it may call those facts which it cannot reconcile with its notion of the divine providence. There must be some such facts, because the imaginative way in which the idea of God is framed, like all intuitive modes of consciousness, must generate an opposite. It is only when God is resolved into the absolute of philosophy that he becomes all-embracing ; and therefore religious history bristles with natural facts, diabolical intrusions, enemies of God and so forth, against which God's actions stand out as miracles. Aesthetic history finds its opposite in the unromantic light of common day, the workaday world, which is not in itself any less dramatic than those things which the artist finds interesting, but is simply that in which he happens not to be interested.

History is the synthesis of all these oppositions. It reconciles drama with hard fact by finding drama everywhere, just because its drama is the drama of fact as such ; its aesthetic joy is the aesthetic joy of seeing not any story, but the truth, taking shape under its hand. That is because, setting truth above everything, it subordinates the element of emotion or immediacy to the element of critical reflection consciously developed. It reconciles providence with chance, divine ordinance with diabolical intervention, because, not being intuition but thought, it takes no sides ; it enters into the joys and griefs, the hopes and fears, of both parties to every struggle, sees them not as saints and devils but as striving and suffering human beings. It reconciles necessity with contingence because it does not abstract ; it does not come to the facts with a ready-made law in its hand and try to force them into it, throwing them away in disgust when they are too hard ; it rejoices in their hardness and finds its satisfaction in their very diversity and uniqueness.

But in superseding and negating the other forms of experience, history does not proceed as if they had never existed. The historian who handles history as if it were mere drama is in a state of deadly sin ; but unless he is enough of an artist to see the dramatic force of it, unless he is cunning in the use of words, a clear and an eloquent writer, easily moved by pity and sympathy, unless the deeds of the past speak with a trumpet tongue to his heart and kindle within him a poet's ardour—without all this, he will never be an historian. Again, if he sees his theme as that of the *gesta Dei per*—whatever his chosen people may be, if he belittles the agency of man before some inscrutable purpose of which God has revealed the secret to him alone, or makes heroes and villains of his personages, he is no better than a liar ; but unless he is saturated with a sense of obscure and mighty forces working in history for ends which no one man completely sees, unless he is prepared boldly to pronounce certain actions right and wrong according as they helped and hindered such forces, and unless he is able to see the course of history as the manifestation of an inexorable and righteous reason, he will never be an historian. And lastly, if he thinks he can lay down laws *a priori* that govern the course of history in the past, present, or future, if he thinks that there is any way of determining a fact except by straightforward historical inquiry, or that history truly repeats itself in any way whatever, large or small, he is merely a fool ; but unless he is prepared to spend years in the inductive study of coins and title-deeds, peculiarities of grammar and idiom, fragments of architecture and pottery, all the pedantic detail of scholarship and antiquarianism in its aspect as basis for possible generalization and hypothesis—he will be at best a transcriber of other people's opinions, not an historian.

§ 2. *The Growth of History*

The object of history is fact as such. To determine facts far distant in space and time is not the essence of history but its climax, the very heroism and bravado of the historical spirit in its defiance of empirical limitations. There is a growth of history, as we have already seen that there is a growth of art and religion and science, which proceeds from perception through annals and memoir to history in this highest sense. In perception we do not, as is sometimes falsely supposed, apprehend merely the immediately given in sense. To perceive is to see what we do not see, to grasp the object as a whole in a synthesis of front and back, top and bottom, past, present, and future ; all this is implied in my perception of the ink-pot I see before me. Thus in perception we have. that very identical process of reconstruction from data which is the essence of history. In the work of the annalist this is extended. He writes what he remembers ; what he remembers, he once perceived. In memory he carries out a further synthesis which is not different in principle from that of perception, for this again is a work of reconstruction from data, the data being now explicitly perceptual. The attempt to give an account of memory as a distinct ' faculty ' is so long out of date that this brief reference to it may suffice. Memory is an implication, not the definition, of the historical consciousness : to be aware of a fact implies being aware of past facts in memory. In perception, memory is already implicit ; unless one could remember, one would not be able to fix one's attention on a single object for long enough to perceive it ; but in perception this memory is not recognized as memory, and thus we get what is called the ' specious present ', which is exactly the implicitness of memory.

Perception in which memory has become explicit is reminiscence, the rehearsing to oneself of past facts. Such an activity is not pure memory, but memory explicit in perception, because it is the perceptual consciousness of here and now remembering. Reminiscence, in its most sustained and coherent form, is the activity of the annalist or writer of memoirs. But in this form it is no longer simply personal reminiscence ; it inevitably develops into collective reminiscence. The historical spirit at this stage of its career becomes the collector of legends or tales, the historian sup-

plementing his own private reminiscence by drawing upon
the reminiscences of other people. These other people are
the ' sources ' or ' authorities ' of which historians speak.
The historian is said to be at the mercy of his authorities,
unable to go behind them and so on. This is quite true,
but only as a description of the stage of historical thought
now under discussion. History in its first childhood, like
other children, is capable of believing almost any nonsense ;
at times it lapses consciously into the aesthetic attitude
with the preface ' this is the tale as I have heard it : of
its truth I say nothing ', at times it falls into this attitude
unconsciously and repeats a story merely because it is
effective. But even at this crude stage of historical development, there is such a thing as scepticism ; and though in
general the ancient historians rose no higher than the ideal
of conflating their own reminiscences with those of others,
they exercised some kind of selection as to the tales they
repeated.

But the most irresponsible retailer of old wives' gossip
does that. Even in the mere rehearsal of one's own memories
one keeps some kind of a hold over oneself in the interests
of the distinction between remembering and imagining.
The collector of legends who compiles them into a history,
so called, does not explicitly ask himself, ' Is this legend
credible, and is the source to which I owe it trustworthy ? '
But none the less he has implicitly answered that question
by the mere accepting of some legends and the rejection of
others. No historian, however innocent, can proceed wholly
without a system of *Quellenkritik*, because his very life as
an historian is the perpetual exercise of some such criterion.
Even if he accepts every legend he hears and rejects nothing,
he has a criterion, namely (it is to be presumed), the principle
that whatever anybody says is likely to be true. That is

a very bad criterion, no doubt ; but it is nevertheless a criterion. .

The historian at this stage has therefore a criterion, but an implicit criterion, of historical truth. The explicit criterion of mature historical thought is nothing but historical fact itself : the historian asks himself, ' Does this fit in with everything I know about the world of facts, the nature of the case, the liability of the informant to error and mendacity, and so forth ? ' [1] Now in the immature stage of historical thought this criterion is implicit, but its very implicitness renders it liable to deformation. An historian who does not formulate his criterion to himself is likely to confuse the criterion of factual coherence (history) with the criterion of aesthetic coherence (picturesqueness) or the like.

It is therefore untrue to say that the ancients had no *Quellenkritik*. It is rather correct to say that they had a confused one : one in which the genuine historical criterion was overlaid by other criteria which necessarily led the historians astray. The same thing happens in all ages when the historical conception of reality is not resolutely maintained in its explicitness. People nowadays believe that their dead friends are speaking to them at ' spiritualistic ' gatherings, not because the evidence would satisfy an historian, still less because they are anxious, on such a matter, to be deceived. They believe things of this kind for the same reason for which women, not long ago, used to believe that they were in communication with the Devil and maintain that belief to the point of dying for it in torment. It is not a matter of deception or fraud, but an

---

[1] If the reader protests that this is a circular criterion and therefore no criterion at all, I can only assure him that I know this as well as he does, and ask him to wait for a later section of this same chapter.

example of the extreme difficulty, even for civilized and educated people, of sticking to the conception of historical fact instead of lapsing into an imaginative attitude. Such a lapse, a mere failure of attention or a partial ' going to sleep ' of the mind, is the true source of all such illusions, and those ' mediums ' and thaumaturgists who really are fraudulent know very well how to induce it and take advantage of it.

It would be too long a task here to detail the growth of historical thought and to show how criteria other than that of historical fact itself have influenced writers at one period or another. But one or two instances may, perhaps, not come amiss. The ancients, when first they began fitting reminiscences and legends together into history, did so under the influence of that religious view of the world which led them to the invention of tragedy, or the unfolding of a divine plan for the overthrow of the proud. It is not an accident that the history of Herodotus described the nemesis that overtook the pride of Xerxes. Herodotus has taken care to point out that it is not an accident, and he has concluded his work with a chapter as pointed as the closing chorus of a tragedy : which indeed it is. Nor is it an accident that Thucydides, in the story of the decline and fall of the Athenian empire, has given us a Sophoclean drama in shaggy prose, a drama whose tragic force has been the wonder of all ages. Are we to suppose that the bare events of the later fifth century, recorded by a writer whose only aim was to state *was eigentlich geschehen ist*, would ever have aroused our pity and fear like the pages of Thucydides ? ' Well, that only shows what a great historian Thucydides was.' Great certainly : one of the greatest writers of all time. But to call him great as an historian is to misdescribe his greatness. What every one admires, and rightly admires, in him is the quality not of a great historian, but of a great tragedian.

To say this is not to accuse Thucydides of lying. When I say that Antony's speech in *Julius Caesar* is great poetry, I do not mean that Antony never delivered any such speech. I mean that Shakespeare wrote it as he did for its beauty, not for its truth. And one need have no hesitation in saying that Thucydides selected and emphasized incidents in his history for the sake of dramatic effect. No one denies it; but every one knows that this is precisely what an historian must not do. An historian must state the facts as they happened, and if he manipulates them into drama, that may make him a great dramatist, but it cannot make him a great historian. The criterion actually employed by Thucydides as the mainspring of his work was intended, certainly, to be historical; but it was actually tragic.

It is no reproach to a religious age that its history should be religious, nor to a scientific age that its history should be scientific. Such forms of history are indeed erroneous forms; but they are better than none, because all error contains some truth, and we are grateful to the most benighted chronicler of an age when other sources fail us. It is only when the concept of fact has become explicit that we can make an end of these erroneous forms and reach, for the first time, historians' history. This is the meaning of the revolution in historical thought which took place in the eighteenth century. The pioneers of that revolution had a very insecure grasp on its principles: even Vico thought that historical facts could be deduced *a priori* in the absence of positive evidence; and it was effected very slowly. The nineteenth century saw, alongside of a vast growth of genuine history, an even vaster mass of scientists' history, history aping the method of inductive inquiry, deducing itself from geographical and racial, climatic and economic, abstractions, which because they are scientific are always matter of personal caprice, and even claiming to foretell the future—that unforgiveable sin which for ever banishes the sinner from the company of genuine historians.

The historian's business is with fact ; and there are no future facts. The whole past and present universe is the field of history, to its remotest parts and in its most distant beginnings. Over this field the historian is absolutely free to range in whatever direction he will, limited not by his ' authorities ' but by his own pleasure. For the maturity of historical thought is the explicit consciousness of the truth that what matters is not an historian's sources but the use he makes of them. If they mislead him, the responsibility for being misled is his. It is his business not to lie down under his authorities, but to criticize them : if they intend to deceive him, to outwit them : if they are silent, to invent means of making them speak. These devices of self-reliant and self-conscious historical thought form what is called historical method.

§ 3. *The World of Fact as the Absolute Object*

We have said that history is the affirmation of fact. The business of history is to state what happens and has happened, and that only. This may cause a difficulty ; for, it may be said, the true historian is not content with stating facts, but endeavours to understand them. He must see not only what happened but why it happened ; he must investigate causes and inquire into motives, discerning the right from the wrong.

This is perfectly true. But it adds nothing to our original definition. The historical fact in its full concreteness—and fact is by definition concrete—already contains all these things within itself. To understand the facts is to affirm them not in arbitrary isolation but in their actual relation to their context. The reason why an event happened is sought by the historian not in an abstract scientific law but in facts, and facts again. The cause of an event in history is its intrinsic relation to other events in history, and the causal nexus is not external to them but lies in their very nature. The motives of historical personages are not psychical forces brooding above the flow of historical events : they are elements in these events, or rather, they are simply these events themselves as purposed and planned by the agents. And the historian cannot escape the necessity of judging the value of actions, not indeed as a partisan but as the impartial spectator and judge whose very impartiality obliges him to pronounce some actions well done and some ill. This judgement is not an alien act performed by the historian for motives outside his historical work ; it is a part of that work which cannot be omitted without turning the whole into a process of false abstraction, the abstraction which separates the event from the act. In this sense the valuation of historical fact is identical with its determination, and the saying is true that *die Weltgeschichte ist das Weltgericht*.

There is thus no feature of experience, no attitude of mind towards its object, which is alien to history. Art rests on the ignoring of reality : religion, on the ignoring of thought : science, on the ignoring of fact ; but with the recognition of fact everything is recognized that is in any sense real. The fact, as historically determined, is the absolute object.

The mark of the absolute object is individuality, for individuality is concreteness. The object as individual is the whole of what exists, and this is concretely articulated into parts each of which is again individual, and so to infinity. Within the cycle of this infinite articulation of the absolute object, the historical spirit moves freely in all directions, never finding anything that is not individual and unique, never finding anything that is not, on the one hand, composed of individual and unique parts, and, on the other, itself a part of an individual and unique whole. The object, as a system of fact so organized, is objective throughout, for every part is a true microcosm, and is truly infinite.

It is this object of which the preceding forms of consciousness have been in search. Each has grasped it, but in such a way as to destroy it. The aesthetic consciousness expresses itself in a single work of art. Here it finds a cosmos which like the world of history is individual and unique, whose organization is a systematic structure of parts each displaying the same individuality, the same uniqueness, in its indispensable contribution to the whole. But it is only by an abstraction that the single work of art is a cosmos. Outside it are other works of art, each a cosmos in itself, and these do not combine into a totality which is itself a single all-embracing work of art. Thus the aesthetic consciousness, instead of systematic, is monadic ; and the monads, being windowless, are not so much reflections of the whole universe as rival claimants to be the whole universe. This rivalry is fatal to all the claims alike. Art is thus even within its own limits a false form of individuality.

Religion goes a step farther and finds exactly the same individuality in God. God is the monad of monads, a cosmos whose structure is that of the absolute object. But God always stands over against a world whose very nature is to be outside him, and thus God forfeits his own absoluteness. As long as the world stands over against him, his own individuality is unattained. And because religion is conscious of this, its search for objectivity is confessed to be vain.

In science the attempt is made to bridge the gulf between God and the world. Instead of God we find the concept or law, which because it is the law of the world no longer stands outside the world. Here what was transcendent has become immanent. But in this very success, failure is revealed ; for it becomes plain that the immanence is a false immanence. The world is not a world of individuals but a world of particulars, and because the concept is indifferent to the various particulars in which it is embodied, their diversity remains meaningless and the world is to that extent a chaos. What is individual and organized as a system of individuals is not the world but only the concept, so that the failure of religion is repeated and the quest for immanence ends in transcendence, but an abstract transcendence more intolerable than the concrete transcendence of religion.

Thus the work of art, God, and the abstract concept are all attempts on the part of thought to reach the organized individuality of history. Art comes nearest to success ; religion fails more openly, and science most openly of all. But this order of relative failure is due to an inverse order of seriousness in facing the problem. Art ignores the real world altogether, and constructs an arbitrary cosmos of its own ; religion contents itself with a cosmos outside the world ; and science alone tries to bring the concrete world into the unity, but destroys its concreteness in the attempt. But because all are agreed that the real object must be an absolute individual, their failure is wholly redeemed by the success of history, which actually achieves the idea of an object beyond which there is nothing and within which every part truly represents the whole.

This absolute whole is the concrete universal ; for concrete universality is individuality, the individual being simply the unity of the universal and the particular. The absolute individual is universal in that it is what it is throughout, and every part of it is as individual as itself. On the other hand it is no mere abstraction, the abstract quality of individualness, but an individual which includes all others. It is the system of systems, the world of worlds. Everything in it is determined by its place in the whole, but this is not determinism because every part determines the whole and therefore by implication every other part : so that each part taken separately may be regarded as the crucial determinant of everything else, just as every separate link bears the whole responsibility for keeping the chain together. Everything in it is as unique as the whole, and the uniqueness of every part is based upon the uniqueness of every other. The principle of its structure is not classification, the abstract concept, but the concrete concept, which is relevance, or implication. The only reason why this notion of a concrete universal is thought puzzling or paradoxical is that our attempts at philosophical theory suffer from the obsession of regarding science as the only possible kind of knowledge. For the concrete universal is the daily bread of every historian, and the logic of history is the logic of the concrete universal.

§ 4. *Duty or Concrete Ethics*

At the scientific or materialistic point of view, man regards himself as a machine. Now to call oneself a machine is to prove that one is not a machine, for no machine calls itself one. By saying ' I am a slave to mechanical law ', man actually lifts himself above such law. But he does so only implicitly ; he does not realize that he is doing it ; and because he grasps his freedom only implicitly he does not really enjoy it. He enjoys only a perverted and abstract freedom, the freedom to make the best of a bad job, the freedom of utility. He becomes an economic agent ; he acts selfishly.

When the concrete or historical point of view is achieved, this is effected by recognizing and so transcending the abstractness of the scientific point of view. Man now sees that even in calling himself a machine he had really been vindicating his own freedom, and in that discovery he grasps this freedom and makes it truly his own. Concrete or historical thought is the discovery of individuality, and individuality is freedom. Abstract thought is always deterministic, because the universal is not contained in the particular but thrown outside it : what determines the particular is not itself but something else, namely, the universal. It is useless to protest that the universal is merely the universal *of* the particular, and therefore not alien to it. The master is the master *of* the slave, and it is just because of the closeness of the relation between the two persons that the slave is a slave and not his own master, that is, free. Separate the universal from the particular, and you hypostatize it into a second particular whose special nature is to be the determinant or tyrant of the first. It is this deterministic or mechanistic tendency of abstract thought which degrades duty into utility ; for utility is simply slave's duty.

Restore the concrete unity of the universal and the particular, and utility is reabsorbed : the means and the end coincide, the means becomes an end in itself and the end becomes the means to itself. Utility, or the transcendence of the end to the means, having disappeared, action is no longer an end to something good which is beyond itself, but is its own good. Action as thus good in itself is not capricious or morally indifferent, for caprice means the annihilation of the end and the sole existence of the means, which is now the means to nothing. Since the end is absorbed in the action, the action becomes that which is done for its own sake and as its own justification.

Every action is an integral element in the complete world of fact, and is determined by its place in that world as the relevant action for the given facts. The existence of a world of fact constitutes the obligation to perform the relevant action, and thus the ' station ' of the agent as a member of the world of fact dictates his ' duties ' as a contributor to that world. But, on the other hand, the action determines in its turn the rest of the world of fact, and hence the agent is free to make his ' station ' what he likes.

Here we meet with a problem which will take us beyond the confines of this chapter. If the world of facts faces the agent as an infinite given whole, this whole determines all its own parts but nothing outside it, for there is nothing outside it. But is not the agent outside it ? If he is, how can it be infinite ? If he is not, he is already in it and his action is already determined by it and reciprocally determinative of it. The facts are said to oblige the agent, as his duty, to perform the action relevant to them. But this is absurd, for if his action is in any sense indeterminate, it renders the whole world of facts indeterminate. If his station dictates his duties, any question as to what his duties are raises a doubt as to what his station is—that is, a doubt as to the nature of the whole which is said to be given in its infinite concreteness.

Historical ethics thus fails to give a clear answer to the question ' What is duty ? ' and in practice vacillates between two contradictory answers.

First, the subjective answer : the will is its own world

and its own law. It has nothing outside it to determine it, but is absolutely autonomous, and duty is simply its pure self-determination.

Secondly, the objective answer : the moral order of the objective world as a given whole is the law which must determine the subjective will.

Both these solutions are doomed to failure precisely because of their distinctness. They are a pair of opposites, as yet unreconciled. The error must lie in their very separateness, and in accordance with the programme of concrete thinking we must try to overcome this separateness. Till we have done so, the conception of liberty or duty which we have achieved is held by the most precarious tenure ; for the whole essence of duty is the reconciliation which it effects between the universal and the particular, and if these are once more separated, as in effect they are by a cleavage between the individual and society, the very conception of duty must fall to the ground. For if my duty is to obey society, I am a slave and my obedience is useful but not good : if my duty is to ignore society and follow my own bent, my defiance of society is precisely the opposite of useful, namely, futile ; for society will crush me, and rightly. The reality of duty therefore depends on over-coming the antithesis between these terms.

The characteristic embodiment of concrete ethics is law. Law is nothing but the structure of society regarded as the source of an obligation on the individual to act in certain determinate ways. The legal mind is not scientific in its attitude towards truth, but historical ; the judge is the 'learned judge'—that is, his qualification is a deep knowledge of concrete fact, and law in its highest and most delicately-organized form consists on the one hand of statutes, and on the other of case-law, these two elements

reacting upon one another in such a way that the body of
law which they together constitute forms an organic whole.
In so far as statutes are generalizations, the legal attitude
is often mistaken for a form of the scientific or abstract
consciousness ; but this is an error, because the generality
of law, like the generality of archaeology, is not an end in
itself but a means to an explicitly-recognized concrete end.
The ideal of law is not the self-identical immobility of this
or that statute, but its interpretation ; and this interpretation means using the law as an aid to the determination of concrete cases, just as the archaeologist uses his
generalized rules for the purpose of fixing the concrete date
of a building or other object. Law is thus parallel to history
in that each explicitly includes the abstract act of generalization within itself as a subsidiary element, not the whole of
its substance.

Further, law is gravely misunderstood if it is regarded as
the field of expediency or utility, as if to obey the law were
merely to act in one's own interests through fear of punishment, as if to legislate were to assert the interests of a
legislative class, and as if government in general were an
economic function. The right to punish, which belongs to
all law, is a right not to maltreat the disobedient but to
require them to obey : it is not terror, but majesty, that is
the true attribute of law. The law punishes the disobedient
not because it can but because it ought ; not as a business
man discharges an untrustworthy clerk, on the principle
' if you won't work for me I won't work with you ', but as
a vindication of its own *laesa maiestas,* because the criminal
owes it obedience as a duty. We are punished not because
we break the law, but because we ought to obey it. The
duty to obey is the correlative of all law ; and obedience
rests on this duty, not on expediency or force or fear of un-

pleasant consequences in case of disobedience. Punishment is only legal when it is deserved ; to confuse it with education, or (last sophistry of a corrupt utilitarianism) degrade it to the level of a bogey, is to miss its essential nature, that concreteness which distinguishes government from business.

If law is not utility, *a fortiori* it is not convention, which is a lower ethical development than utility. And yet to identify law with convention is in a way more excusable than to identify it with utility. This is because the relation between play and convention is repeated in the relation between utility and law : in both cases we have an abstract, individualistic point of view set over against a social or concrete point of view. But as the individualism of play is an intuitive individualism while that of utility is an intellectual, so the concreteness of convention is an intuitive concreteness, that of law an intellectual concreteness. We obey conventions intuitively, unreflectively : we obey laws reflectively, recognizing it, on thinking the matter over, as a duty whose neglect deserves punishment. In the same way we institute a convention intuitively, just because we choose that things shall be so done ; but we institute a law reflectively, because we think that things ought to be so done. To defy a convention is merely to break with one's company, to pick a quarrel with friends ; to defy a law is to commit a crime.

Law in its whole extent includes the entire life of affairs, as distinct from business : politics in all its legislative and administrative branches, large and small. This field, in virtue of its concreteness, is far out of the reach of abstract scientific thought, which revenges itself upon it by at once despising it for its illogicality and trying to reduce it to order by sheer mutilation. That real life is illogical every one admits ; but that is the fault not of life but of logic, of abstract thinking. The scientist wants actual fact to behave as if it were a mere example of some abstract law ; but it is never simply this, and the elements he has deliberately ignored upset all his calculations. He then calls the fact irrational, or contingent, meaning unintelligible to him because too solid and hard to be forced into his moulds, too heavy for his scales, too full of its own concrete logic to listen to his abstractions. Even the life of convention resists his methods, precisely as religion resists reduction into terms of theology. The merest conventions, fashion in dress, etiquette and ceremonial, are lumped together by abstract thought as irrational ; but to the eye of concrete historical thought they reveal themselves as informed by the most delightfully subtle intelligence, as inevitable as the plot of a drama and as little capable of scientific or abstract analysis : differing from the rationality of law only in being implicit. Paris dressmakers could not tell you why they alter a certain fashion in a certain way this autumn, or if they did the reason would be a wrong one ; but there is a reason, and it can be traced if the problem is approached from an historical point of view.

What is true of the proverbial caprices of fashion is *a fortiori* true of law and politics. The attempt of abstract thought to mutilate these historical facts appears theoretically in the attempt to construct a sociology, or science intended to reduce history to a pattern of abstract concepts, and practically in the attempt to oust the lawyer and the statesman from public life and replace them with the business man and the scientist. Thus the state, which in its historical reality is a fabric of law, is reduced to a business concern by an ' economic interpretation of history ' which destroys the concreteness of legal fact and replaces it by the abstractions of utilitarian ethics ; and we get socialism or the substitution of economics for justice, with its natural corollary, the destruction of that internal ' king's peace ' which the political spirit has guarded through centuries as the very flame of its domestic altar, and the declaration of a class war which is the explicit negation of the state. Similarly the family, just because it is a concrete spiritual reality whose foundation is the act of spontaneous choice in which, moved by some spirit certainly not born in the counting-house or laboratory, one man and one woman greet one another as co-parents of the world's future ; just because it is the tree on which new souls grow in a manner unpredictable to scientific calculation ; just because it is these things, the family is the object of attack by eugenists,[1]

[1] I do not wish it to appear that my remarks on eugenics are hasty or that they proceed from any doubts as to the value of medical science. I therefore beg leave to add :

(i) That because it is obviously every one's duty to do what he can for the welfare of his unborn children, I approached eugenics with a prepossession in its favour, and have only changed my mind as a result of studying the utterances of its friends.

(ii) That in so far as it consists in repeating the pious wish that people would recognize that duty, I sympathize with its propaganda.

(iii) But that it neither is nor promises to become an adequate guide towards determining what actually can be done, because all its facts are arbitrarily selected to support its dogmas, like ghost-stories, which indeed they resemble in more ways than one, as designed to produce horror rather than conviction of anything definite; its generalizations are almost invariably, even when so favourably founded, matter of dispute among experts ; and its arguments, regarded as argument, are, when they exist at all, usually sophistical.

(iv) That I should warmly support compulsory vaccination for small-pox, and that if eugenics could ever produce a practical legislative scheme as well supported by expert opinion and as workable as compulsory vaccination, on that day I should begin treating it with respect. At present, I confess, I look upon it as an aberration on the part of certain biological speculations into a political field from which their best friends can only wish to rescue them, and return them to their laboratories.

who are quite sure that professors of science could mate young men and young women a great deal better than the poor ignorant things can do it for themselves, with the amateurish assistance of their friends and relations ; and have the effrontery to bolster up their propaganda with facts concerning the failure of this or that marriage, arbitrarily selected to suit their purposes, as if a fanatic who wished to make gramophones compulsory by law should produce statistics showing that some people sing out of tune. For love and marriage and the procreation of children are, every time they happen, a voyage of discovery ; and when scientists have discovered the logic which will infallibly produce true discoveries, it will be time enough for them to usurp that chosen province of intuition, the business of matchmaking. The same fallacy recurs in militarism, or the seizure of the state by that science of war which the state has devised to serve its own ends ; commercialism, or the overthrow of law by profit and the replacement of statesmen by business men ; and other ailments of the body politic, whose common nature is to deny the very essence of the state, which is concrete freedom in the guise of justice or right, and its replacement by one form or another of expediency. They are alternative forms of that abstractness, that hatred of concrete historical fact, which is the fountain of all political corruption.

Yet this corruption is no external enemy ; it is inherent in the very fabric of the political life itself. The perfect concreteness of pure justice, of absolute right, is unattainable in the sphere of law, for law regarded as an objective reality over against the individual already shows the mark of that last abstraction which divides subject from object. Society, as distinct from the individual, is already an abstraction, and as such cannot have that claim upon the individual which is possessed only by an absolutely concrete principle. Law is not the will of the individual himself ; it is a command laid upon him from without, and therefore his obedience to it is always tainted with utilitarianism. Hence all those utilitarian degradations of law to which we have referred are in a sense inevitable. For law—and the same, we shall see, is true of history as a whole—is an incomplete realization of concrete thought : it is essentially a step, but an imperfect step, from abstract to concrete, from utility to responsibility. The very externality of law to the agent binds it down to the world of abstract or scientific thought, and necessitates a contradiction by which, on the one hand, the law itself claims to embody right, while on the other the individual conscience claims to defy the law in the name of right. It is useless to debate the issue between the disputants ; granted their common initial error, each is equally justified in his position. The same contradiction reappears in external relations, where the very fact that the state is law makes the inevitable conflict of state with state a conflict not of mere interest but of right against right, and therefore gives rise not to economic rivalry but to war.

We shall see that history is an unstable attitude which leads either back into science or forward into philosophy, according as the intellectual vigour of the historian is exhausted or stimulated by his attempt to get rid of the abstractions of science. So law is an unstable attitude, and either leads on to the position of absolute ethics, in which the law becomes simply the act of the individual's own will and its abstract objectivity disappears, or else leads back to the position of abstract or utilitarian ethics and the politics of the scientist and the business man. The later nineteenth century, as we shall see later on, appears to have been a time when an historical attitude, insecurely reached, was relapsing into the abstractness of a new scientific phase of thought ; a retrograde movement in the history of the human mind, though one which, perhaps, served only to lay the foundation of a more secure advance. If this was so, it is no ground for surprise that socialism, eugenics, militarism, commercialism, and their like should have especially flourished during that period, as parasites upon the political life of the civilized world. Nor is it improbable that each one of them may prove in time to have justified its existence and contributed something of value to the advancement of human life.

§ 5. *The Breakdown of History*

History is the knowledge of the infinite world of facts. It is therefore itself an infinite whole of thought : history is essentially universal history, a whole in which the knowledge of every fact is included.

This whole, universal history, is never achieved. All history is fragmentary. The historian—he cannot help it— is a specialist, and no one takes all history for his province unless he is content to show everywhere an equal ignorance, an equal falsification of fact. But this is a fatal objection to the claims of historical thought as we have, without favour or exaggeration, stated them. History is the knowledge of an infinite whole whose parts, repeating the plan of the whole in their structure, are only known by reference to their context. But since this context is always incomplete, we can never know a single part as it actually is.

It may be said that this is hypercritical. The historical specialist admits that where his period begins and ends there are loose threads in his knowledge, and that these recur where his period trenches on contemporary events of which his knowledge is imperfect. No doubt, he will continue, the looseness of these threads may affect the stability of his patterns even in that part of his period in which he feels most at home. A misconception as to the facts preceding those of which he deals will falsify his approach to many of the central questions of his period, and so falsify to some extent his answers. But this, he may say, cannot destroy very much of the value of his work, and to suggest that it destroys the whole is fantastic.

But it is important to recognize the nature of the dilemma with which we are here faced. If universal history is an absolute and perfectly-organized individual whole, such that every part in it determines every other part, there is no escape from the conclusion that ignorance or error concerning any one part involves an essential and radical ignorance or error concerning every other. If we are to escape this inference it can only be by withdrawing everything we have said about the structure of historical fact and substituting a new theory.

It is easy to see what this new theory will be. The individuality of historical facts, we must now say, is not systematic but atomic. Each fact is what it is irrespective of all others. The relations of each to the rest do nothing to affect their nature ; for each is wholly closed within itself and is knowable as ·a perfectly isolated atom. This being so, we can apprehend the atomic facts of history one by one, and thus build up ever-increasing structures of fact which have nothing to fear from any unrevealed fact that may lurk in the surrounding darkness. Thus the possibility of historical knowledge is saved.

We may perhaps venture to ask what will be the price of this salvation ; and this with peculiar interest and anxiety at a time when some of our most distinguished

philosophers are advocating it as the one basis for knowledge. What is called the ' theory of external relations '
has been deliberately invented in recent years as an escape
from the difficulty just expressed. If the object is an infinite
whole whose parts are mutually interdependent and conditioned, then, it is recognized, knowledge of this object or
any part of it is impossible. Let us therefore surrender the
whole, and resolve every part into a mere agglomeration of
atoms, each untouched in its real nature by any relation in
which it may stand to any other. Such is the proposal.
Now these atoms, as the word suggests, are nothing new in
the history of thought. On the contrary, they represent
a very old idea, and one from which the modern conception
of critical history has but lately and with difficulty emerged.
They are precisely the *instances* of an abstract law : that
is to say, they belong, together with the allied notions of
agglomeration or addition, infinite series, and externality,
to the sphere of science. Historical atomism saves history
by surrendering the whole thing and plunging back into the
scientific consciousness. After recognizing this, we are the
less surprised to see that its advocates are almost exclusively
mathematicians. For it is simply a proposal to purge history
of everything historical and reduce it to mathematics. It is,
in fact, only the latest and most fashionable of a large
number of attempts to ' reduce history to a science '. To
these in their general principle and features we have already
referred, and we need not here waste time on discussing the
merits of this latest comer. We must observe merely that
there is no question of arguing as to whether the theory of
external relations is ' true '. For a scientist, of course it is
true : to be a scientist is to commit yourself to abstracting
the concept from the individual and leaving bare particulars
to which their interrelations are external. For an historian

it is of course false : history is nothing but conceiving the object as concrete fact, fact to which its context is not irrelevant but essential.[1] But since history only comes into being because of the breakdown of science, to suggest that an historian should get rid of his difficulties by embracing the theory of external relations is like suggesting to a gunner that he might escape the problems of gunnery by adopting the catapult.

We are therefore thrown back on the dilemma with which we were originally faced. If history exists, its object is an infinite whole which is unknowable and renders all its parts unknowable. If its parts are atoms, then history does not exist and we are thrown back on science, whose bankruptcy we have already accepted.

There is a natural temptation to escape between the horns of this dilemma by arguing as follows : Universal history, as an infinite whole, is plainly inaccessible. Let us face this fact. What have we left ? Individual histories, histories of this or that special period or single state. These individuals are not atoms, nor are they composed of atoms ; they are genuine individuals, microcosms of the whole. But the whole does not exist, and these individuals do exist : here then we find the nature of the historical object truly expressed, none the less truly for the non-existence of that chimerical whole whose part they are falsely imagined to be.

This argument takes us even farther back into darkness than the last. For it reduces history to the level of art. To be a monad, as opposed to an atom ; to be a world in itself unconnected with an indefinite number of other such

---

[1] Lest the reader should suspect me of teasing him, let me hasten to add that, because neither science nor history is tenable, neither the theory of external relations nor that of internal relations is *really* true.

worlds, each windowless and ignorant of a whole whose parts they nevertheless are—this is to be a work of art. Take away the conception of a universal history in which every special history finds its place and its justification, and you have committed the first and deepest sin against history, you have confused it with art : you have denied it any concern with truth and made it a mere thing of the imagination.

To translate our difficulty into empirical terms, we have already seen that periods of history thus individualized are necessarily beset by ' loose ends ' and fallacies arising from ignorance or error of their context. Now there is and can be no limit to the extent to which a ' special history ' may be falsified by these elements. The writer insists upon this difficulty not as a hostile and unsympathetic critic of historians, but as an historian himself, one who takes a special delight in historical research and inquiry ; not only in the reading of history-books but in the attempt to solve problems which the writers of history-books do not attack. But as a specialist in one particular period he is acutely conscious that his ignorance of the antecedents of that period introduces a coefficient of error into his work of whose magnitude he can never be aware. He sees how radically the work of others in the same field has been vitiated by faults of the kind which he knows he must himself be committing daily, and he knows that if these faults were removed others would of necessity remain. Nor is it mere despair, as when one dismisses an historical problem as insoluble on our present evidence, that induces him to assent to the paradox that all history is quite certainly in some respects false, but what these respects are we can never know. To believe the contrary is simply to let oneself be hypnotized by the repetition of statements in one book after another, to allow oneself to argue that because authors are unanimous they must be right, instead of confessing the truth, that they are unanimous because of the depth of their ignorance. Wherever a number of people have detailed information about any fact, their summary accounts of it will certainly be different, according to the differential importance which they find in this detail or that : it is only when they know nothing, or next to nothing, that they begin to agree. Ancient history is easy not because its facts are certain but because we are at the mercy of Herodotus or some other writer, whose story we cannot check ; contemporary history is unwritable because we know so much about it, and it is only when all the Balaclava survivors have died that we can begin to reach an ' accepted version ' of the battle's history. Contemporary history embarrasses a writer not only because he knows too much, but also because what he knows is too undigested, too unconnected, too atomic. It is only after close and prolonged reflection that we begin to see what was essential and what unimportant, to see why things happened as they did, and to write history instead of newspapers. We can never see the bones of historical fact till the flesh has dropped off them, and then it is too late. History, which seems to be essentially remembrance, is only possible through forgetfulness, a forgetfulness which in destroying what it takes away makes it impossible for us ever to understand what is left.

This fundamental self-contradiction in which all history— and therefore all perception—is involved takes us far beyond certain comparatively simple objections to history based on its alleged dependence on testimony. How, it is asked, can truth be claimed for a narrative which depends in every detail upon stories handed down to us which may have been, and indeed almost always are, falsified by the passions of their authors ? All our historical sources are based in this way on testimony : all testimony tells us not what happened but what its author wanted us to believe, or wanted to believe himself. In this way the uncertainty of history is contrasted with the certainty of perception and memory. But neither the criticism nor the contrast is well founded. Granting that we cannot get the truth from our authorities, we can at least get the expression of their own personalities, the expression of their prejudices and desires, and this too is history, and history of a kind not to be despised. And further, in so far as history rests on other things beside the actual statements of authors, upon archaeological data, upon charters and statutes, upon analysis of the institutions of to-day, and so forth, to this extent we have access to sources not falsified by the prejudice of any informant. But the real prejudice against which we have to guard is still left at large, and is the more dangerous for the scientific rigour upon which we plume ourselves when reconstructing history from these more recondite sources. It is precisely our own prejudice. If ancient historians give way to drama or edification in their narrative, are we exempt from the same temptations in our own ? We know that this is not so. We know that just as we remember not what happened but what we want to remember, as we perceive not what is ' there ' but what we attend to, so we reconstruct history not as it was but as we choose to think it was. We are all ready to see this fault in other historians, but we all commit it ourselves, none of us more so than those who pride themselves on the ' objectivity ' of their methods.

And yet to surrender this ' objectivity ', to confess frankly that our histories are nothing but an expression of personal points of view, this is the very cynicism of history, the conscious acquiescence in what has now become a deliberate fraud. If every history is an historical romance, we may leave out the adjective and frankly identify history with art. As long as we pretend to write history, we must claim access to the fact as it really was. This fact, we have seen, is inaccessible. History as a form of knowledge cannot exist.

Thus history is the crown and the *reductio ad absurdum* of all knowledge considered as knowledge of an objective reality independent of the knowing mind. Here for the first time we place before ourselves an object which satisfies the mind ; an object individual, concrete, infinite, no arbitrary abstraction or unreal fiction, but reality itself in its completeness. This object is what we have tried and failed to find in art, in religion, and in science. In history we have found it ; and we have found it to be an illusion. In its perfect reality it is perfectly unknowable, and our efforts to achieve it can do nothing but frustrate themselves. In art, the individual work is actually enjoyed ; the mind grasps it in its wholeness, clasps it to its bosom and becomes one with it. In religion, God is glorified and enjoyed in a mystic union which achieves the same intimacy, but the clamour of the world outside is never wholly forgotten and the union is always therefore imperfect. In science the mind grasps the concept in an act of *a priori* thought, but the concept is a mere phantom and thought recognizes its own impotence to clothe it with reality. The progressive alienation of the mind from its object is in history complete. The world is triumphantly unified as object, only to find itself separated from the mind by a gulf which no thought can traverse.

But in this process, which seems to travel at every step farther from that intimacy of subject with object which constitutes knowledge, the indispensable condition of knowledge is progressively and inversely realized. We know at last in history what we never knew before, namely, what kind of object it must be that is alone knowable. It must be an object not merely of imagination, like the work of art, but of thought ; but, like the work of art, it must be concrete and individual. It must be, like the object of religion, absolute and eternal ; but unlike this again, it must be a real object and not the imaginative or metaphorical presentation of an object. It must be conceived, like the object of science ; but it must not be an abstraction. And like the object of history, it must be fact, an absolute concrete individual ; but it must be accessible to the knowing mind.

§ 6. *The Transition from History to Philosophy*

We have been discussing history on the assumption that it was knowledge of fact—that is, concrete thought. This assumption has not failed us ; it yielded every actual mark of historical thought and of its object, and it is not open to us to suggest that our starting-point was an error. Nevertheless it has brought us face to face with the difficulty that if the object of history is such as we have described, it cannot be known.

For an infinite given whole of fact cannot at any point be grasped by the mind. Every part implies the whole, and the whole is presupposed by every part. No part can therefore be known first. No process of thought with respect to such a whole is possible. We cannot come to know it. We must have known it all from the beginning, have known it as a whole before we began to learn any given part ; and once the whole is known any given part must be known too, and therefore cannot be learnt.   There is no learning anything.[1]

This cannot be avoided by saying that the whole is roughly or confusedly known at first and by degrees known more precisely or adequately.   It is no more possible to know a single aspect of the whole by itself than to know a single part of it by itself.   To know anything about it whatever must be to know all about it.

Nor can it be avoided by placing the whole in time and calling it a progressing, developing, or changing whole.   This merely adds a new difficulty.   If its progress is such that its present state implies or necessitates its future states, then these states merely augment the number of implications which any knowledge of the whole, however superficial, involves.   But if its progress is such that its future states are not implied in its present, then it is no longer a perfect individual all of whose parts imply one another.

We are therefore unable to escape the dilemma that either this infinite whole of fact is known perfectly and always by any given mind, or else it can never by that mind be known at all.

Now this is an old dilemma.   It is exactly the famous crux of the *Meno*, which Plato solved in the only possible way, by accepting the first alternative.   The Platonic ' form ' is just such an infinite whole, and Plato saw that on that account the mind could never come to know it. Every mind must have known it from eternity.   But Plato added to this a qualification.   The mind must indeed know the form, but it need not know that it knows it.   Its knowledge may be implicit at any given moment, and what we call learning may be only the bringing of this implicit knowledge into explicitness.

[1] This is the truth anticipated on p. 214, where we pointed out the vicious circle of the historical criterion.

Plato's solution is powerless to save the validity of historical knowledge. For the absolute whole of which we are speaking is the entire world of fact, and if it is a fact that I know something—whether I know it implicitly or explicitly—this fact is included in the world of fact, and therefore the entire world of fact is changed by my coming to know it, for that event is a new fact and *ex hypothesi* changes the world of fact, however slightly, from top to bottom, like any other addition to it. Therefore the facts as I know them are by that very knowledge made different from the same facts as I do not know them ; and this applies to the conversion of knowledge from implicit to explicit. The universe of fact which is implicitly known becomes objectively different by being explicitly known, because our knowledge is part of it.

Now in the course of our inquiry the truth has from time to time forced itself upon us that there is one object at least of which it can be said that its nature is altered by being known, without entailing the consequence that error concerning it is impossible. This object is the knowing mind. In this case, we saw, an error reacts on the mind itself, and alters its behaviour, which (in the case of a mind) is its nature ; for a mind is what it does. If therefore the infinite given whole of fact is *the nature of the knowing mind as such*, our problem is solved, and the possibility of knowledge is vindicated.

We must not accept this escape rashly. It is advisable to follow up another hint derived from the comparison with Plato.

The difficulty in the *Meno* arises from the abstractness of the Platonic logic. If the universal is really nothing but the structure of the individual, there is no special difficulty as to how we come to know it. That same experience, historical and perceptual experience, which reveals the individual, reveals its structure. But Plato had not attained to the conception of historical experience or perception, and split up its object, the individual, into the sensuous particular and the intelligible universal. Hence the universal, set outside the particular, transcending sensuous experience, was set outside time and process, and therefore the cognition of it had to be similarly thrown outside time. Now our conception of a world of facts had led us back to Plato's dilemma. But Plato's dilemma is due to the abstractness of his thought. Can it be that our own thought has relapsed into abstractness?

We have permitted ourselves to hold somewhat boastful language about the absolute concreteness of historical thought ; but we find it now behaving exactly as if it were the victim of an abstraction. And this is not the first symptom of the disorder. At the end of section 4 we found that history left us with an unreconciled opposition between the individual and the community, and these are opposites, and therefore terms which history as concrete thought is bound to reconcile in a synthesis.

We have hitherto been uniformly searching for an object of knowledge. We have found that in art we get no true object, because the ostensible object, the work of art, points beyond itself to some hidden mystery as the real object of which it is the symbol. In other words, art pretends to be pure imagination but is not ; it is the implicit assertion of something which is not explicitly asserted, and this is its real object. But what the nature of this real object may be, art cannot say. We went on to religion. Here again we found that the ostensible object, God, was not the real object. The mythology of religion does not say what it means. It points beyond itself, even more unmistakably than the work of art, to a concealed mystery, a truth which is not stated. The real object of religion is not grasped by religion itself. We tried science, and here we found that the ostensible object, the abstract concept, which is indifferently called the physical or material world, the realm of (abstract) thought, pure being, or the like, is confessedly an arbitrary construction, an expedient of thought, not the object of thought. In history alone we found a type of thought which, to all appearances, meant what it said, and when it pointed to fact as its object really meant that fact was its object. We therefore ventured to assume that fact, this same fact which comes face to face with the mind in history, is the hidden object not only of science—that is admitted—but of religion and art also. But what is this fact : fact about what ?

We have assumed that it was 'about' an object other than the thinking mind. We have assumed that the imagery of art, the mythology of religion, the mechanism of science, are successive veils hung between the mind and this object, and that when they were torn down we should see the object as it is in itself. That is to say, we have assumed, without justifying or criticizing it, a distinction between subject and object ; and not only a distinction but a separation, a relation of difference without identity.

Difference without identity is the abstract concept. Have we all the time been vitiating the historical consciousness by the retention in it of one relic of abstraction ?

The suggested answer to this will perhaps be, that if subject and object are opposites, then we must indeed assert their synthesis and deny that they can be separated ; but if they are merely different individuals, then their relation will be a relation of distinct concrete facts to one another, and they will not coalesce into a unity.

But this is a question of heads I win, tails you lose. If subject and object are opposites, then they can only exist in synthesis: well and good. But if they are distinct concrete facts, they both fall within the world of fact, and if of this world it remains true that everything in it determines the whole and everything else, it follows that subject and object are just as inseparable on this hypothesis as on the other. For the concept of the world of fact as the concrete universal has destroyed any distinction between a logic of opposition and a logic of difference.

The fundamental principle of history itself, namely, the concreteness of the object, thus makes it impossible for the object to ignore the subject, and compels us to recognize an object to which the subject is organic, in the sense that the subject's consciousness of it makes a real difference to it as a whole and to all its parts. The subject is thus no mere separable part of the world of fact, but an essential element which penetrates its whole fabric, a constitutive element in the object itself. Being known, whether truly known or erroneously known, must make a difference to the object: to deny this, we can now see, is to turn one's back on concrete thought and revert to the fallacies of abstraction.

This does not reduce the object of knowledge to the position of a figment of imagination. On the contrary, a figment of imagination is created by imagining it, not by knowing it, and exists—in the only sense in which it does exist—precisely as it is imagined, so that there is in its case no such thing as error, just as there is no such thing as truth. The conception of an object which we have now reached is the conception of something determined by the knowing it, in the sense that error deranges it, though not so far as to bring it into harmony with the erroneous judgement ; because this would then cease to be erroneous. This object can only be the knowing mind itself. A mind's error about itself, we have seen, actually deranges it and causes it to behave abnormally ; and it is only by correcting this error that the mind can regain its true nature.

The world of fact which is explicitly studied in history is therefore implicitly nothing but the knowing mind as such. This is no strange or unfamiliar notion, repugnant to plain and simple minds. It is, on the contrary, a theme reiterated not only in all philosophy but in the implicit philosophizing of religion and popular proverbs. The union of God with man is the burden of all religion, and ' know thyself ' is the epitome of all proverbs. Philosophies preach it unanimously, only differing in that some preach it, as it were, backwards and in a riddle, like the materialists, who after all are only trying to define knowledge as the self-knowledge of the only reality, namely, matter, or the realists, some of whom argue that reality gets itself known without the intervention of anything called a mind, while some believe that mind is only a peculiar conformation of space-time which is able to know other such conformations, the self-knowledge of space-time ; while others again preach it explicitly, like Socrates and Aristotle and Descartes and almost all philosophers of the first rank, whether ancient or modern : who with strange unanimity and for the most various reasons [1] have held that in the last resort nothing but the knower can be known.

The transition thus effected from history to philosophy is, like our other transitions, merely the making explicit of

[1] This clause may puzzle the reader, unless he reflects that a concrete truth has an infinity of reasons (*rationes cognoscendi*, and for that matter *rationes essendi* as well). For instance, there is no one mark by which one recognizes one's own face in the glass, and the most various reasons may be given without disagreement.

what was implicit already. But in every case the implicit is made explicit in the teeth of a certain resistance. It is only unwillingly that art realizes its own immanent logic, or religion its mythological character, or science its nature as arbitrary supposal. This is because the stability of these activities depends on their refusal to face these facts about their own nature. When the facts are faced the artist becomes a critic, the religious man a theologian, the scientist a philosopher. Similarly the realization that history or perception is an activity which affects its own object in such a way that the hope of discovering *was eigentlich geschehen ist* is foredoomed to failure, is the breakdown of history, its collapse before an historical scepticism to which there is no answer.

But though, in the transition from history to philosophy, history as such is destroyed, the transition is so brief and so inevitable that much belonging to the historical frame of mind is taken over almost unchanged by the philosophical. Philosophy, like history, is essentially the assertion of concrete reality, the denial of all abstraction, all generality, everything in the nature of a law or formula. For this and similar reasons the identification of philosophy with history is far less violent and misleading than its identification with science, religion, or art. But all such identifications are barren abstractions, for all these activities are in a sense identical with philosophy and in a sense different from it. To assert the identity without the difference or the difference without the identity is to turn one's back on reality and amuse oneself with paradoxes.

VII

PHILOSOPHY

§ 1. *Philosophy as Self-consciousness*

THERE are two current definitions of philosophy. In the first place it is regarded as the return of thought upon itself, thought ceasing to contemplate an external object and studying the process by which it comes to be aware of such an object : thought become self-conscious. In the second place it is regarded as the self-liberation of thought from uncriticized assumptions, the determined attempt to believe nothing except on good grounds, the surrender of all dogma, hypothesis, or opinion, and the pursuit of the ideal of knowledge as rational through and through. The first definition defines philosophy by reference to its object : the second by reference to its method.

Each of these definitions, taken singly, is unsatisfactory. The first appears to imply that among the various objects in the world are objects called minds, and that philosophy is the study of these. But so described, philosophy becomes psychology, which is in aim and method scientific and not philosophical. The second merely states an ideal, and does not tell us how to set about realizing it : indeed, we cannot realize it, and therefore, so described, philosophy does not exist at all.

But we have now seen that taken together these two definitions explain each other and give a coherent result. Philosophy is self-consciousness, but this does not mean that there is a self standing in abstract isolation over against a world of objects and that philosophy ignores the latter

and studies the former.   The self and its world are correlative.   I am the self that I am, simply because of the
nature of the world : by studying a certain kind of world
and living in it as my environment, I develop my own
mind in a determinate way.   And conversely, my world is
the world of my mind : I see in it what I am able to see,
trace in it the kind of structure which my powers qualify
me for tracing, and thus determine my world as it determines me.   The abstract psychology which would study
a thing called mind, having a structure and nature of its
own irrespective of what it owes to the world, is as unphilo-
sophical a quest as the abstract ontology which would study
objective reality irrespective of its debt to any and every
mind.   Thus philosophy as self-consciousness includes all
possible knowledge in itself : to know what I am includes
knowing what I think.

On the other hand, the determination to think coherently
and rationally has led us to self-consciousness as to a foreordained and not wholly unforeseen goal.   Nothing but this
determination has led us past art, religion, science, and
history in turn : we abandoned each on discovering that
the object of each lacked something of intelligibility and
that therefore each itself lacked something of intelligence ;
each in turn was in part an unintelligent attitude towards
an unintelligible object.   And this defect was only redeemed
by the conviction, which has reappeared at every turn, that
the unintelligible object was not the real object but only
an ostensible object which pointed to a real object but did
not wholly reveal it.   Of this real object we have been in
continual search ; and we seem now to have arrived at the
conclusion that it is nothing but the mind itself.   Thus
the two definitions of philosophy seem to coincide.   Intelligence alone is absolutely intelligible, and therefore absolute

knowledge can only be the knowledge of a knowing mind by itself.

This identification of subject and object is no mere abstract indifference or *coincidentia oppositorum*. We have left the region of abstract thought behind, and are now in the region of concrete thought where differences are supported by unity, not swamped and lost in that unity. Mind is here its own object; but the mind which is at once subject and object does not cease to mean anything by that distinction. That which is subject is also object : it is only the one because it is the other ; but the two terms retain, and indeed now for the first time acquire, really distinct meanings. For it is only in the synthesis of opposites that these opposites can be distinguished. It is only by comparing and contrasting A with not-A, which means holding them together in a single unity, that one can see the difference between them.

In philosophy subject and object are identified, and this is the differentia of philosophy ; but if that were all, philosophy would be only a freak of the mind, a demonstration that subject and object can on occasion be identified, leaving us puzzled as to why, if this can happen at all, it happens so seldom. Philosophy is only important and worth cultivating if this identity is an all-pervading principle, present in every phase of experience but only becoming explicit in philosophy. But this is exactly the position which we must now maintain. In art, religion, science, and history the true object is always the mind itself : it is only the ostensible object that is other than the mind. That is to say, art and the rest are themselves philosophy, but implicit philosophy. Their true nature is to be philosophy, but this nature is concealed beneath an error in self-knowledge whose peculiar character produces the peculiar *facies* of the artistic or other

consciousness. Art and the rest are the unconscious philosophies of a mind *nescientis se philosophari*; and this
ignorance, which is the difference between the artist and
the philosopher, is what prevents art, religion, and so forth
from consciously studying their real object, the mind, and
compels them to believe that their true aim is to contemplate
those images and abstractions which are their ostensible
objects. We have shown how any error in a mind's knowledge of itself necessitates this result. The erroneous conception of itself is judged, falsely, to be real: that is the
ostensible object. But the reality—its own true nature—
is still the real object, though hidden as it were behind the
ostensible object. Now if error could ever be pure and
unadulterated error, the opacity of the ostensible object
would be complete; but in fact every error is partly true
and therefore inconsistent with itself, and therefore these
inconsistencies in the ostensible object are, as it were,
rifts in the veil of illusion through which truth is always
breaking in. Or, to state it in a less metaphorical way, the
mind, having formed a false conception of itself, tries to
live up to that conception. But the falseness of the conception just means that it cannot be ' lived up to '. There
is therefore a permanent discord between what the mind
thinks it is and what, on the strength of that conception,
it does: even though this behaviour is not at all the same
thing as the behaviour of a mind that knows itself truly. The
result is an open inconsistency between theory and practice;
and this inconsistency, as ground for dissatisfaction, is the
starting-point of the attempt at truer self-knowledge.

Art, religion, science, and history are thus philosophical
errors, and owe all their characteristics, and the characteristics attributed by them to their ostensible objects, to
the initial error on which each is based. None is a mere

or complete error, for such a thing does not exist. Each grasps 'one aspect of the truth', as we say, forgetting that truth is a whole whose aspects cannot be thus separated : each is true, even while it is false ; and only its truth enables it to effect that self-criticism which leads to something better. If there were a complete error, the person who fell into it could never by any means escape it, and no one could ever tell which of two rival views was true and which false.

All error is inconsistent with itself, and owes this inconsistency to the fact that it is not merely erroneous but partly true. Truth and error are opposites which only a false abstraction can so separate as to speak of mere truth and mere error. All error is based on, and implicitly contains, truth, and is therefore never quite false. All truth, it might be hastily inferred, contains error and is never quite true. But to say this would be to fall into the sophism of the little boy who, on expressing a wish to marry his grandmother and being told by his father that this was impossible, replied, ' You married my mother, so why shouldn't I marry yours ? ' Error is always present in truth, but negatively present, that is to say, it is present as that which is denied : as drunkenness is present to the mind of a temperance preacher : as the enemy whose dispositions and tactics condition every element in the plans of a general. Every truth, that is to say, takes the form which it does take in order to refute or deny a particular error. This negative presence of error in truth must not be confused either with positive presence or with mere absence.

This interdependence of truth and error, error containing truth positively and truth containing error negatively, is not only a fact easily verified in empirical observation and

well known as an article of worldly wisdom even to those
who in their philosophies try to deny it, but it is a corollary
of the fact that all knowledge is self-knowledge, and every
error an error about the knowing mind. Hence the abstraction which separates subject and object also separates truth
and error (good and evil, and so on), and, with the melodramatic taste of unsophisticated youth, paints its truths
and its heroes pure white and its errors and villains pure
black. Such a melodramatic view of life is a logical consequence of realism, for if there were a world of real objects
completely other than the mind, absolute errors could no
doubt be made concerning them. Only, by an inevitable
coincidentia oppositorum, no one could possibly distinguish
an absolute error from an absolute truth.

§ 2. *Realistic or Dogmatic Philosophy in general*

Art, religion, science, history, and whatever other forms
of thought may be distinguished, are not autonomous forms
of experience but philosophical errors. They are, that is
to say, the forms of philosophical error, and in order to
study this phenomenon we must look not at philosophy but
art and the rest.

This is, as stated, an obvious paradox. It is a half-truth
which, unqualified, is a whole falsehood. Its falsity is based
on the fact of its being an abstraction : the abstraction of
truth from falsehood. Art as such is not a simple error,
any more than, say, neo-Platonism as such is a simple
error. Each—to use a common but metaphorical phrase—
makes an indispensable contribution to the body of truth
as a whole. But each has its own besetting sin, its own
characteristic way of misstating the truth. We have
hitherto allowed ourselves to say that in art, religion, and
so forth the substance of truth was present, but was con-

cealed by an inadequate form : that, for instance, religion actually solved the riddle of life but presented its solution in a mythological form. This implies that the task of philosophy, regarded as the philosophy of religion, is the simple translation of this solution of the riddle of life out of the language of mythology into that of philosophy. In a sense this is a true account of the matter, but it is not wholly true. It implies that matter and form are indifferent to one another, and that the meaning is indistinguishably the same however it is stated. If that were so, why restate it ? Translation itself is based on the fact that the meaning takes new colour and shines with a new light when we express it in different words. To set the meaning as an abstract self-identity over against the language makes translation pointless : to swamp it in a mere immediate union with the language itself makes translation impossible. Meaning and language are simply the universal and the particular. Abstract logic, the false theory of science, sets them outside one another. Abstract aesthetic, the false theory of art and religion, swamps the one in the other. Concrete logic sees them as distinct yet inseparable.

For this reason thought in its concrete form is not indifferent to its own choice of language. It realizes that an unsuitable linguistic form affects its own inmost being, and that what we have called merely formal error is in reality material and essential error. Our distinction between formal error and material truth was, in fact, only an abstract way of stating the very important fact that no error is wholly erroneous, but is always capable of a dialectical development into truth by simply bringing to light what is already implicit in it : what the thinker, as we para-doxically say, ' *really* means ', but ' does not know that he means ' This process of translation into progressively adequate language is simply the dialectical self-criticism of thought.

A distinction has been made between dogmatic and critical philosophy. Dogmatic philosophy is described as the procedure of thought without inquiry into its own powers ; critical philosophy as the investigation by thought itself of the limitations of its capacity. It is easy to be clever at the expense of this distinction, by pointing out that, because to discover a limit to one's thought is to transcend that limit, therefore critical philosophy is impossible, since one can never get outside one's own mind. But the people who actually made the distinction were not attempting to get outside their own minds. They were attempting to criticize, not thought in general, but a peculiar form of thought, namely, what we have called abstract thought or science : they were struggling to achieve concrete thought by criticizing abstract thought. And because they had not yet fully achieved concrete thought, their criticism of abstract thought necessarily took the form of a dialectical criticism of abstract thought by itself. Not to realize this was a venial sin in themselves ; it is culpable stupidity in their modern critics.

There is not only one dogmatism ; there are as many types of dogmatism as there are types of abstraction. There is only one type of concrete thought, namely, what we call philosophy, the mind's explicit consciousness of itself ; but this may be reduced to a dogmatism by dogmatizing or abstracting in an infinite variety of ways. In point of fact we have already reviewed some of these ways. Art, religion, science, and history are themselves precisely forms of dogmatic philosophy. The mind recognizing its own character as thought but affirming this thought abstractly in opposition to sensation is science, which as a kind of philosophy

is scientific dogmatism ; and so on. But in all these dogmatisms there is a distinction between the direct form of
consciousness (art, religion, &c.) and the reflective form
(aestheticism, theism, &c.), and this appears as the distinction between direct or primary experience, as the
apprehension of the object and reflective or secondary
experience, as the return of the mind upon itself to study
its own primary experience. Such a distinction between
primary and secondary experience is the infallible mark of
dogmatism in all its varieties. It is indeed the logical consequence of philosophical error in general, because if philosophy is self-knowledge, an error in self-knowledge generates
an object other than the subject (namely, the erroneous
conception of the subject), and thus sets up a distinction
between knowledge of this object and knowledge of the
subject, or primary and secondary experience. But because
the object is nothing but an error about the subject, the
knowledge (so called) of the subject will itself be affected
by this error, and hence the secondary experience will turn
out a mere reduplication of the primary, a *coincidentia
oppositorum*. Thus, for instance, formal logic and metaphysics are the scientific mind's account of itself and its
object respectively, and it is easy to see that they are the
same thing. On the other hand, this identity of primary
with secondary experience is necessarily concealed from the
mind affected by it, by the mere fact of its dogmatism.
The philosophical system called theism or philosophical
theology is not recognized by the simple religious consciousness as identical with itself, but as its own opposite, reflective thought as opposed to immediate intuition : yet
all theology tries to do is to think what in religion is
intuited.

Thus each of the various types of experience which we

have analysed is, as we have said, a philosophy and an erroneous philosophy ; but it is a necessary result of their error that they do not recognize themselves as philosophies. Their character as philosophies is essential to their being, but it is hidden within themselves, implicit ; and comes out into explicitness only when, from contemplating their ostensible object, they turn back to contemplate their ostensible selves. I say ostensible selves, for the error which deforms the object deforms the subject too, and hence the account they give of themselves when they reflect upon themselves cannot be a true account.

It is therefore inevitable that there should be an aesthetic philosophy, a religious philosophy, a scientific philosophy, and an historical philosophy, not to mention others corresponding to any form of experience which our analysis has passed by. The necessity of these philosophies is sophistically denied by the point of view which argues that philosophy is the business of philosophers and ought to be left in their professional and qualified hands. This academic trade-unionism is contemptible, not because it is trade-unionism, which in its own sphere, the economic life, is a good and necessary thing, but because it is trade-unionism hypocritically posing as philosophy, or in other words the error of conceiving philosophy as one specialized form of experience, instead of realizing that it is merely the self-consciousness of experience in general.

‘ The world really is what, errors apart, we take it to be.’ From this unexceptionable major premiss, dogmatism gets conclusions by framing the minor premiss ‘ in such and such a type of experience there is no error ’. For instance, in a newspaper review that catches my eye to-day, an able young writer is pompously reprimanded for ‘ not understanding that Mr. Blank ’—one of our leading realists—

' is concerned with the analysis of propositions (like, this is a table) which are quite certainly true, and that the business of philosophy is to discover what these propositions mean '. Not, that is, to ask whether they are true : that is guaranteed by something other than philosophy, whose infallibility philosophy has to take for granted. This is the programme of all dogmatism. An infallible non-philosophical source vouchsafes a revelation of absolute truth, ' quite certainly true ', which philosophy is not asked to justify and is not allowed to criticize ; and philosophy is granted the privilege of expounding and commenting on this revelation.

On this programme we would remark that the alleged non-philosophical form of experience is, as we now know, always a form of philosophy, but philosophy in its implicit form, at the mercy of abstraction and prejudice. Hence the form of thought which is placed above philosophy differs from philosophy only for the worse—only by being philosophical dogma, philosophical prejudice instead of philosophy willing to explain and if necessary modify itself. Thus, the proposition ' this is a table ' is, even at best, a mere expression of abstract classification, and false just as far as it is abstract. The assumption that we have in our hands an actually achieved cognition which is ' quite certainly true ', which is wholly exempt from error, cuts the ground from under any further process of thought heterogeneous from that by which this revelation was gained : philosophy, if that is the name of this further process, is thrown out of work, for if we already know that a given proposition is ' quite certainly true ', it argues an unnatural simplicity of mind to suppose that there can still be room for inquiry as to ' what it means '.

The form of experience which has here been dogmatically asserted as infallible is perception, regarded as implying classification. This is a modern type of dogmatism, and to call it dogmatic is therefore unsafe ; but the exactly parallel dogmatism of the religious experience is sufficiently out of date to be analysed with impunity. When philosophy assumes the infallibility of religion and, accepting that as its fixed point, constitutes itself the *ancilla fidei*, such a philosophy must be false, and the hard things that have been said about philosophy in bondage to religion are not at all undeserved. But the warmest critics of such a philosophy generally fail to see that its fault lies not in its choice of masters but in its admitting a master at all, and they lift up their voices in a plaintive protest if in their own day philosophy refuses to swallow whole the worlds of science and perception. They can only account for such a refusal by accusing philosophy of ' malice ' towards science, precisely as the philosophy which broke with religious dogmatism was accused of malice towards religion. In a sense, these accusations are just. Reasoning can be met by criticism, but dogmatism cannot. You can only argue with a willing disputant. If you say to a convinced dogmatist, whether religious or scientific, ' Come, let us reason together ', and offer to criticize his fundamental dogmas, he can only, as a consistent dogmatist, refuse ; and if you then, like a wise man, shake the dust of his city from your shoes, he is acting within the recognized conventions of abuse if he calls you malicious, because you are refusing to share his comfortable pigsty for no reason which he can see to be valid.

Dogmatic philosophies cannot be refuted, because the dogmatist has a trump card in his hand all the time, namely, his own dogmatism or imperviousness to argument. Thus any and every attack on a religious view of the world can be annihilated by the reply ' God knows best '. There is no answer to that ; you can only circumvent it by drawing the dogmatist out and getting him to discuss the question 'What do you mean by God?' Similarly, modern realism can crush any critic by pointing out that everything he says has already presupposed its own pre-existent object, so that all his best arguments turn to his own destruction. But this realistic 'Open Sesame' is only the original act of abstraction whose validity is in question, and which, in answer to any doubts as to its value, is simply repeated.

But dogmatic philosophies, though they cannot be refuted —a truth which dogmatism, grown fat and cynical, publishes in the form of the doctrine that all argument is circular— can and do refute themselves. Every such philosophy contains the seeds of its own destruction, and these fail to germinate only when they are planted in a barren mind. For a dogmatic philosophy is really nothing but a single, blind, abstract act of will : it is the determination to remain within the circle of a specific form of experience. Religious dogmatism only consists in repeating to oneself 'I *will* remain at the religious point of view', and in reasserting this point of view in all its abstractness against all comers. Modern realism says to itself 'I *will* on every occasion separate the object from the subject', and that is all it does. Now this attitude is one of resistance ; but resistance to what ? The dogmatist thinks that he is resisting 'malicious' external enemies, but that is part of his self-deception. He is resisting his own doubts.

Dogmatism is simply the resistance which a given form of experience presents to its own destruction by an inner dialectic. Perhaps it would be truer to say that it is the dead body of such a form which, as living experience, has already been so destroyed. It is only when a given form of experience can no longer justify itself by a vigorous and

healthy life that it shrinks into a crust of dogmatism to
die. The dogmatic philosophy which, on the face of it,
serves a tyrannical master is really nothing but the collapse
of that master's own life into the repetitive mumblings of
senility. In his vigour he needs no such help. Then, his
justification of his own existence is that the blind receive
their sight, and the lame walk; the lepers are cleansed,
and the deaf hear; the dead are raised up, and the poor
have the gospel preached to them.

Yet senility is a part of the dispensation of nature, and
a thing venerable and not without sanctity. And since we
are commanded to honour our fathers and mothers, we
ought to treat dogmatic philosophy with reverence and
eschew the sin of Ham. For it is only by the gate of dogmatism that any one can set forth upon the road of philosophy; and the critic of dogmatism inevitably looks back
on it not only as upon the Egypt of his bondage but as the
pit whence he was digged and the home of his youth;
home, too, of all those who, young now, may one day go
out into the wilderness as he has gone and as his fathers
went before him.

§ 3. *Aesthetic Philosophy*

The first of the dogmatic philosophies which we shall
briefly review is the philosophical self-assertion of the
aesthetic consciousness. This is aesthetic philosophy or
the philosophy of art, the reasoned vindication of the
aesthetic experience. All works which treat of ' aesthetics '
as a separate philosophical science belong to this class; for
the possibility of separating aesthetics from other philosophical sciences implies a correlative separation of art from
other activities of the mind, the assertion of art as a self-
contained and autonomous form of experience. But art is

really no more than the aesthetic side of all knowledge, unintelligible in abstraction from knowledge as a whole; and therefore the only intelligible philosophy of art is a philosophy which places the aesthetic side of knowledge in its right place, and this can only be a complete philosophy of knowledge. The act of drawing a ring-fence round the aesthetic consciousness and regarding it as a thing to itself is an abstraction which gives birth at once to art, as a specific experience, and aesthetic philosophy as the study of that experience.

Aesthetic philosophy in its most primitive form is simply art-criticism, the talk of artists about art. This is a necessary development of art itself, and is of high interest to the philosopher, very much as the conversation of farmers and shepherds, with their deep knowledge of hill and dale, is of interest to the surveyor. But as the surveyor must rely on his own measurements for the drawing of his map, so the philosopher must form his conclusions upon art from his own reflection, and cannot undertake to believe all that the artist tells him. This is not because the artist is an amateur in philosophy. There is no such thing in philosophy as amateur or professional. It is because his very profession as an artist takes its rise in a philosophical error concerning the nature of experience in general, which necessarily vitiates everything he says whether about art or about life.

In all forms of philosophical dogmatism, the point is not that the dogmatist may be right in his dogmatically-expressed philosophy, by a lucky guess or the grace of heaven; the point is that the dogmatic form is itself only the expression of a material and positive error which affects by an iron necessity everything couched in that form. The dogmatist is not, as it were, shooting in the dark by 'instinct' at a target which with luck he may hit; what

we call his ' instinct ' is a self-frustrated form of ' reason ',
and the blindness of his aim is nothing but the fact that he
is aiming away from the target. These metaphors, however,
must be corrected by the proviso that in thinking there is
no such thing as a real miss, a wholly erroneous error.

Even in its simplest form, as the artist's theory of art,
aesthetic philosophy is implicitly a theory of life as a whole
and tends to flood, so to speak, that part of life which lies
outside the aesthetic experience. When this happens we
get a true aesthetic philosophy. This is a philosophy which
reduces all philosophical problems to terms of imagination
or intuition. For such a philosophy everything is monadic,
unique in the sense of abstractly unique or free from any
taint of continuity with everything else ; every event is
abstractly new, not concretely new like the facts of history,
but new in the sense of irrelevant to what went before.
Such being the real world, a world of pure change, the only
attitude which is adequate to it is the intuition of the artist
with its monadic structure or negation of structure. Philosophies of this kind appear at various points of history, but
the best-known modern example represents the positive
proposal following on a destructive criticism of science.
Such a denial of the scientific intellect, followed by an
assertion of intuition as the opposite of intellect, clearly
betrays a failure to pass beyond science itself ; for this
denial of A and assertion of not-A is based on logical presuppositions which are precisely those of the scientific intellect. A real repudiation of science would involve the
repudiation of that repudiation itself, and the absorption
of science into a concrete historical whole. The modern
philosophy of intuition is a backward eddy in the stream
of thought.

Aesthetic philosophy is the abstract assertion of immediacy, the denial of thought. ' Don't think, feel,' is its maxim. It is therefore, as the denial of thought, the denial of philosophy and of itself : if, as it declares, feeling were enough, the explicit principle which recommends feeling would be unnecessary. A person who has to remind himself to act on impulse has ceased to act on impulse ; and one who advises others to follow their impulses is really advising them to follow his advice. Thus aesthetic philosophy is the formal denial of its own existence ; and yet, in that very denial, it exists, but only because it shows itself, by its denial, to be doing precisely what it denies it is doing, namely, thinking. Aesthetic philosophy is thus a living example of the so-called ' Fallacy of Pseudomenos '. Like all forms of that fallacy, it is dissipated by the discovery that its very denial is implicitly an assertion.

It may here be observed that there is no dialectical transition from aesthetic philosophy to religious philosophy and so forth. These dogmatisms are only the negative moments of the dialectic of experience, dead by-products of the forms of consciousness which produce them, blind-alleys in the process of thought. You cannot work forward out of them : you must retreat backwards from them and begin afresh from another form of experience. Aesthetic philosophy is not the mother of religious philosophy but the corpse of art. This is the truth for which those are contending who say that philosophies do not come, and cannot be emended, by reasoning ; and that they depend not on argument but upon conviction, temperament, or experience. Such a contention is in substance true enough : it is only false because it insists upon substituting one error for another and interpreting ' temperament ' or the like in a mythological and superstitious way.

§ 4. *Religious Philosophy*

The second type of dogmatic philosophy which we have to consider is that which takes its cue from the religious consciousness. Religion affirms God as its object, and we have seen that this affirmation is a misunderstanding of its own true nature. For though religion expresses itself in terms which, taken literally, imply the objective existence of God, its meaning is only apprehended when we make up our mind to regard these expressions as metaphorical statements of something else, something which is never by religion actually stated in literal terms, though it is capable of being so stated.

The peculiar kind of dogmatism which we call religious philosophy is a philosophical analysis of religion conducted on the assumption that in the language of its creeds religion is expressing itself not metaphorically but literally. These creeds are then examined as if they were literal statements of fact ; and the result is a conflict between two canons of interpretation. First, because the religious consciousness actually exists and finds the belief in these statements necessary to its own existence, it is argued that they must be true. Hence arises philosophical theism, or the attempt to show that the statements of a creed are literally true ; and of this the most powerful weapon is the ontological argument. It is shown that religion is not the mere assumption of God as an hypothesis or probable theory, but the actual living contact of the soul with God. Hence, to state the argument in its simplest form, God must exist or religion could not exist. And this argument is incontrovertible in the sense that, since religion certainly exists, that which it means by the term God must also exist ; but what it means by God is not what it says, and hence the recurring objection

to the ontological proof that what it proves is indeed the
existence of something, but not of the religious man's God
(the literal God, God as an image), rather of the philosopher's
absolute (the concept which the image of God metaphorically
means).

Such is the first canon of interpretation. The second is
the principle that because God, as naïvely represented in
religion, is clearly a mere imagination, a figment of mythological fancy, therefore religion, which is so intimately bound
up with his existence, is an illusion. This also can be proved
by a method which we might describe as the converse ontological argument ; but here again the proof always misses
the point. Religion always replies to the arguments of
atheism that its God is wholly unaffected by such arguments,
that its own living contact with the object of its devotion
is far too close and far too convincing an experience to be
dispelled by any kind of reasoning. This is why, as we
have already seen, atheistical arguments are a peculiarly
futile and unintelligent form of sophistry, and one not
actually cultivated by any one above the intellectual level
of the tub-thumpers in public parks ; who, however, may
be pardoned for their eccentricities if we remember that
their arguments, however silly, are at least incapable of
refutation by those against whom they are directed. For
atheism assumes at the start that religion means what it
says, and on this basis it is all too easy to prove the non-
existence of an infinite God who because he is distinct from
finite beings is finite ; an omnipotent being who, because
his existence leaves man free to act, is not omnipotent ;
a loving and good being who because he does not exert
himself to protect us against calamity is no true friend ;
a ruler of the universe whose actual methods of rule, so far
as we can see them, are those of a mentally deranged tyrant.

Hence atheism has no difficulty in proving the absurd and irrational character of religion and the desirability of stamping it out. Characteristically of a negative form of thought, it does not trouble itself with the question why religion exists. It contents itself with attacking, and does not aim at understanding.

This is because atheism is the negative side of religious dogmatism. A dogmatic philosophy does not aim at understanding a form of thought, and hence it falls necessarily into two opposed halves: on the one side it asserts that form, on the other it attacks it. The positive side of religious dogmatism, namely theism, and the negative side, namely atheism, are at one in not trying to understand religion, and taking up a dogmatic attitude towards it.

Theism is much in favour at the present time, and is defended by many writers of distinction as the last word in philosophy. It is especially taken to be the crown and completion of something called idealism, namely, the explanation of the entire universe in terms of mind. Idealism, in the sense in which it leads to theism, is the doctrine that the world is made, so to speak, of mind; and is regarded as the opposite of materialism or the doctrine that the world is made of matter. Both these theories begin by abstracting the object of knowledge from the subject, and both go on by inquiring into the nature of the object in this abstraction, regarded as a thing in itself. Both agree in committing the fundamental error of separating the metaphysical inquiry as to what the world is in itself from the psychological inquiry as to how we come to know it. Idealism in this sense leaves unreconciled the opposition between subject and object, and therefore sets the object outside the subject; but, feeling that this opposition must somehow be reconciled, it tries to bridge the gap by ascribing to the object some kind of consubstantiality with the subject, turning it into another mind, a society of minds (spiritual pluralism) or an infinite mind (theism).

With anything which deserves the name of idealism in this sense, we have nothing to do except to reject it. We do not ask whether the world, considered in isolation from our mind, is material or mental, because we are engaged on a consistent attempt to get rid of these abstract separations and antitheses. We hold that the scientist's world, so far as it exists, really is material, in the sense that, so far as he is a scientist, he believes in its reality as material, and that, so far as he succeeds in being a scientist, he is right so to believe. But we hold that this material world, regarded as material, is not fully intelligible, and that to describe it as the object of scientific thought is to fall into the error of supposing that scientific thought can maintain itself as a stable attitude towards a real object. The scientific attitude cannot be thus maintained : when we try to grasp it, it dissolves in our grasp. Hence the theory that the world or any part of the world is material is not so much a false theory as a theory that nobody holds, though some people delude themselves into thinking that they hold it. The material world of science is thus not in the last resort a world of animate objects or minds or the like : it is in the last resort an illusion, and its ' mental ' character is just the fact that, like all illusions, it is a figment of the mind which tries to conceive it. In the same way, any object considered in abstraction from a mind which knows it is neither material nor mental, but an illusion, a false abstraction. Thus we certainly do not say that the objective world *in itself* is mental. If we are asked what it is apart from a mind that knows it, we shall answer that it is not ' apart from ' such a mind ; it is ' with ' it in the sense of being known by it. If we are asked what it *would be* apart from such a mind, we shall answer that the very question implies the *suggestio falsi* that we can describe that which by definition is unknown.

Our enemy is abstraction. We object to materialism only because it represents a claim to ultimate truth made on behalf of a concept which is flagrantly abstract. For the same reason we object to theism. Theism is a form of realism, of the abstract separation between the knower and the known. Philosophically, we object to it for this reason, because it fails to live up to the ideal of concrete thought ; but we object to it on religious grounds as well. Religion cares nothing for philosophical theism, because religion is not interested in argument. The existence of its God does not require, and does not even admit, proof. For since religion does not define what it means by God, it is impossible to discover what we are to prove. We have to offer our own definition of the term, and whatever definition we offer will necessarily be rejected by religion, because the refusal to admit that God can be defined is vital to the religious consciousness, and to attempt such a definition is already to pass outside the sphere of religion and to falsify, from the religious point of view, our relation to God. For the true God, the object of love and worship, we have set up a false God, the object of understanding, and what we prove is always this false God, never the true. Thus religion rejects its would-be friend, theism, as decisively as its would-be enemy, atheism. They fight over its head, and it goes calmly on its way ignoring them, knowing that the only God in whom it is interested is safe in his heaven and unaffected by the storms of controversy raging round his empty name.

But theism, outcast from religion, is no less definitely an outcast from philosophy. This, in spite of repeated attempts

to deny it, is notorious enough. Every one whose intellectual conscience is keen and untainted by sophistry, every
one who has a fine sense of values in philosophical work,
knows instinctively that the importation of God into an
argument breaks the rules of the game, upsets the table
instead of working the moves out to a finish. Philosophers
drag in the idea of God when they are conscious of coming
to the end of their tether, and not before : so that the
entry of God into a philosophical system marks unerringly
the point at which the system breaks down. Every candid
philosopher knows that this is so ; and it is easy to see the
reason for it. Since the religious idea of God differs from
the philosophical concept of an ultimate reality in leaving
itself undefined, that idea may in a philosophy stand for
any concept whatever. To expound a philosophy in terms
of God is like evaluating a quantity in terms of x and
leaving x undefined. In the concrete life of religion God is
given a content by the way in which we worship him ; our
attitude to him shows what sort of a God we take him to
be. But a philosophy whose ultimate appeal is to God
gives him no content whatever, and he remains a mere
cipher, an unknown which renders valueless every formula
in which it appears—that is, the whole philosophy. Thus
the word God might be replaced by any other word so far
as its philosophical value is concerned, and the controversy
between theism and atheism turns out to be a meaningless
dispute over a word. And in proportion as the idea of God
is accurately defined, so as to remove this difficulty, the
name God becomes progressively less and less applicable,
more of a misnomer.

None the less, the development of theism and atheism
out of religion seems to be inevitable. As long as religion
so far misunderstands itself as to affirm the image instead

of the meaning, it must happen that this misunderstanding will be perpetuated and bear fruit. This is the only way in which it can be removed. Hence religion must give rise to theology, a form of thought which elaborates the assertions of religion on the assumption that they say what they mean, and is therefore a science ; and theology, or the scientific elaboration of religious expressions, must give rise to the philosophical question whether these expressions, so elaborated, are true or false. The two dogmatic answers to this question are theism and atheism. Each is equally tenable ; for the theistic case that religion itself guarantees their truth precisely balances the atheistic case that they are nonsensical. The clash between these two, however, naturally leads to the reconsideration of the original question. This is the critical attitude, which instead of asking whether religion is true or false asks what it means. The result will be the discovery of the metaphorical character of religion, and hence the destruction of both theism and atheism, as misinterpretations of the religious consciousness. From this critical point of view it will be possible for the first time to do justice to the spirit of religion instead of quarrelling over the letter. But the critical point of view cannot be reached by any direct path from dogmatic theism or atheism. These empty wranglings over a dead word which is, in fact, the corpse of the religious consciousness must be swept aside by a resolute and open-eyed conversion of the soul to the discipline of thought. Only in the daylight of explicit thought, however distressingly that daylight reveals the poverty and squalor of both disputants, can the theist and atheist finish their battle and sign a treaty of peace. That daylight will not come of itself. It can only be won by rigorous training in scientific, historical, and philosophical thought.

§ 5. *Scientific Philosophy*

If science is the affirmation of the abstract concept, scientific philosophy is this affirmation raised to the level of a philosophy, that is to say, become explicitly self-conscious. The scientist as such assumes that in describing the world in terms of abstract concepts he is, in principle, describing it correctly : scientific philosophy raises this assumption to the level of a definite assertion consciously made and defended against criticism. The scientist thinks abstractly : the scientific philosopher justifies him in so doing.

This justification of the scientific attitude takes a double form. In the first place, it is logic (which throughout this section means formal logic) : in the second, metaphysics. In the first place, it is an account of scientific thinking, an exposition of its principles, structure, and methodology : in the second place, it vindicates the objective validity of this type of thinking by showing that the real world is constructed in such a way that, in thinking of it scientifically, we are thinking of it as it really is. Logic and metaphysics are necessary to each other. Without metaphysics, logic can only show that thought has principles and abides by them ; but these principles might be such as to falsify, instead of verifying, the thought which obeys them. Without logic, metaphysics can only show what the real world is like ; but it may be such a world as, to our thinking faculties, must remain unknown and unknowable.

Now if the scientific consciousness is to be affirmed as valid, logic and metaphysics must themselves be scientific ; for if their fruit is the conclusion that abstract thought is in principle sound, they must conform to the standard which they set up or pronounce themselves bankrupt. Logic and metaphysics are thus the vindication of science from its own point of view ; science in them is justifying itself. Hence logic, including metaphysics as its implied correlative, is correctly described as *scientia scientiarum*, the scientific theory of science. Thus we at once reach a position superior to that of the aesthetic or religious type of philosophy ; for in these the justification of art or religion is entrusted to something which is other than art or religion itself, and is therefore invalidated by the fact that to argue in defence of a form of experience which itself cannot or will not argue, is implicitly to assert not the autonomy or finality of that form of experience but precisely its weakness, its inability to justify itself. The aesthetician and theologian, in ostensibly defending art and religion, are really laying bare their defects ; but in the person of the logician it is science itself that undertakes its own defence. Thus science achieves the very important feat of becoming self-conscious and still remaining itself, thereby exhibiting a stability and self-reliance which are beyond the reach of art and religion. This it can do because in it thought has become explicit.

But thought is in science merely abstract, and therefore the scientific philosophy which emerges from it is abstract also. The universal and the particular still stand over against one another in an unreconciled dualism : hence thought in the primary sense, or science, is merely an object to thought in the secondary sense, or logic. As the chemist studies the general nature of the physical elements, so the logician studies the general nature of thought. But as the chemist's thought is distinct from its own object, so the logician's thought is distinct from that ' thought in general ' which is the object of logical analysis ; for this separation of thinking from the object thought about is presupposed in all science. It follows that the thinking which goes on in the logician's mind cannot be the thought which he is studying and describing. His object is said to be thought, but it is by definition an object of thought—the object of *his* thought—and therefore, because thought and its object are by definition separate, he can never by his logical analysis grasp the thought that is actually going on within his own mind.

This difficulty cannot be evaded by protesting that, in so far as he studies the general nature of thought, he is implicitly studying his own thought as an instance of thought in general. For thought in general is no thought in particular : it is the mere abstraction of a thought which nobody thinks, and is therefore simply not thought but the rules which thought, when it is valid, obeys. Thought in general thus turns out to mean the object of thought in general, and logic is the description not of thinking as it actually goes on, but of the general characteristics of objective reality as such.

Thus, by an inevitable *coincidentia oppositorum*, the initial abstractness of scientific procedure converts the analysis of thought as such into an analysis of its object as such : thought comes to mean the abstract object of thought and logic passes over into metaphysics.

But this transition only makes matters worse. Logic distinguishes valid from invalid inferences, and lays down certain canons which thought must obey if it is to be valid. But these canons depend on metaphysics. It is only because they are deduced from the structure of the real world that they are canons at all ; apart from this, they may be laws of thinking but they are not laws of true thinking. They may be ways in which we cannot help thinking, but that does not prove that in thinking thus we think the truth. Therefore we must justify them metaphysically : we must demonstrate that what we have hitherto called logic or the theory of thought is really metaphysics or the theory of reality, and that what we have called the laws of thought are the laws of being.

But this is precisely what we cannot do. Metaphysics is impossible ; for its task is to vindicate the objective validity of the ways in which we think, and if there are any flaws in our methods of thought, these will affect our metaphysical theory of reality and introduce into it the very mistakes which by its help we had hoped to eradicate. Hence the theory of being as distinct from thinking (metaphysics) will only be the theory of thinking as distinct from being (logic) expressed in a different terminology but subject to the same fatal weakness, namely that just as logic can never analyse real thinking—the thinking that, going on in the logician's mind, always lies behind his analysis—so metaphysics can never analyse real being, being as it is in itself untainted by thought.

All that is left at this point is psychology : that is to say the study of thought as a mere phenomenon, without attempting to raise the question whether a given thought is true or false, valid or invalid. The distinction between truth and falsehood, already waived by logic in so far as logic ignores the truth of the premises and attends only to the validity of the inference from them, is by psychology banished altogether, and thought now becomes something that happens and nothing more. It is a mere event, whose claim to be an act of knowledge is ignored. This abstraction of thought from its own truth or falsity is the characteristic mark of the psychology of knowledge; a similar abstraction marks the psychology of conduct and so forth.

The limitations of psychology are quite clear and consistent, but are not always recognized by those who practise it or by those who, not being themselves psychologists, hope to derive certain results from its pursuit. Because psychology ignores the distinction between truth and falsehood, it gives us laws of thought which apply indifferently to both : all its distinctions, that is to say, cut across the distinction between truth and falsehood, and when psychology has classified a certain process as one of association or whatever it may be, no result ever follows as to whether this process yields a truth or an error. It is a fallacy, but an exceedingly common fallacy, to imagine that by giving a psychological analysis of any ' mental event ' we have done anything whatever towards either discrediting or commending it as an attempt at achieving truth, goodness, beauty or the like. Its character as such an attempt is precisely what psychology ignores ; and hence thinking, as such an attempt, is not even recognized by psychology to exist. In behaviourism, psychology becomes aware of this self-imposed rule, and asserts it explicitly. Hence it is idle to protest against the behaviouristic tendency to regard thought as a mechanism ; we ought rather to be grateful to the behaviourists for revealing the true nature of psychology and pushing it to its logical conclusion.

But this logical conclusion is nothing more nor less than a *reductio ad absurdum.* If psychology is a correct account of thinking, it is a correct account of the thinking of psychologists ; that is to say, psychology itself is only a kind of event which goes on in the minds of people called psychologists, a complex of mental idiosyncrasies innocent of any distinction between truth and falsehood. But no psychologist believes that his own psychological theories and inquiries can be described in this way. He tacitly excepts his own activity of scientific thinking from the analysis which he is giving of mind in general : [1] that is to say, the mind which

[1] Behaviourism reduces thought to behaviour ; but the existence of behaviourism implies that behaviour not only exists but is

he is describing is not the mind which is doing the description, but something not merely different but absolutely heterogeneous. What in his psychological works he calls mind is not mind at all in the sense in which he is mind. It is mind de-mentalized, materialized, and having over against it something untouched by his analysis, namely mind itself, as it exists in him. Thus psychology is self-condemned as the description of a wholly fictitious entity. In ignoring the distinction between truth and falsehood, the psychologist has not ignored something alien to thought, namely its accidental relation to an object other than itself, he has simply ignored thought; for thought is nothing whatever but the drawing of this distinction. And yet, in ignoring the distinction, he has asserted it implicitly in his own person, and is thus the living refutation of his own principles. Psychology is refuted by the psychology of psychology.

The moral of this is not that we ought to abandon psychology and return to the old logic and metaphysics. Those sciences have been once for all criticized by and absorbed into psychology, which has made a real advance upon them. They were based upon a foundation incapable of supporting them, but in the course of their existence they collected a vast body of valuable and sound doctrine transcending in a sense the fallacious principles on which it was ostensibly founded. They were not pure errors, but bodies of truth shot through with erroneous interpretations

observed. If behaviourism told us how behaviour got itself observed, the behaviour of behaviourists would begin to be worth observing. But at present we are put off with inanities like this: 'Behaviourists say that the talk they have to listen to can be explained without supposing that people think.' Why not 'the books they write'? Only because the writer quoted is too keen on his joke to see that, sauce for the goose being sauce for the gander, the joke recoils automatically on the behaviourist.

and implications. The same is true of psychology. Its basis is radically unsound, and this defect becomes progressively important as it deals with more and more fundamental problems ; in saying this we say no more than what is said by the most distinguished psychologists themselves. But the work which it has done and is doing in detail is of the greatest value, and no one wishes to deny the fact. What we want is not a clean sweep of psychology but a psychology bent upon overcoming its own abstractness, a psychology of concrete mind ; and, in a sense, that is the aim of this book. It is all to the good that psychology attempts to conceive mind as a self-contained system, working by its own laws and not determined by relation to anything outside itself. Its error is to regard this system not as thought itself but as an object of thought, external to the psychologist as a thing to be observed, not living in him as a thing to be enjoyed. By this error it reasserts the very fallacy which it is trying to avoid.

Scientific philosophy or the self-justification of the scientific consciousness fails because its self eludes it at every turn. Abstractive by its own chosen nature, it throws the object outside the subject in the form of a law, a universal, over against its own instances ; and therefore when it tries to return upon itself it can only study, not itself, but the abstract law of its own operations regarded as something objective and not subjective, not itself but some alien determinant of itself. This alien determinant, which it calls nature or the objective world, is in reality a pure fiction, the fiction of the hypostatized or abstract universal. Science itself bridges the gulf between the abstract and the concrete by its interest in empirical fact ; but scientific philosophy has no such mitigating influence, for it simply asserts and reasserts the gulf. This is why science hates philosophy, and why most people regard philosophy as the acme of futility, the abstraction of abstraction. Science hates philosophy because what it calls by that name—scientific philosophy—is the discovery of its own abstractness, its own self-refutation and death. Common sense despises philosophy for the same reason; because in ' philosophy '—scientific philosophy—the abstractness which in science is only provisional and partial becomes absolute. This is that ' philosophy ' which beats in vain against problems like that of body and soul, mind and matter, evil, and so forth, which are insoluble because they simply express its own abstractness.

The reason why the name philosophy is almost invariably applied to what we call scientific philosophy is that, from the days of the early Greeks to the eighteenth century, the main effort of European thought was concentrated upon the development and perfecfion of science. During this period, therefore, philosophy meant the reflection of science upon itself, or scientific philosophy; and the popular opinion of philosophy is a valuation, and in the main a just valuation, of scientific philosophy and therefore implicitly of science. For the philosophy of the scientific consciousness—logic, metaphysics, and psychology—is the quintessence of that consciousness, which here for the first time realizes to the full its own abstract nature, and in realizing it rejects it as a foolish error.

This rejection is visible enough in the greatest philosophers of what we may call the scientific epoch of thought. The lesser philosophers have been content to set up the abstract concept as the goal of thought, the supreme reality; but the greatest have risen above this dogmatism and, as it were piercing the clouds with their summits, penetrated if only for a moment into the clear air of concrete thought. Thus Socrates, the very father of formal logic, based his whole

life's work on the discovery that the only true knowledge was to know one's own ignorance ; thus Plato,
whose doctrine of forms, with its mathematical colouring,
is the sheet-anchor of scientific dogmatism to this day,
discovered that beyond the sciences there was something
called dialectic, the conversation of the soul with itself,
whose function was precisely to annihilate the hypotheses
on which the sciences were built ; thus Aristotle, in whose
name whole armies of dogmatists have fought, worked out
the concept of a pure activity knowing no law and no end
outside itself, and found this realized in the absolute self-
knowledge of God. To these great discoveries the scientific
dogmatism of the Greeks was a mere background, a foil
which lesser disciples have mistaken for the jewel. And the
same struggle between scientific dogmatism and the concept
of self-knowledge is the key to all modern philosophy and
notoriously that of Kant, who tried with one hand to
justify the existence of science, and with the other, by
refusing to give up the thing in itself, to maintain the
possibility of a philosophy transcending the limitations of
science, a reality which in his paradoxical phrase ' we can
think but not know '.

This phrase gives the very essence of scientific dogmatism,
even while breaking through it. The essence of this dogmatism is to regard generalizing, abstracting, as synonymous
with knowing, which implies the conception of the ultimate
reality as an abstract reality. In the Platonic doctrine of
forms, this identification is explicitly made. It was already
abandoned in effect by Aristotle when he constructed his
theology, but only abandoned to be reasserted, for his God
was a transcendent God whose relation to the world was that
of an abstract law. It was abandoned again by Descartes
when he found ultimate reality in the act of thinking, and

subsequent philosophers, so far as they have effected a real advance, have simply given body and life to Descartes' conception. At the present day, scientific philosophy is an anachronism; but an anachronism that still walks the streets and seems in no haste to die. The error of asserting an abstract generalization as lying behind and conditioning concrete fact still takes a vast variety of shapes. It appears in formal logic, whether that of the old text-books or that of the mathematical logisticians; it appears in psychology, rational and empirical, normal and abnormal; it appears in the attempt to draw up a table of 'categories' or necessary forms of thought, whether regarded as a cycle of *a priori* concepts, a series of predetermined dialectical phases of experience, or a system of distinct and separate forms of the spirit; it would appear in this book if, as we assumed at the outset to be legitimate, we regarded art, religion, and the rest as permanent and necessary distinctions instead of shifting and indeterminate manifestations of thought which might be rearranged, subdivided and grouped in ways other than that in which we have here treated them. In fact, it is the error of formalism in every possible shape, and its shapes are infinite.

But formalism is not overcome by merely issuing a general warning against it. Those who pride themselves on being unconventional are as a rule not only snobs but hypocrites; they do not let themselves see how miserably conventional they are. Formalism, like conventionality, is only the defect of a good quality. All conduct is in part conventional, and all thought is in part formal or systematic. The aim of good thinking is not to evade system but to become the master of one's system instead of its slave; and one learns to rule by learning to obey. Thus scientific dogmatism is not altogether an error. It is a discipline. Hegel said that every philosopher ought to pass through a phase of Spinozism, which is little but a scientific dogmatism of a peculiarly rigid kind. So the technicalities of abstract thought, though they are not philosophy, are a gymnastic without which the philosopher is likely to be a slack-jointed and flabby creature.

But the reverse is to-day far more important. The cry that philosophy must accept the results of science and adopt scientific methods is quite sufficiently heard among us. In fact, it is the prime obstacle to the healthy development of modern philosophy. Philosophy has its own problems and its own methods, and must look for its own results. Science is the scene of remarkable triumphs ; so is agriculture ; that does not prove either that surgeons ought to perform their operations with a plough or that philosophers ought to attack their problems with the weapons of the scientist. The philosophy current to-day is almost without exception riddled with fallacies arising out of the uncritical application to philosophical questions of methods and results derived from the sciences ; and the progress of modern philosophy is intimately bound up with its liberation from a scientific dogmatism which has long ago exhausted its contribution to philosophical thought. Happily, the very petulance with which our dogmatists preach the gospel of scientific method in philosophy is an indication that the battle is going against them and that they know it.

§ 6. *Historical Philosophy*

The historical form of dogmatism is that represented by modern realism. Although realism itself is as old as thought, being in fact identical with dogmatism or error in general, the authors of modern realism are right in claiming that it is a new invention. It is that form of error which results from discovering the concept of fact.

We shall make no attempt here at a detailed discussion of the modern realistic school of thought. Controversy is no part of this book's purpose, and it does not even set out to describe in detail the philosophy of any one except its author. If this resembles arrogance, it is at least intended in the spirit of a witness who, once in the box and on oath, feels bound to tell his story as plainly as possible to the exclusion of all else.

Historical dogmatism is the assertion of fact as ultimately real, and fact means not only the facts of 'history' but the facts of perception. Such a dogmatism may take a considerable variety of forms. It may concentrate on perception and describe the world as a spatial whole composed of 'things', variations within which are produced by a system of perspectives ; it may refine upon this and conceive a spatio-temporal world whose structure is made up of events or point-instants ; it may, on the other hand, concentrate on history and biography and treat reality as a mind or a system of minds coexisting with a material world or creating the material world out of itself. Or, obsessed by the pseudo-problem of mind and matter and unable to realize that materialism is a logical phenomenon, it may describe the ultimate ground of both mind and matter as a non-material and non-mental 'neutral stuff', matter with a nonsense name ; or it may work upwards instead of downwards, and find reality in an absolute whole which cannot be called this rather than that, because in it all differences are included ; a whole which is non-spatial, non-temporal, non-moral, non-material, and non-spiritual but somehow the ground and source of all these distinctions. That which unites all these divergent views is their common assertion of the positivity of the object : that is, their denial that the object is conditioned or affected by becoming known to any thinking mind or to what, with a question-begging epithet, is sometimes called finite mind : its finiteness being just this indifference to it on the part of its object. Such a realistic account of the object, as positive fact indifferent to its being known, is at first sight compatible with any theory as to what the ultimate nature of this object may be ; and so we get all manner of realisms, monistic and pluralistic, intuition-ist and intellectualist, materialist and spiritualist, all equally capable of being held in combination with the fundamental thesis of realism, which is distinguished from them as ' theory of knowledge ' from ' metaphysics '.

Such was, at least, and to some extent still is, the belief of eminent realists, who sum up their own position in the negative formula that knowledge can make no difference to its object. On the other hand, it is not possible to assert so much as this without asserting more, namely the principle of abstract thought ; for what is explicitly asserted is the complete separateness of subject and object, their independ-ence of one another : and this implies that there are facts in existence which are thus completely independent. It is therefore correct to maintain that realism commits its author to the principle of pluralism ; and pluralism only means the scientific abstraction of the universal from its particulars. This path, therefore, leads from historical dogmatism back to scientific dogmatism.

If, on the other hand, we concentrate on the positive statement of realism, the concrete reality of its object, we arrive at the opposite conclusion. All facts fall into their place in a single all-embracing system of fact, and this system is the absolute, the ultimate reality. Thus we arrive at a monistic instead of a pluralistic realism. But it is equally self-contradictory. For either the thinker himself falls inside the absolute whole or he does not. If he does, then differences in his thought about it make a difference to it, and the more concretely real—that is, organized and interconnected in all its parts—it is, the more fundamental these differences will be and the more completely the positivity of fact is lost. If he does not, then the monistic doctrine is surrendered and we return to pluralism.

In spite of the simplicity of these difficulties, they have as yet not been fairly faced by a single realist with whose work the present writer is acquainted. In practice, realists merely play a kind of puss-in-the-corner with these problems, running across from one alternative to the other when it seems to be safe, and adopting whichever view suits the need of the moment. They are just pluralistic enough to distinguish anything from anything else when they want to do so, and just monistic enough to assert relations whenever relations are required. They are not to be blamed for this. It is inevitable ; unless they did it, their philosophy would extinguish itself and they would have to take to another occupation ; but the observer of their movements is affected with some astonishment when he finds that these movements are quite unconscious. The reason why he is surprised is that the whole essence and heart of the realistic position is the logic of abstraction which denounces as a stupid and trivial confusion anything in the nature of a synthesis of opposites. In point of fact, it is perfectly harmless to be a monist and a pluralist in alternate half-minutes, because they are the same thing : there is no reason why one should not insist on the objectivity of fact and yet argue for the subjectivity of value, because objectivity and subjectivity are as inseparable as fact and value ; but the realist is a realist precisely by denying this and setting up for himself a whole entanglement of abstract dilemmas on the understanding that he is to wriggle through them on one horn of each. It cannot be done, and no realist makes even a sporting attempt at bringing it off ; but he is so deeply in love with the rigour of his own game 'that if one points out that these old dilemmas, monism and pluralism, objective and subjective, appearance and reality, perception and conception, are on a level with the question of the hen and the egg, he feels morally outraged and regards one as little better than a pickpocket.

The fact is that modern realism is essentially inconsistent. It is a halt, or rather a confused running to and fro, between two principles, the abstract concept and the concrete fact. It springs from the scientific realism which asserts reality in the form of the abstract concept and, by implication, reduces the opposite of the concept, namely immediacy or sensation, to the level of mere appearance. This one-sided rationalism inevitably recoiled into a one-sided sensational-ism which regarded immediate sensation as the only reality and treated the concept as a mere figment of the understand-ing. It was the merit of Kant to see that each of these opposites succeeded in existing only by implicitly assuming the other, and to show that what they both aimed at was a view in which sensation and thought existed together in an inseparable unity. But this unity was for Kant an attribute of ' consciousness in general ', and this generality of the notion of consciousness marked the collapse of Kant's philosophy into another abstract rationalism, by his failure to identify the ' empirical ego ' with the ' transcendental ego ', mind in its immediacy with mind in its ideal perfection. Hegel succeeded in bridging this gulf, but the very act by which he bridged it became for him a transcendent norm or ideal of all experience, and this meant once more parting the actuality of mind from its own true nature. No subsequent philosopher improved on Hegel's solution, of which modern realism is indeed the child, though not a child of the kind which proverbially knows its own father. The Kantian synthesis of intuition and conception enriched philosophy with one priceless possession, historical fact or the concrete universal. But the failure of Kant and his successors to effect the further synthesis of mind in its empirical immediacy with mind in its ideal perfection deprived their legacy of half its value by setting this fact over against the conscious mind as a transcendent object. The result was that one of two things was bound to happen. Either the concreteness of the fact, or its transcendence, was bound to go ; for its concreteness implied the absolute immanence of every reality in every other, and its transcendence was simply a reaffirmation of the principle of abstraction.

In the sequel, the historical positivism of the nineteenth century stuck to the transcendence of the historical fact and let its concreteness go. It became, from Marx and Comte onwards, less and less historical, more and more scientific, till in the modern realists only the slightest traces of historical concreteness remain, and in a very large number of them these traces are practically invisible. We are back in a pure scientific dogmatism.

This relapse of historical idealism into a realism almost wholly scientific seems to underlie the tragedy of the nineteenth century, its slide backwards into materialism and superstition, and the breakdown of its political life into that international and social chaos to which no one nowadays is blind. But it is fair to remember, when we complain of the reactionary and obscurantist character of most modern philosophy, that it is due in the last resort to the unsoundness of the foundations laid by the great German idealists. Their achievement of the concrete universal was one of the supreme events in the history of thought. It meant the foundation of modern science, of modern history, and of modern philosophy, at a single blow. It initiated in the minds of men like Hegel, Darwin or Mommsen a truceless war against all abstractions, a hatred of all formalism, an attention to facts in all their detail, which have never been equalled. The very decay and senility of this movement, in men like Herbert Spencer and the positivists, is impressive in its passion for facts, even doubtful facts, and for gigantic, even if top-heavy, structures. But the movement was vitiated from the first by the failure to live up to the example of Descartes and see the objective fact as the inseparable correlative of the subject's thought. The abstract, formalistic positivism which so soon dominated the followers of Hegel was present, sorely against his own better judgement, in Hegel himself; and hence the modern realist, if he takes the trouble to investigate the history of his own thought, need not fear the reproach of degeneracy. For he can reply that the principles on which he takes his stand were never effectively denied even by the idealists of the past ; that these were idealists only in name, in fact crypto-realists; and that the idealism which they reject has actually never been maintained.

We shall not try to refute such allegations. On the contrary, we wish to support them whole-heartedly. But we do not agree with the implication that realism is the only possible philosophy. German idealism may have been unsuccessful as a positive movement, but as a negative movement we venture to think it was final. It killed scientific realism—the popular philosophy of to-day—as dead as a door-nail. Ghosts walk, of course. They walk when the survivors have no healthy occupation for their minds. But they can be exorcised. Only you do not exorcise a ghost by arguing with it : ghosts rely for effectiveness not on argument but on their victims' quite unfounded timidity.

§ 7. *The Theory of the Forms of Error*

We are now in a position to realize more clearly than hitherto the meaning and value of our list of dogmatisms.

The dogmatic philosophies are identical with philosophical errors. Every error is a lapse from concreteness into abstraction, and all abstraction is dogmatism. We err because we dogmatize—because we do not criticize our own assumptions—and we dogmatize because we err, because we think they are not assumptions.

To compile an exhaustive table of errors, a list of all the possible forms of false philosophy, is a programme whose very attractiveness reveals its weakness. Such a table would be a system of pigeon-holes in which we could without more ado arrange all philosophies except our own, and so excuse ourselves from any further criticism of them : ' So-and-so is a scientific dogmatist : fundamental error, abstraction of universal from particular : necessary consequences, this and that ' : nothing more need be said. So-and-so's philosophy is thus disposed of because it is a mere instance of a type, not an individual but an abstract particular. But so to regard any concrete fact is to falsify it and to lapse into the most vicious kind of abstract formalism. The pigeon-hole table of errors is itself an example of what we have condemned as scientific philosophy. It is a labour-saving device, like all abstraction ; but in philosophy the saving of labour means the saving of thought, and that implies the deliberate abandonment of the possibility of truth.

Nor is this fallacy avoided if we rearrange our list of errors so as to form a series of errors through which thought in general must necessarily pass on its way to the truth. Such a view has the merit of recognizing that errors have some mutual connexion, that one leads to another ; but the ' phenomenology of error ' so achieved is only a labyrinth instead of a set of pigeon-holes, and this labyrinth forms a kind of predetermined scheme, ordained before any actual thinking begins, in which thought is to play the game of pigs in clover. This is simply the error of deducing history *a priori* and expecting the facts to come to heel, which they can never be trained to do.

There are two senses, and only two, in which a table of errors can be legitimately drawn up. First, as a history of thought. In its actual course, thinking moves by the dialectical criticism of errors—the criticism of an error by itself, its break-up under the stress of its internal contradictions—to their denial : this denial is a truth, so framed as to negate the error just exploded, but generally falling into a new and opposite error by an exaggerated fear of the old. Any element of error in this new truth will, if thinking goes vigorously forward, initiate a new dialectical criticism and the process will be repeated on a higher plane. Thus thought in its progress—a progress not mechanical or predestined but simply effected by the hard work of thinking —moves through a series of phases each of which is a truth and yet an error, but, so far as the progress is real, each a triumph of truth over a preceding error and an advance to what may be called a truer truth. Such a progress, however diversified by stagnant backwaters and crosscurrents, has actually been exemplified at least in the history of European thought as known to us ; and a history of this thought shows the unfolding of a dialectical drama in which every phase has grown out of its predecessor with a kind of dramatic inevitability. But this inevitability is not abstract or predetermined necessity : it is only the inevitability of a well-constructed plot or fugue, the in-

T

evitability of concrete rational fact. A history of thought, then, gives a series of errors not exhausting the possibilities of unreason nor forming a predetermined scheme for thought, but recounting the errors that have actually been made and showing how each has contributed something to the state of knowledge to-day : a *felix culpa*, in so far as it has been the occasion of our rise to higher things.

Secondly, a table of errors may mean a critical review of the philosophies now current and a summary of results, in which it is shown that certain types of thought found among ourselves are subject to certain types of fallacy. The word type need not frighten us with an accusation of abstractness ; for we need not forget that every philosophy is more than a mere example of a type, is an individual creation which exemplifies even its typical error in a unique and instructive way.

But these two legitimate senses of a table of errors are not mutually exclusive. Modern philosophy is based on its own past, and modern errors are always to a great extent atavistic reversions to type, recurrences of mistakes which have been made before and which the progress of thought has already in principle refuted. In criticizing a contemporary error one always finds it to be based on ignorance or superficial knowledge of the history of thought : it is always at bottom a view which somebody has already worked out and somebody has already refuted. It is, of course, always more than this. But this at least it is ; and hence the criticism of contemporary error is simply the application to modern problems of lessons learnt in the school of philosophical history.

Our own table of errors is primarily intended as a review of the erroneous tendencies in modern thought. But this review is undertaken in no spirit of controversy. It is undertaken for our own guidance. The writer is aware of certain temptations to error, certain ways of thinking which, though they attract him, do not satisfy him. In order to arrive at his own philosophy he must face these temptations, think them out, and discover what it is in them that is attractive. This, on pain of certain shipwreck, he must absorb into his own philosophy while rejecting the elements which make them unsatisfactory. Hence a table of errors is the philosopher's personal confession of sin.

§ 8. *Philosophy as Absolute Knowledge*

To describe philosophy as the mind's knowledge of itself is only a formal or abstract description, and likely to cause misunderstanding. We shall not blame the reader if he sees a picture, first of a mind contemplating an entire universe, rich in detail of every kind—the picture being entitled ' Realism ' ; secondly, the universe blotted ruthlessly out and the mind reflecting on its own forlorn condition, this picture bearing the title ' Idealism '. The mind, as conceived by the idealist, seems to have lost everything that makes life worth living.

But the reader who feels this difficulty must not be offended if he is answered as people answer a child who says ' When I am in heaven, I shall want a Rolls-Royce and a salmon-rod '. The correct answer is, we understand, ' If you want them when you get to heaven, you shall have them '. If the mind feels cold without an object other than itself, nothing is simpler for it than to create a palace of art, a world of mythology, a cosmos of abstract conceptual machinery, and so forth. In fact that is precisely what it does when it cannot achieve what it really wants—self-knowledge—without the help of these things. But it is not these things that it wants : it is self-knowledge. *For*

T 2

when it has its works of art, what it values in them is not
themselves but the glimpses they give it of hidden and
mysterious beauty. What it worships in the figures of its
gods is not these figures themselves in their externality to
itself but the revelation through them of something really
divine ; and so on. If then any one feels that the ideal of
knowledge, as we present it, is cold and unattractive,
abstract and barren, we reply : How would you like to
enjoy for ever what in the highest art you glimpse, half-
concealed in the torrent of sensation ? How would you
like to live face to face with that which now and then you
have felt stir your heart in moments of worship and prayer ?
And if he is so simple as to believe that the very evanescence
of these moments is what gives them their value, the answer
is that to prefer them in the form of evanescent emotion is
just to create the world of art and religion. To feel the
need of an external world is already to possess such a world ;
for the error of thinking one needs it is the same as the error
of thinking that it exists. This is parallel to the familiar
truth that to look on virtue as cold and unattractive is not
to wish one were vicious, but to be vicious.

Not that such creation of an external object is capricious.
The mind cannot simply think whatever it pleases, or even
imagine whatever it pleases. It is bound by the laws of its
own nature to this extent, that even though it can deform
its nature by misconceiving it, it can never deform it out of
recognition, because misconceiving is after all a kind of
conceiving. Its scientific concepts, its religious imagery,
its aesthetic imaginings must grow out of the soil of fact,
and that fact is just its own nature as that stands for the
time being. This necessity of all its actions, ignored in the
life of imagination, is though ignored not done away. It is
transformed, by being ignored, from a rational necessity to

the blind necessity of instinct, obedient to a law which it does not understand. The discovery of necessity—not indeed an alien necessity, but the necessity of its own nature, which appears as external only so long as the figment of an external world remains—is the achievement of the religious consciousness ; but this necessity is there from the first.

All externality is imaginary ; for externality—a mutual outsideness in the abstract sense of the denial of a mutual insideness—is as such abstraction, and abstraction is always intuition or imagination. It is only to the imagination that the mind is *ever* outside its object ; but to the imagination it is *always* outside its object, even when that object is itself, as in fact it always is. Therefore, since the externality of the object is only imaginary, the act by which we create the object is never capricious : we only imagine it to be capricious : in point of fact it is necessary and an integral part of the life of reason.

Philosophy therefore does not mean the negation of all other forms of experience and the reduction of all life to the dead-level of cold ' thinking '. That, no doubt, would ' strike as chill as the coldest materialism ' ; in fact it would simply *be* materialism, for it would be the assertion of the abstract concept. The progressive reduction of art, religion, science and history to philosophy means nothing but the exposition of the life of philosophy as the lives of art, religion, science and history. In a sense, each one of these lives disappears ; but philosophy itself disappears as completely as any   Certainly, it is not our doctrine that professional ' philosophers ' are the only people who are really alive !

Art has turned out to be philosophy ; and concrete philosophy is therefore art. That beauty which is the fleeting quarry of the artist is no stranger to the philosopher. His thought must clothe itself in speech, and to him all the quire of heaven and the furniture of earth becomes a divine language, symbolizing in sensuous imagery the eternal truths of thought. Nor is this imagery to him mere art; for art in his mind is enriched and deepened into religion in the knowledge that what he was taught in his youth, and in his haste perhaps rejected as fable, is true: that God really lives and is his father, that the voice that speaks in nature is truly the voice of her creator, and that this very God became man to die for him and to atone by a full, perfect and sufficient sacrifice for the sins of the whole world. And this knowledge is not, for him, in any conflict with the regularity and uniformity of nature, with the fact that he can and does abstract, generalize, conceive everything as matter and motion or in modern language as space-time; for this abstract conception of the world is to him only the schematic order which, without doing it violence, he detects in that infinite whole which is at once spirit and nature, the whole of which the starry heavens above him and the moral law within him are parts. And in learning to know this whole, a whole of truly objective fact in which art and religion and science all play their parts—so, and only so, he comes to know himself. Its true objectivity is not the abstract objectivity of a world in which the knower himself has no place, but the concrete objectivity which is only the correlative of his own subjectivity. It is *his* world that he knows in this way: if he were not, this world of reality as he sees it would not be. Other worlds would no doubt exist, and in their very difference these would be in a sense identical with his, versions of it; but they could never replace it.

This enjoyment of the entire world of fact, released alike

from the intermittence of art and religion, the abstractness of science and the indifferent externality of history, is the life of philosophy. The philosopher can be a philosopher all his life, not only in his moments of inspiration. Everything, not merely the selected experiment, comes as grist to his mill, for his philosophical thought is infinite in its application. And he knows what the historian does not know, that his own knowledge of facts is organic to the facts themselves, that his mind is these facts knowing themselves and these facts are his mind knowing itself. Everybody enjoys this life, and enjoys it unceasingly ; but those who do not know that they are doing so, and give a false account to themselves of their own experience, so deform that experience that it loses its highest qualities and actually becomes something not altogether unlike what they falsely think it.

This is called the life of absolute knowledge not because it is secure from error : that is impossible ; but because in it there is no element of necessary and insurmountable error, as there is in the lives of art, religion, science and history in the restrictive sense. In these lives the mind is by its very self-determination as aesthetic, religious, and so on, committed to certain errors and forced—always by its own act—to distort any truth it achieves, however great this truth may be, into conformity with them. In the life of philosophy such distorting media are done away : the mind here says what it means, and therefore can for the first time say what is absolutely true. If it errs, the smallest error as to a matter of fact infects to some extent its whole life : to misjudge the tiniest fact is as if a cloud went over the sun and darkened the face of the world. And since every error is abstraction, this darkening of its world is the self-alienation of the philosophical mind, its degradation into the life of history or even lower. Consequently there is no such thing as a mere error of fact. Any such error distorts the whole mind and must be eradicated not by the correction of a detail but by the recovery of the balance of the whole.

It follows that the concrete life of philosophy is no mere haven of rest, but a ceaseless act of achieving this balance. The balance is achieved not by the static contemplation by mind of its own fixed given nature—mind has no fixed given nature—but by the self-creation of this nature in a perpetual discovery of fact which is at the same time the creation of fact : the creation of the fact of its discovery, which is only the indispensable subjective side of the fact itself. The life of absolute knowledge is thus the conscious self-creation of the mind, no mere discovery of what it is, but the making of itself what it is.

Now in error (and the same is true, of course, in wrong-doing) the mind also creates itself : determines itself in this way, just as in knowledge it determines itself in that. Whatever the mind does, therefore, it cannot escape that self-creation which is moral responsibility. But in error it creates in itself a nature which it conceals from itself : quite literally, error and evil are the mind knowing not what it does, creating itself in one shape while it thinks of itself in another. Thus it cannot be said that an idealistic view of mind finds no place for error and evil. On the contrary, it requires their continual presence in the form of that which, by conscious reflection, the mind in knowledge and in duty rejects ; and inasmuch as its whole life is a process of self-determination, the past in any such process is the evil which is rejected, good when it was brought into being but now outworn and therefore evil if it had been retained.

But what is most fundamental is that the mind can not

only commit error but can redeem itself from error. This is because any error it makes concerning its own nature (and every error is that) creates two conflicting results : a new state of itself, and a new notion of itself. But because its own state is a state of consciousness, this new state, even though only implicitly, contradicts the newly formed notion. Thus there are two conflicting notions of itself in the mind, and this conflict is the mark of error and the signal that a return to the road of truth is required. Thus the equilibrium of thought is a stable equilibrium like that of a gyroscope ; but it is only the energy of the gyroscope that keeps it upright.

§ 9. *The Absolute Mind*

It is customary to ask people who speak as we have been speaking about ' the mind ', what mind are you talking about ?

It is no reply to say, that mind which is at once subject and object of the absolute experience. It remains to be asked what this mind is.

In the first place we may reasonably reply : We are speaking of any mind you please, mind in general. We are discussing the behaviour of the mind as you might discuss the behaviour of the trout or the potentilla. What we have said is true of every mind that exists, wherever and whenever you please, and by whatever name it is known.

That might stand as a provisional answer ; but it evades the real problem. For it implies that we are discussing the abstract common nature of all minds as such, irrespectively of the question what minds, if any, there are. And we may very well be asked, are there any minds in your sense of the word ? And if so, where are they to be found ? Thus our ' theory of knowledge ' is referred beyond itself to a ' metaphysics ', or statement as to the nature of real existence. But this is a flagrant collapse into the scientific fallacy and a fall from even the historical standard of truth. Mind in general is merely an abstract concept, and in appealing to it we are convicted of psychology.

The absolute mind, then, must be an historical fact, not a generalization. Is it the world-spirit, the mind whose life is gradually being developed as the universe evolves ? Hardly, for the world-spirit is mere mythology. If there is such a thing, we know nothing of it. Moreover, a world-spirit embodied in the universe ' whose body nature is, and God the soul ' is a quite confused conception belonging to a primitive dualism of body and soul which history, and *a fortiori* philosophy, cannot for a moment tolerate.

The mind of which we are speaking is an absolute fact, one of which there can never in anybody's mind be any doubt. That is to say, it must at least be the mind of each one of us, for each his own particular mind. But if it is my own particular mind, it is not the same mind as yours ; and hence my philosophy of it is a description not of mind as such but of my own individual mind, and all my knowledge is of my own mind and not of anything other than my own mind ; and philosophy becomes mere autobiography.

This is solipsism ; the answer to which is, from the idealistic point of view, easy. Realists are always afraid of solipsism, because it is a difficulty which they cannot answer except by an arbitrary refusal to listen to it. It alarms them because it contains two elements, a realistic background and an idealistic foreground, and these cannot be brought into focus together. The realist cannot explain away the idealistic element, but the idealist can point out that the realistic element is a false abstraction and so lay the spectre. The background is the realistic separation of subject and object into two independent things ; the fore-ground, the idealistic principle of self-knowledge. Put them together, and you get the disastrous consequence that the self-knowledge of the mind excludes all knowledge of any-thing else. The realist is helpless before this suggestion, and it drives him to all sorts of strange expedients such as denying the reality of self-knowledge ; but the idealistic answer (as Kant once for all pointed out) is that the mind's knowledge of itself is its knowledge of everything else : in knowing itself it knows its world, and in knowing its world it knows itself. Thus solipsism, which is a disease endemic among realists—as is clear from their morbid interest in its symptoms—leaves our withers unwrung. In knowing my mind, I know yours and other people's : these reveal me to myself and I simultaneously explain them to myself. My mind is obviously a product of society, and conversely the society I know is the product of my mind, as thinking it according to its lights.

The absolute mind, then, unites the differences of my mind and other people's, but not as the abstract universal unites : rather as the concrete universal of history unites. The absolute mind is an historical whole of which mine is a part.

Yet the category of whole and part is false, for the part in its externality to other parts is but a reassertion of abstract difference. The absolute mind is not ' one stupendous whole '. It lives in its entirety in every individual and every act of every individual, yet not indifferently, as triangularity is indifferently present in every triangle, but expressing itself in every individual uniquely and irreplaceably. This is its necessary nature as concrete : it cares, so to speak, how many individual reduplications of itself there are, and will have so many as form a real organic whole in which every element is essential to the being of the whole.

To demonstrate in detail this necessity of every individual to the whole is precisely the work of history. It is in the nature of the case a work permanently incomplete ; but that is only because it grows upon itself and every fresh thought is a fresh individual fact.

The philosophical conception of such an absolute mind requires that we should see it as concrete, that is, to banish solipsism and pantheism (abstract assertion and abstract denial of the individual), determinism and indeterminism (abstract assertion and abstract denial of the whole), and in general every form of the two complementary abstractions one of which denies the whole to assert the part, while the other denies the part to assert the whole. It requires us to conceive the whole as *totum in toto et totum in qualibet parte,* and the part as performing a function in the whole without which the whole would simply not exist. This is not a difficult feat, except to minds hide-bound in the habits of abstract thought : it is simply thinking historically, and every historian enjoys it as the very breath of his life.

The absolute mind has nothing over against itself as a necessity by which it is bound : not even the laws of its own nature. These laws it creates by acting upon them, and this creation is not the arbitrary act of a divine tyrant who could make twice two into five if he pleased—as if that could mean anything—but the necessity of reason itself. The thoughts of this absolute mind, in so far as they are true, are known as true not by any so-called correspondence with fact but simply by being justifiable under criticism, which of course is always self-criticism, and from which there can be no appeal. Anything which is by definition non-mental is an object of this mind which it creates by lapsing into error concerning its own nature.

Thus, the reader may have imagined that when we spoke

of the process of thought we were presupposing the reality
of time, since every process is a process in time. Hence
time would appear to be something external to the absolute
mind, the necessity which stands over Zeus himself. But
so to regard time is to forget that the process of which we
are speaking is a process not of mechanical change but of
thought : a self-knowing process. A mind which knows its
own change is by that very knowledge lifted above change.
History—and the same is true of memory and even perception—is the mind's triumph over time. It is a commonplace of philosophy that whereas sensation is temporal,
thought is eternal or extra-temporal : sensation apprehends
the here and now, thought apprehends the everywhere
and the always. Hence the abstract psychology which splits
the mind up into a sensitive and an intellectual faculty
paradoxically presents us with a picture of man as standing
with one foot in time and the other in eternity. This is
mythology, but true mythology. All concrete thought is,
in its immediacy, temporal, but in its mediation extra-
temporal. The mind in its actual thinking at once recognizes and defies temporal (and spatial) limitations. The
opposites, time and eternity, are necessary to one another.
Time is not a mere appearance ; it is perfectly real ; but
like all opposites it can be real only as the correlative of its
equally real opposite, eternity. Time in fact is the abstraction of the externality to one another of the phases of
a process : eternity is the opposite abstraction of the continuity of this process, the identity of the whole in its
process. To describe the life of man as temporal or finite
and the life of God as eternal or infinite is only a way of
saying that time is not real in abstraction, but real only in
relation to its opposite. In the absolute process of thought
the past lives in the present, not as a mere ' trace ' or effect

of itself in the physical or psychical organism, but as the object of the mind's historical knowledge of itself in an eternal present.

This is the solution of all those problems concerning finitude and infinity which have so vexed abstract thought. Man recognizes himself as finite and knows that, if he really is finite, he is thereby debarred from that infinity to which he aspires. But just as a being really limited in time could not know of its own limitation—for it could have no conception of a past and a future if it lived wholly in the present —so a being really finite could not know itself as finite. The self-knowledge of man as finite is already his assertion of himself as infinite. In the very act of abstraction by which psychology asserts the existence of finite centres of consciousness it is rising above its own theory and making a concrete act of thought which refutes its own ostensible content.

Religious imagery cannot prove the truth of any philosophy, because the interpretation put upon such imagery is already the work of philosophy ; but it will illustrate, if it does not help to demonstrate, our conception of the absolute mind to point out the way in which one religion at least has expressed itself, when dealing with the ultimate questions which here concern us.

God is conceived as the absolute spirit, alpha and omega, the beginning and the end. Behind him, beyond him, apart from him, there is nothing : neither matter nor law, neither earth nor heaven, neither space nor time. In the beginning, by an absolute act which was not itself subject to any determination of time or space, God created the heavens and the earth : the visible world, with all its order and furniture, even the very space in which it floats and the time in which it endures and changes, is the work of this absolute act. But this world is no mere toy shaped by

God and thrown off from himself in contemptuous alienation. His spirit moves upon the face of the waters, even the
waters of chaos, and this same breath becomes the soul of
life in the man whom he creates in his own image. Man
is one with God, no mere part of a whole, but informed by
the indwelling of the divine spirit. Now man, by his mis-
guided thirst for knowledge, partakes of that knowledge
which is forbidden, namely error, or the human wisdom
which negates God's wisdom. This error deforms his own
true, that is divine, nature, and the deformation takes
the shape of banishment from the presence of God into the
wilderness of the visible world. Having thus lost even the
sight of God, the knowledge of what he himself ought to be,
he cannot recover his lost perfection until he comes to know
himself as he actually is. But not knowing himself as he
ought to be, he cannot know himself as he is. His error is
implicit just because it is complete. It can only become
explicit if God reveals himself afresh, if the true ideal breaks
in upon the soul clouded by error. This, in the fullness of
time, is granted. Human nature sunk in error is confronted
by the confutation of its own error, and thus, through a fresh
dialectical process, redeemed.

Now in this imagery there is one flaw, namely the transcendence of God. God standing aloof from the drama of
human sin and redemption, a mere stage manager, is no
true symbol of the absolute mind in its concreteness. But
this is exactly where the truth of our religious imagery
shines most brilliantly. It is God who accepts the burden
of error, takes upon himself the moral responsibility for the
fall, and so redeems not his creature but himself.

The absolute mind, if our account of it is true, can never
be more profoundly or impressively pictured than in this
drama of the fall and redemption of man.

§ 10. *Absolute Ethics*

With the disappearance of the last remnant of abstraction
in the form of the distinction between the individual and
society, the obstacle to the realization of perfect freedom is
removed. The agent is now conscious of himself as absolute
mind, and of every other agent, whether in agreement with
himself or not, as coequal with himself. This means that
he ceases to regard himself or his country or his party as in
the right and everybody else in the wrong, but he regards
all actions as manifestations of a will which is always and
necessarily rational even when ' in the wrong ', and therefore
never wholly in the wrong. He thus sympathizes even with
his opponents, and in proportion as he becomes truly
rational he ceases to regard any one as an unmitigated
opponent, but sees in every one a fellow-worker with himself
in the cause of the good.

This is the attitude of which universal love is the intuitive
or emotional expression. In itself, however, it is not emotional but rational. Caricatured by abstract thought, it
becomes humanitarianism or the mere indifference of
people's actual aims and performances to the way in which
they are regarded (abstract equality, rights of man, &c.).
Such abstract humanitarianism is the true object of criticism
when realists fulminate against concrete or idealistic ethics
as taking away all motive to action, destroying the distinction between good and evil, and so forth. There is in point
of fact all the difference in the world between the concrete
attitude which determines what precisely a man has done and
judges it as in certain ways right and in certain ways wrong,
and the abstract attitude which says that what he has done
and whether it is right or wrong does not matter. The former
attitude is the only possible basis for just and appropriate

action: the latter cannot be the basis of any action what-ever.

In absolute ethics the agent identifies himself with the entire world of fact, and in coming to understand this world prepares himself for the action appropriate to the unique situation. This is not an act of duty, because the sense of an objective and abstract law, whether lodged in the indi-vidual 'conscience' or in the political 'sovereign', has disappeared. The agent acts with full responsibility as embodying and identifying himself with the absolute mind, and his act is therefore the pure act of self-creation. This act is identical with self-knowledge, and thus the abstract distinction of the will and the intellect is transcended.

The claim to have attained this position is the essence of the claim made by and on behalf of 'conscientious objectors' and similar persons who on the strength of an immediate divine mandate defy the laws of the society to which they belong. The falsity of their claim is evident from the fact that they regard the law of the land as an irrational external object, and call it 'force' and the like (force being the false abstraction of will seen from the outside). They are thus by their own confession inhabitants not of the heaven of freedom, but of the earth of bondage and heteronomy, and differ from others only in their failure to recognize the fact. To recognize the fact—to obey the law in the spirit of intelligent and cheerful co-operation—is to transcend it, and to have reached, if only implicitly, the position of absolute ethics.

VIII

SPECULUM SPECULI

WE set out to construct a map of knowledge on which every legitimate form of human experience should be laid down, its boundaries determined, and its relations with its neighbours set forth. We assumed that such a map could be made : imperfect and abstract, like all maps, but none the less valuable to those whose task it is to explore and cultivate the country of the mind. We assumed, that is to say, the real existence of art, religion, and so forth as distinct forms of experience, forms not wholly separable or independent, but at least mutually exclusive, relatively autonomous and capable of some kind of delimitation.

Such a map of knowledge is impossible ; and our trouble is well spent if it produces no other result than the recognition that this is so. There are no autonomous and mutually exclusive forms of experience, and, what is more, it is in no one's interest to assume that there are.

The artist does not want a map of knowledge : he only wants a map of art, and this map is art itself. For him art and life are the same thing : art is long and life is short, his own actual span of work lies wholly within the all-embracing universe of art. The religious man, again, just in so far as he is really religious, in his truly religious moments, knows that nothing but religion exists. All experience is religious experience, even that of the heathen and the atheist. He does not ask for a holiday from his religion : his holiday would be to dwell in the house of the Lord for ever. The moralist, again, sees the whole of life as duty. Every claim is for him the claim of duty, and he is not to be deceived when the devil offers him a ' moral holiday ' or poses him with sophistries about the relation of morality to art. For him, art, when it ought to be pursued, is a duty : when it ought not, it is a crime. That is all. The scientist again is by the principles of his own thought compelled to interpret everything in scientific terms, as the working of abstract and iron laws. Any one who pleads for the least little bit of back-lash in the working of his machine, an *exiguum clinamen*, at certain moments and at certain points *une certaine élasticité*, is simply as a publican and a sinner : a stink in the nostrils of the scientific conscience. The scientist does not want a map of the forms of knowledge. There is for him only one legitimate form, science ; and that is its own map. All other forms are not other territories but false maps of the same territory.

Every person who is actually absorbed in any given form of experience is by this very absorption committed to the opinion that no other form is valid, that his form is the only one adequate to the comprehension of reality. Hence arise discords ; for when artists and scientists, who after all do inhabit a common world of fact, meet and discuss their aims, each is apt to accuse the other of wasting his life on a world of illusions. The ' ancient quarrel between poetry and philosophy ' is only one of a whole series of such quarrels in a ceaseless international war in which every country on our map is eternally embroiled with every other ; for all, ' because of their independency, are in continual jealousies and in the state and posture of gladiators, having their weapons pointing, and their eyes fixed on one another . . . which is a posture of war '. This war is complete even down to the existence of pacificists of the mind, getting between the legs of the combatants and kindly offering to explain to ' religion and science ', or whatever the combatants may be, that they are fighting about nothing.

On this scene of international warfare the philosopher pictures himself as looking down calmly, enthroned on a cloud *audessus de la mêlée*, seeing perhaps that it is God's will for these deluded mortals to fly at one another's throats, or perhaps, in a voice of authority, bidding them be still, with a result suggestive rather of Canute than of Christ. For they, poor things, do not recognize the philosopher's superhuman status : they actually think he is one of the combatants. ' Philosophers ', wrote a great historian to a young friend appointed to a philosophical tutorship, ' are my natural enemies.' And this is perfectly just ; for the philosopher asserts philosophy as the only legitimate form of experience, and not only condemns the others as illusory but adds insult to injury by giving reasons for his condemnation, which goes against all the maxims of civilized warfare. Philosophers are justly, therefore, the objects of universal dislike. They fight their own professional battle and claim to be defending the ark of God.

This, roughly speaking, is the situation with which we began. We hoped that the proper construction of a map of knowledge, by a kind of international boundary commission, might do something to stop the fighting. It was a vain hope. Plenty of such maps have been made already, in the form of philosophies of the human mind and so forth, and they only arouse suspicion, because they are not international documents but the propaganda of one combatant.

Beginning, then, with our assumption of the separateness and autonomy of the various forms of experience, we have found that this separateness is an illusion. Each form is at bottom identical with all the others. It is only an error that makes some people ignore one element of their experience and others ignore another, and thus come to the conclusion that their experiences are of a fundamentally different kind.

They are different, but it is only the error of thinking they are different that makes them different. Artists and scientists must fight ; it is their nature to ; but they have acquired this nature by committing themselves to the error of regarding art and science as independent things.

The various countries on our initial map, then, turn out to be variously-distorted versions of one and the same country. No one accustomed to maps compiled from travellers' reports will be surprised at that. What, then, is this one country ? It is the world of historical fact, seen as the mind's knowledge of itself. Can we, then, sketch this country's features in outline ?

We cannot. To explore that country is the endless task of the mind ; and it only exists in being explored. Of such a country there is no map, for it is itself its own map. The explorer, the country explored, and the map are one and the same thing.

There is and can be no map of knowledge, for a map means an abstract of the main features of a country, laid before the traveller in advance of his experience of the country itself. Now no one can describe life to a person who stands on the threshold of life. The maxims given by age to youth are valueless not because age means nothing by them but because what it means is just its own past life. To youth they are empty words. The life of the spirit cannot be described except by repeating it : an account of it would just be itself. This is equally the case whether we present our map in the form of a group of categories or concepts which are supposed to reappear as units of thought in the texture of experience ; or a group of laws somehow suspended above it which govern its course ; or a group of presuppositions which lie beyond' and behind its very beginning, and condition, through its beginning, its whole development ; or a world of objects over against it, in beating itself against which it comes to the use of its own powers ; or a series of stages through which, as along a railway line, it necessarily runs. All these assertions of something other than the absolute mind itself are versions of a single error : the error of abstraction, of failing to realize that subject and object, condition and conditioned, ground and consequence, particular and universal, can only be distinctions which fall within one and the same whole, and that this whole can only be the infinite fact which is the absolute mind. A fact which has anything outside it is not the concrete fact. If that which falls outside it is its own law or nature, we have fallen into the abstraction which tears apart the individual into particular and universal ; if another fact, we have torn apart the individual into two individuals unrelated and therefore both fictitious.

Our inquiry has not only abolished the notion of a map of knowledge distinct from knowledge itself: it has also abolished the notion of an external world other than the mind. It has not, of course, abolished the distinction between subject and object : on the contrary, it has established our right to use that distinction by showing its necessity in the life of thought. It is no more abolished than are the distinctions between truth and error, good and evil, particular and universal : these distinctions are only abolished by the *coincidentia oppositorum* which is the suicide of abstract thought, and conserved by the synthesis of opposites which is the life of concrete thought. Just as we began by assuming a map of knowledge, so we began by assuming an external world, a world of which we could say with the realists that it really is what, errors apart, we think it to be : a world of which we could even say that it was what it was quite irrespective of any ignorance or error of our own about it.

Our position at the start was wholly realistic, and there is a sense in which it is realistic to the end. But we did not—and this is where realists tend to go wrong—assume that ' errors apart ' is a clause which need not be taken seriously. We did not assume that any one form of experience could be accepted as already, in its main lines, wholly free from error. Led by this principle, we found that the real world was implied, but not asserted, in art ; asserted, but not thought out, in religion ; thought out, but only subject to fictitious assumptions, in science ; and therefore in all these we found an ostensible object—the work of art, God, the material universe—which was confessedly a figment and not the real object. The real object is the mind itself, as we now know.

But in abolishing the notion of an external world other than the mind we do not assert any of the silly nonsense usually described by unintelligent critics as idealism. We do not assert that the trees and hills and people of our world are ' unreal ', or ' mere ideas in my mind ', still less that matter is nothing but a swarm of mind-particles. The very essence of trees and hills and people is that they should be not myself but my objects in perception : they are not subjective but objective, not states of myself but facts that I know. None the less, my knowing them is organic to them : it is because they are what they are that I can know them, because I know them that they can be what to me they really are. They and I alike are members of one whole, a whole which the destruction of one part would in a sense destroy throughout, as the death of our dearest friend darkens for us the very light of the sun.

A philosopher once refuted idealism by begging his audience to watch his desk and see whether, when he left the room, it continued to exist or not. It was a pretty piece of buffoonery, whose chief merit was to show that he imagined

them to see in his desk everything that he saw in it himself :
in other words, that he took his stand firmly on the abstract
point of view which cannot see that any given fact makes
any difference to the whole. Now such an act of abstraction,
error though it is, really creates its own world, though not
a wholly rational world. To dispose of this world by calling
it a mere idea is no more intelligent than to call a temptation
to sin, or a nightmare, or a toothache, a mere idea in the
hope of dispelling it. The world of abstract concepts—the
material world—is an objective world called into existence
indeed by an error of the mind, but by that very error
asserted as real. Hence to make the abstraction and to
regard the reality of its object as self-evident are one and
the same thing, and these 'farcical refutations of idealism
are only successful as showing, what nobody doubts, that
it is as possible to put your blind eye to a microscope as to
a telescope.

Now the construction of such an abstract world is not
a pointless or purposeless waste of energy on the part of the
mind. To suppose that this is so, that religion is *only* a fiction
and science *only* an arbitrary play of abstractions, is the
error of those critics, whether of religion or science, who
unintelligently praise one by unintelligently condemning the
other. In the toil of art, the agony of religion, and the
relentless labour of science, actual truth is being won and
the mind is coming to its own true stature. This is simply
because the ostensible object whose apparent articulations
are being so patiently traced is not the real object, and
because every new touch given to the determination of the
former does not obscure, but rather illustrates, the latter.
For the true object is not concealed behind the ostensible as
behind a veil. Had that been so, the elaboration of the veil
could but make its density deeper, and religion or science

would be the prison-house of a self-frustrated mind whose very effort to see the world only resulted in its enclosure within a thicker and thicker crust of illusion. But the true object is not

> our great roof, its gilt carving and groining,
> Under yon spider-webs lying.

It is the mind itself. And thus the external world is not a veil between it and its object, but a picture of itself, drawn to aid its own self-vision ; a picture which as it grows firmer and harder, takes surface and polish and steadiness, becomes the Mirror of the Mind ; and all the detail visible in it is seen by the mind to be the reflection of its own face.

Knowledge polarizes itself into abstract or erroneous and concrete or true. Abstract knowledge is the same as error, because, separating what is thought to be from what is, it erects that which it thinks into a false object over against itself, an external world. To err, and to believe in an external world over against the mind, are one and the same thing. Now if error were mere error, the mind would merely assert the external object, which is what it thinks itself to be, and thereby deny itself, and resolve the dualism. But all error contains an element of truth, and the conflict between the truth and the error appears as the externality of the object, its otherness with respect to the mind. Because these two are really one, all knowledge of the external object is really the mind's knowledge of itself. But all this knowledge, however true it may be, is affected by the fact that it is projected upon an external world : it is, so to speak, reversed like the face we see in the glass. This reversal constitutes its falsity ; as long as we do not know that we are looking at our own reflection, we see not ourselves but a distorted caricature of ourselves, in some ways strangely like, in some ways opposite. Hence we can never resolve the

doubt whether nature is our tender mother or a tigerish
Kali ; whether God is love or tyranny ; whether matter is
embodied reason or embodied irrationality. This doubt is
the mind's wonder whether the face it sees is that of its twin
brother or its opposite. All externality breeds this ambiguity,
for the ambiguity is the equivocation of error as such.

To see in a glass and to see darkly are the same. But in
concrete knowledge the mind sees itself face to face, and
knows even as it is known. Here the object is the subject,
not in the sense of a *that is thou* which is the mere negation
of individual distinction, but in the sense that the object
finds its very life in being known by the subject, the subject
in knowing the object. Of this experience it is said that
number here in love is slain : not distinction, not individuality, but separateness, the externality of abstract units
to one another. The whole objective world is concentrating
its energies into the creation of this one act of consciousness,
and this one act greets the whole world as its own world, not
because it cannot see the difference between one thing and
another, which is precisely the attitude of the abstract
concept, but because it can see the identity which is the
basis of this difference.

This absolute experience of concrete knowledge has
nothing to do with any professional distinctions, any more
than with distinctions of social class or physical race. The
enjoyment of it has nothing to do with that ' philosophy ',
a confused mixture of scientific abstractions and historical
facts, which is professionally expounded by people called
philosophers. It lives in a unity above all professional
distinctions, and the philosopher may well achieve it in
greater perfection when sailing a boat or telling stories to
a child than when discoursing technicalities to a class. But
it is not an intuitive or emotional experience, a mood whose

precious visits illuminate the waste of life : it is just life itself in its infinite self-conscious development, a development which sees every detail of itself as organic to the whole.

This life has no map and no object other than itself : if it had such an object, that would be its map, for the features of the object would be its own features. Thus the external world, whose origin, growth, and structure we have been, throughout this book, investigating, is the Mirror of the Mind and the Map of Knowledge in one.

But to make such a cleavage as we have suggested between concrete and abstract knowledge, truth and error, is to commit another abstraction. Concrete knowledge is not generically different from abstract knowledge, it is abstract knowledge freed from its own abstractness by simply recognizing that abstractness. The mind is not one among a number of objects of knowledge, which possesses the peculiarity of being alone fully knowable : it is that which is really known in the ostensible knowing of any object whatever. In an immediate and direct way, the mind can never know itself : it can only know itself through the mediation of an external world, know that what it sees in the external world is its own reflection. Hence the construction of external worlds—works of art, religions, sciences, structures of historical fact, codes of law, systems of philosophy and so forth *ad infinitum*—is the only way by which the mind can possibly come to that self-knowledge which is its end. Such a constructive process is one of abstraction and error so long as the external world in question is not realized to be the mind's own work. It is perhaps not possible to carry out this process in the full consciousness of what one is doing : the illusion of abstract objectivity is essential to it : it must be done in good faith, in the belief that one is now at last discovering the ultimate truth, coming into

contact with a pre-existent and absolute reality.   But when
it is done, when the work of art or system of philosophy or
what not is achieved, the mind, in so far as this exercise has
really strengthened instead of exhausting it, realizes that
it has been not exploring an external world but tracing its
own lineaments in a mirror.   In this realization it sees the
abstraction of its previous work to be an abstraction and
nothing more, and the abstraction, the error, is thus van-
quished.   The truth is not some perfect system of philosophy :
it is simply the way in which all systems, however perfect,
collapse into nothingness on the discovery that they are
only systems, only external worlds over against the knowing
mind and not that mind itself.

This process of the creation and destruction of external
worlds might appear, to superficial criticism, a mere futile
weaving and unweaving of Penelope's web, a declaration of
the mind's inability to produce solid assets, and thus the
bankruptcy of philosophy.   And this it would be if knowledge were the same thing as information, something stored
in encyclopaedias and laid on like so much gas and water in
schools and universities.   But education does not mean
stuffing a mind with information ; it means helping a mind
to create itself, to grow into an active and vigorous contributor to the life of the world.   The information given in such
a process is meant to be absorbed into the life of the mind
itself, and a boy leaving school with a memory full of facts
is thereby no more educated than one who leaves table with
his hands full of food is thereby fed.   At the completion of
its education, if that event ever happened, a mind would step
forth as naked as a new-born babe, knowing nothing, but
having acquired the mastery over its own weaknesses, its
own desires, its own ignorance, and able therefore to face any
danger unarmed.

The collapse of a system of thought is therefore not equivalent to the cancellation of the process by which it came into being. It collapses, but it does not perish. In constructing and destroying it, the mind has learnt a permanent lesson : it has triumphed over an error and so discovered a truth. The destroyed system collapses not into bare nothingness but into immediacy, into a characteristic or attribute of the mind itself, passes as it were into the muscle and bone of the mind, becomes an element in the point of view from which the mind raises its next problem.

For the life of the mind consists of raising and solving problems, problems in art, religion, science, commerce, politics, and so forth. The solution of these problems does not leave behind it a sediment of ascertained fact, which grows and solidifies as the mind's work goes on. Such a sediment is nothing but the externality of a half-solved problem : when the problem is fully solved the sediment of information disappears and the mind is left at liberty to go on. Philosophy, therefore, is not a prerogative kind of knowledge immune from this reabsorption into the mind's being : it is nothing but the recognition that this reabsorption is necessary and is indeed the end and crown of all knowledge, the self-recognition of the mind in its own mirror.

·INDEX [1]

[1] For the compilation of this Index the author is indebted to the kindness of Mr. T. M. Knox.

truth of, guaranteed by mathematics 166, 185
physics, modern 167
'picture thinking' 141
Plato 66, 81, 104, 188, 199
his dialectic 77, 279
his theory of art 50, 58, 73, 86
forms 180, 191, 196, 240–2, 279
science 162, 164, 176, 178, 183–4, 201
play 102–7, 170, 226
pleasure 104
pluralism 190–1, 283–5
poetry 50, 58
and philosophy 307
polarization of aesthetic experience 63
holiness 120
religion 114, 119
politics 226, 229–30
Pope quoted 298
positivism 286–7
pragmatism 78, 182.
prayer 121, 130
primary and secondary experience 255, 272
primitive religion 114, 117
process of thought 301
history 56
(*see also* dialectic)
professional and amateur in philosophy 261
progress 54
Prologue (of Chaucer) 60
proofs of the existence of God 151, 264
psycho-analysis 75, 92–4
psychology 168, 181, 195, 247–8, 274–8, 280, 298, 302
error of 277
(*see also* faculty-psychology)
punishment 225–6
puritanism 31

Quellenkritik 213–14
questioning, its relation to fact 79
knowledge 76–80
supposal 78, 186

rationalism 137, 146–8, 172, 265–6, 269–70
realism 201, 245, 252, 259, 268, 281–7, 291, 298–9
realistic art 61–2, 76
reality, Greek scientific view of 161–3, 169

and appearance 285
as matter 267
as object independent of knower 238
Kant's view of 279
modern realistic view of 285
reason 131, 195–200, 300
reconciliation 139, 142
redemption 37, 130
Reformation 31
refutations of idealism 312
relations, external 233, 234 (note)
internal 234 (note)
relevance, concept of, and art 98–9
RELIGION 108–53 *passim* (*see* Table of Contents)
act of will in 259
and art 154–5
and children 50
and fact 209
and language 154
and science 40, 49, 193, 307
claims truth 39
dogma in 259
God as the object of 48, 116–22, 158–9, 219–20, 238, 242–3, 264, 268, 311
imagery of 302–3
individuality of 219
life of 295
medieval 27–8, 30
present state of 16, 19, 33–4, 145–6
supposed illusory nature of 265
Religion and Philosophy 108 note
religious agnosticism 131
art, opposed to secular 27, 122
controversy 116
cosmology 115, 258
ethics 171
history 209, 216
morality 134
philosophy 28, 258, 264–70 (*see also* theism)
reminiscence 212
Renaissance, aftermath of 33–4, 74
Christianity of 38
freedom of 30–1
laughter of 32
life of 36–7, 47
science 177–8, 184–5, 187, 201–
view of art 31, 73
Republic (of Plato) 178
resurrection 37
Revelation, Book of 132, 139
Rhodes, Cecil 147
rights of man 304

PRINTED IN GREAT BRITAIN
AT THE UNIVERSITY PRESS, OXFORD
BY VIVIAN RIDLER
PRINTER TO THE UNIVERSITY

PRINTED IN GREAT BRITAIN
AT THE UNIVERSITY PRESS, OXFORD
BY VIVIAN RIDLER
PRINTER TO THE UNIVERSITY